# Refugee Talk

'A wide-ranging, erudite and multi-faceted analyses of the fundamental problem of who gets to be counted as human in a planet under stress.'
—Kate Evans, award-winning cartoonist and activist, and author of *Red Rosa*

'In *Refugee Talk*, the authors tell us that they "align [themselves] with what Edward Said labels 'amateurism' – 'the desire to be moved [by] unquenchable interest in the larger picture, in making connections across lines and barriers." In this absorbing book, they manage to do exactly that: They combine the rigors of academic argument with Said's broad-minded, and deeply-felt, intellectual generosity, focusing on the moral, aesthetic, sociopolitical, and narrative aspects of the phenomenologies of migration. As a work of anti-reductive complexity that engages both urgently and unflinchingly with the refugee crisis, *Refugee Talk* is aimed not just at scholars of migration studies, philosophers, sociologists, political theorists, narrativists, and others, but at those looking to better understand the plight of refugees in terms of what the authors call "a new humanism for the twenty-first century". It is indeed this humanism, urging us all to take seriously not only refugee justice, but our shared, and fragile, humanity, that is at the core of this remarkable book.'
—Anna Gotlib, Associate Professor of Philosophy at Brooklyn College,
City University of New York

'This book is built around that which is absent from most books of this kind: the voices of the refugee. Eva Rask Knudsen and Ulla Rahbek deploy a rich blend of theory and textual analysis, complemented in a distinctive way by a range of original conversations with writers, journalists, critical theorists, and refugees themselves. The book challenges those of us working in the field to rethink the existing refugee lexicon and to open up fresh debates about the ethics, aesthetics, and politics of representation. What is particularly heartening about the book is the way in which, at a time of such negativity, the authors attempt to frame their overall approach in a context of hope.'
—Roger Bromley, Emeritus Professor of Cultural Studies,
University of Nottingham

'Deftly weaving theoretical analysis with conversations from journalists, activists, and exiles themselves, *Refugee Talk* stunningly accomplishes what responsible critique demands of us all: nuanced, ethical and material engagement with those to whom our thought is indebted.'
—Sabeen Ahmed, Assistant Professor of Philosophy, Swarthmore College

'In the midst of political conflicts concerning refugees, *Refugee Talk* steps back from the immediate fray to reflect on the ethical character of "refugee talk" in academic, media, activist artistic, and literary contexts. The result is a genuinely thoughtful – and engagingly conversational – work that re-orients us to the recognition of hope as a common human dynamic and to a critical humanism expressed in acknowledging the dignity of refugees. Highly recommended.'
—David Owen, Professor of Politics and International Relations,
University of Southampton

# Refugee Talk

## Propositions on Ethics and Aesthetics

Eva Rask Knudsen and Ulla Rahbek

PLUTO  PRESS

First published 2022 by Pluto Press
New Wing, Somerset House, Strand, London WC2R 1LA

www.plutobooks.com

British Library Cataloguing in Publication Data
A catalogue record for this book is available from the British Library

ISBN  978 0 7453 4443 0   Hardback
ISBN  978 0 7453 4442 3   Paperback
ISBN  978 0 7453 4446 1   PDF
ISBN  978 0 7453 4444 7   EPUB

Typeset by Stanford DTP Services, Northampton, England

Simultaneously printed in the United Kingdom and United States of America

# Contents

# Acknowledgements

This book was written during the pandemic years of 2020 and 2021. As travel was restricted, we had to resort to a variety of venues and platforms to make meetings with our conversational partners possible. But we made it. Our warmest thanks go to Homi K. Bhabha, Brad Evans, Kate Evans, Simon Gikandi, Mohsin Hamid, Patrick Kingsley, Dina Nayeri, Gulwali Passarlay, and Daniel Trilling for stimulating conversations in person, on Zoom, via Voxer and email. Your generosity and interest in our project as well as your spot-on, thought-provoking contributions energised the writing process throughout.

Thank you also to Stine Lundgaard Schnor for efficiently transcribing all the conversations and for editorial assistance in getting the manuscript ready for submission – and to our engaged and enthusiastic students at Copenhagen University for their participation in our classes on refugee literature. We have learned a lot from you!

The Carlsberg Foundation awarded us a 'Semper Ardens' monograph fellowship in 2020 and funded the open access publication. We are truly grateful for the Foundation's support which allowed us time off from teaching so that we could devote all our energy to this book.

# Framing Crisis

The refugee crisis literally arrived on Europe's doorstep in 2015. In the late summer of that year, when long trails of people in flight walked along highways from south to north in search of safe haven, we were on our way back to Denmark from a conference in Germany. At a train stop close to Frankfurt, a group of Middle-Eastern men entered the crowded cabin, looked around in bewilderment and quickly made their way to other parts of the train. But one paused to point to a map on his mobile phone and ask in broken English to have the northward direction confirmed, and as he did so his ramshackle suitcase sprang open to reveal that there was nothing inside. The young man pretended to be a regular traveller but his empty luggage betrayed him. We exchanged brief glances, the suitcase was quickly closed and he moved on. This chance moment carried significance. He could not possibly register as a distant stranger – he was simply a young man in close proximity and in need of help on our 'home' turf. Yet everything about his demeanour suggested he was unsure if he would receive it. He appeared to have lost his place in the world and for a brief instant we witnessed it and were short of a response. It was an almost wordless encounter made anxious by a tellingly empty suitcase and a story we would never hear. In retrospect, it was the moment that began this book.

Even if the term 'refugee crisis' did not become common parlance in Europe until 2015 when a record number of 1.3 million people requested asylum within the EU – with the millions of the previous and subsequent years making it the largest population movement since World War II – it is nevertheless an overlooked fact that the European crisis is part of a much larger global crisis. Across the world, 83 million people are currently forcibly displaced and, among them, more than 26 million refugees are seeking international protection from life-threatening circumstances. The fact that 80 per cent of these refugees are hosted by the world's poorer nations puts the European crisis into perspective and begs the question why Europe, global numbers considered, has failed to respond to the local crisis in an apposite manner. The number of pending asylum applications in the EU is close to a million, with many asylum seekers confined to camps, reception or deportation centres where they are made to wait in limbo. With rejection rates ranging in some EU nations between 60 and 80 per cent, the prospects for life to begin again look bleak. Moreover, as is well known without having prompted responsible action, thousands of refugees have died on their clandestine journey to a continent whose outer borders are scrupulously patrolled to prevent them from entering. Human rights are frequently violated when unwanted asylum seekers are pushed back, now more forcefully than ever. Alexander Betts and Paul Collier observed already in 2018 that the 1951 Geneva Convention is 'silent on both where and with what resources refuge should be provided' (2018: 47) with the result that 'it is politics – and more specifically power – rather than law or principle that primarily determines who takes responsibility for refugees and on what basis' (47–8). This is still the case. Even if the EU officially declared in 2019 that the crisis is over, this is, in Daniel Trilling's succinct observation, merely a sign that 'the cameras have gone – but the suffering endures' (2018b). The numbers are still grim, camp situations continue to be devastating and the prospects of resettlement are limited. The refugee crisis is still ongoing.

This book, however, is not about numbers, statistics, rejection rates and EU or state politics. Rather, it is about our variegated cultural responses to people in need of protection. It is written against the backdrop of the current refugee crisis in Europe, but it also draws more generally on experiences of being, or responding to, refugees in previous moments of crisis when this will help shed light on recurring patterns in contemporary responses. *Refugee Talk* acts on the call that academics refrain from engaging with the refugee crisis from 'an arm's length' dispassionate perspective and provide instead 'a narrative of the "crisis" wherein the moral and ethical commitment to doing *something* lies not in the background but the forefront of the "story" we relay' (Sen, 2018: 102). As fellow human beings *and* as academics, we cannot *not* care about what is, in a very real sense, a crisis for refugees, but now increasingly evident as also 'humanity's crisis' (Evans and Bauman, 2016). In this book we are acutely aware that the very word 'crisis' needs to be properly unpacked. In the public debate it pushes the point that refugees have brought Europe into a state of crisis with less focus on the crisis that refugees experience in their encounter with an unwelcoming continent. In fact, 'crisis' is an immensely ambiguous word. Rather than proceed by consistently putting the term refugee crisis in scare quotes, we explore its ambiguity. It is thus pertinent to begin by recognising that the so-called refugee crisis is also a crisis in representation, of words and their meanings. As Neske Baerwaldt argues: 'When there is talk of crisis, we ought immediately to ask: Crisis for whom?' and when the dominant representation of the crisis conveys often indiscriminately 'the idea that "we" are being flooded by "them" [… then] an innocent We and a threatening Them are brought into existence' and this calls for attention, 'for it is precisely through such distortions that some forms of human life are positioned outside of society's sphere of empathy' (2018). Adding to this, Didier Fassin's point that the difference between asylum seeker and refugee 'is not just one of terminology or even status; it is a fundamental difference of recognition' (2016), this book needs to begin by considering definitions of 'refugee' and specify its own usage of the term. According to the 1951 Geneva Convention, a refugee is a person who:

> owing to well-founded fear of being persecuted for reasons of race, religion, nationality, membership of a particular social group or political opinion is outside the country of his nationality and is unable or, owing to such fear, unwilling to avail himself of the protection of that country; or who, not having a nationality and being outside the country of his former habitual residence as a result of such events, is unable, or owing to such fear, is unwilling to return to it. (UNHCR)

Designed to protect the millions of Europeans displaced during World War II or at the onset of the Cold War in the late 1940s, the Convention, even with the amendment of the 1967 Protocol, has since proved to be insufficient in coverage. It is, in Betts and

Collier's words, 'ever less appropriate for modern needs' (2018: 5). Not only is 'well-founded fear of being persecuted' sufficiently open to interpretation to facilitate rejection at state level, it is also contingent on documentation which, in William Maley's words, may be difficult to provide for refugees who 'often have to flee their homes without a neat portfolio of documents to establish their identities and circumstances' (2016: 32–3). As the European refugee crisis has brought to light, this means that the human rights of asylum seekers are often compromised. Maley therefore warns that '[t]he deeper threat to the 1951 Convention is that countries will profess loyalty to its provisions, but in practice either violate them or interpret them in a deliberately rigid or narrow fashion' (27). As the Convention has 'generated normative understandings of refugeehood that can be problematic for the inclusivity of similarly vulnerable persons [in the contemporary moment …] whose political and, above all, *existential* experiences of displacement render them similarly deprived of resources for "bare life"' (Ahmed and Madura in Oliver et al., 2019: 3–4), this has prompted the suggestion that in today's world 'other kinds of definition may be required to identify the classes of persons to whom moral responsibility may be owed' (Maley, 2016: 41). Alexander Betts is concerned with 'survival migration', a term that 'highlight[s] the situation of people whose own countries are unable or unwilling to ensure their most fundamental human rights and yet who fall outside the framework of the refugee regime' (2013: 5). With obvious reference to the shortcomings of the Geneva Convention, Betts proposes to substitute 'persecution' with the more comprehensive notion of 'existential threat' arguing that 'what matters is not privileging particular causes of movement but rather clearly identifying a threshold of fundamental rights which, when unavailable in a country of origin, requires that the international community allow people to cross an international border and receive access to temporary or permanent sanctuary' (5).

In Betts' view, '[r]efugees are one type of survival migrant, but many people who are not recognized as refugees also fall within the category' as they, too, have 'no access to a domestic remedy or solution' (5) to their existential plight and are forced to seek international protection as their 'last resort' (4). Following a similar line of inquiry, Andrew Shacknove has proposed that while persecution is 'an essential criterion of refugeehood' (1985: 275), it is but 'one manifestation of the absence of physical security' (279) and 'state protection of the citizen's basic needs' (277). For Shacknove, then, 'refugees are, in essence, persons whose basic needs are unprotected by their country of origin, who have no remaining recourse other than to seek international restitution of their needs' (277). While 'basic needs' are insufficiently defined in Shacknove's formulation, they do hinge on the contractual 'minimal relation' between nation and citizen of 'rights and duties ... the negation of which engenders refugees' (275). Both Betts' and Shacknove's interventions are based on international human rights and they speak directly into the current refugee crisis where a large number of asylum seekers are rejected precisely because environmental or survival refugees fall outside of the UN provision of protection. Just like an 'overly inclusive conception' of the refugee can admittedly become 'morally suspect' and 'financially exhaust relief programs' (Shacknove, 1985: 276), an overly narrow definition of eligibility can result in violations of basic human rights (Betts, 2013). But what stands, according to Betts and Collier, is the fact that the current refugee 'regime' is 'no longer fit for purpose', it evidently 'fails to engage adequately with contemporary challenges' (2018: 35) and '[t]he moment for a rethink is long overdue' (9).

Such a rethink remains an unresolved matter pending an international acknowledgement of the need for reform and wide-ranging political consensus to overcome the 'inertia, self-interest, and cynicism by which the status quo has been preserved' (Betts and Collier, 2018: 236). In the meantime, our contribution to a reformulation is to concede that 'refugee' is a sliding signifier that carries both legal, political and affective meanings and that this must be recognised. Our heuristic rather than legalistic employment of the term is therefore deliberate. We lean on the contributors in *Refugees Now* who employ the term as 'a generalized marker for statelessness and displacement' (Ahmed and Madura in Oliver et al., 2019: 3). Ahmed and Madura specify that such a formulation is not intended 'to ignore or undermine the particularities' (3) of UN legal definitions, but to address 'the full scope of statelessness as an existential, phenomenological, ethical, and, ultimately, *human* experience' (1). This underscores, we believe, the need for a more inclusive conception of the term 'refugee' as part of the rethink Betts and Collier call for. Our approach to the concept of refugee is to think of the term along both theoretical and experiential lines. Thus, we engage in the 'figure of the refugee' as a theoretical construct and the refugee as a lived reality albeit fully aware that this usage cannot always be maintained as distinct approaches and also that this may sometimes eclipse the gendered, generational, religious and ethnic diversity that is obviously part of such lived realities.

As book title *Refugee Talk* resonates with appropriate ambiguity because it is a commodious and elastic term that refers to a densely saturated discourse spanning everything from quotidian chats and public mediations of the ongoing crisis to serious socio-political theories and philosophical reflection. All such contexts pivot on the meaning-making power of language and it is important to stress the significance of this, especially when refugee talk is about people in precarious situations who regularly experience that they are being talked about, but rarely with. Jenny Erpenbeck writes that '[m]any concepts have suddenly become acute, as it were, and it might be worthwhile to consider their meaning once again from a fresh perspective' (2018b). Elif Shafak goes a step further. She diagnoses the present moment as a 'threshold moment' (2020: 26) profoundly marked by 'one term that frequently appears in our daily lives: crisis' (59). We are particularly concerned with what Shafak calls 'a crisis of meanings' (37): 'For far too long, in our social and political dealings', she writes, 'we have consulted the same old leather-bound dictionary' (37) and become so familiar with it 'that we no longer feel the need to look up rudimentary words' (37). But now heated opinions have turned 'the pages too fast' (37) and set some in flames. This dictionary, which in Shafak's poetic vision is also a collection of ideas and ideals, is now so 'badly scorched' that we must 'save what we can' and reconsider 'some of our fundamental concepts' (38). The latter is what we set out to do in this book.

The focus on discourse and representation is deeply embedded in our approach to the refugee crisis. In the following chapters we therefore distinguish between *vocabularies*, referring to the prevalent circulation of words and images (good and bad) used in representations of, and cultural responses to, refugees and the refugee crisis, and *lexicon*, referring to ideas and ideals (familiar but 'badly scorched') that are employed in representations and responses. Among them are humanity, responsibility, solidarity, and the value of recognition. These are, we contend, along the lines of Shafak's diagnosis of the present moment, indisputably terms in crisis and our ambition is to rehabilitate them. Accordingly, we both unpack antagonistic vocabularies and repack what we call *the refugee lexicon* so that we are better equipped to come to grips with the challenges of the current crisis and respond to them with informed understanding. This, too, is a long overdue project. We are, in short, particularly interested in 'cultural responses' as they index a reaction to the crisis and to the 'refugee talk' that is *also* an answer in its own right. These responses come in the shape of socio-political theory, media reportage, art and activism, and literary narratives. Since we privilege language and perception, aesthetics needs to be an integral part of *our* refugee talk. We approach a myriad of cultural responses, including detailed analysis of case studies, from a perspective that combines ethics and aesthetics with the political, broadly understood.

Nöelle McAfee rethinks the political in the context of the current refugee moment. Pursuing a 'more radically democratic politics', she advocates 'a new imaginary of politics that is not centered on the state or the usual apparati of power', but that 'attends to the kind of power that is created horizontally among people in association' (McAfee in Oliver et al., 2019: 35). Such a new imaginary 'sees the world in a way in which politics is not only what governments do but also what all involved and affected engage in' (35). This reorientation accords with Zygmunt Bauman's comment that global problems – a refugee crisis – cannot be solved on the local level. He insists: 'The integrity of the political body in its currently most common form of a nation-state is in trouble, and so an alternative legitimation is urgently needed and sought' (2012: 15). Bauman calls it a bewildering paradox that 'on the fast *globalizing* planet politics tends to be passionate and self-consciously *local*' (82). To think of human vulnerabilities in planetary terms, and to invoke a more inclusive political imaginary of mobility, also beckons a rethinking of ethics. Judith Butler's ethico-political project on precarity and solidarity in *Precarious Life* (2006) and *The Force of Nonviolence* (2020) is inspirational. According to Butler, precarity names 'a lived reality' and 'a politically induced condition in which certain populations suffer from failing social and economic networks of support more than others, and become differentially exposed to injury, violence and death' (Butler and Berbec, 2017). Our task is to 'maintain an obligation' to people who seem different from us (2017) and to recognise the 'ways in which our lives are profoundly implicated in the lives of others' (Butler, 2006: 7), locally and globally. Thinking beyond local contexts demands that we engage in a 'hearing beyond what we are able to hear' and open up to 'narration that decenters us from our supremacy, in both its right- and left-wing forms' (18).

Rethinking the political in such ethical ways asks us 'to critically evaluate and oppose the conditions under which certain human lives are more vulnerable than others, and thus certain human lives are more grievable than others' (30). In *The Force of Nonviolence* Butler develops her project on precarity with references to the current refugee crisis and is adamant that ethics and the political cannot be severed in questions that concern vulnerable lives. One issue Butler keeps returning to in 'a set of questions that belong to our time' is: 'What makes a life valuable?' (2020: 28). In order to answer this from the perspective of solidary we need 'to formulate an egalitarian imaginary' (28) of human reciprocity. Such a 'relational understanding of vulnerability shows that we are not altogether separable from the conditions that make our lives possible or impossible' (46). If we consider the current refugee crisis also to be humanity's crisis and remember 'that we inhabit the world together in relations of interdependency' (51), then this demands 'global obligations' that are 'post-national in character … since populations at the border or crossing the border (stateless people, refugees) are included in the larger network of interrelationships implied by global obligations' (47). Butler calls for 'a thoroughly *egalitarian approach to the preservation of life*' (56). She thus wants to contribute to 'the formulation of a political imaginary of the radical equality of grievability' (74), that is, of humanity. In Butler's argument, this stance is descriptive, since every life is grievable, and normative, since every life should be grievable (106). This radical 'politics of equality' (202) informs 'an egalitarian imaginary that apprehends the interdependency of lives [... and] in such a world, each life would deserve to be treated as the other's equal' (203). This normative thrust is indispensable to the exploration of what Evans and Bauman (2016) call 'a new humanism for the 21st century'.

Such rethinking of the political is poignant. We want to consider ethics, too, in a broad sense, as a means of opening up and inviting in ideas that are not bound up in any particular school of thought. Geoffrey Galt Harpham answers the question 'What is ethics?' by taking us into 'a history of debates' (1995: 395), since '[a]rticulating perplexity ... is what ethics is all about' (395). To Harpham, '[e]thics is the arena in which the claims of otherness – the moral law, the human other, cultural norms, the Good-itself, etc. – are articulated and negotiated' (394). Ethical inquiries ask two questions, pivoting on the 'one indispensable word in ethics, *ought*' (395): 'How ought one to live?' and 'What ought I to do?' (395). On this view, then, ethics is 'where thought itself experiences an obligation to form a relation with its other' (404). In *Refugee Talk*, we explore how cultural responses to the refugee crisis negotiate the otherness that the figure of the refugee conjures up concomitantly with the perplexity of how we ought to explore such responses, whether they take us into the arena of philosophy, media representations, art and activism or literary narratives.

Inspired by Emmanuel Levinas' comment that 'ethics is an optics' (1969: 23) and that ethics is 'an orientation and an attitude' (Madura in Oliver et al., 2019: 66), we also consider ethics in the all-encompassing sense of Simon Blackburn's 'ethical environment' consisting of a 'climate of ideas about how to live' (2003: 1), with idea understood as 'a tendency to accept routes of thought and feeling that we may not recognize in ourselves, or even be able to articulate' (3). Such an ethical environment 'shapes our emotional responses' and 'gives us ... our standards of behaviour' (1). As 'ethical animals' human beings 'grade and evaluate ... claim and justify' (4) and that explains why ethics can be 'disturbing' (7). Still, an ethical investigation is needed, however uncomfortable it may prove to be considering the fact that in refugee debates, ethics and politics tend to become separate domains. This book, then, is part of a larger ethical conversation, and although ethical conversations can be disturbing and we might feel that it is a good idea to stop, Blackburn insists that '[s]ometimes we shouldn't stop, and sometimes we cannot risk stopping' (25). In this conversation we do not assume that refugees are a homogeneous group of people in the same state of precarity. Nor do we speak on behalf of, but rather about and with refugees. We are deliberately out of our comfort zone in the writing of this book, reaching out beyond our own discipline in conversation with academics, artists, activists, reporters and writers who work with refugee issues or who have refugee experiences. Samples from our extensive conversations are integrated into the chapters as a conversational web, supplementing and challenging our own propositions – that is to say, our suggestions and ideas, typically formulated as arguments pursued in the subsequent chapters on the notions of humanity, responsibility, solidarity, recognition and, indeed, hope.

This conversational web traces a thinking-aloud process that does not intend to be conclusive, but rather tentative and thought-provoking. By assembling responses from significant participants in the refugee debate, we wish to highlight the dialogic nature of this book. We take our cue from Hannah Arendt's elaboration on thinking aloud as a 'quest for meaning' that 'demands a stop-and-think' (1978: 78). *Refugee Talk* is such an extended stop-and-think, where we wonder about what we *really* talk about when we talk about the refugee crisis. Thinking is a form of voiced conversation, between ourselves and with others, in the belief that the harvest of ideas to come from this will illuminate 'refugee talk'. Thinking aloud can unfreeze frozen concepts, a metaphor Arendt uses to describe the potentially destructive effect of thinking (171, 174): thinking is 'dangerous' (176) because the 'quest for meaning ... dissolves and examines anew all accepted doctrines and rules' (176). *Refugee Talk*, then, is an inconclusive conversation about the ongoing refugee crisis. Lyndsey Stonebridge explains that for Arendt, 'to think in dark times is not to retreat from the business of being human, but to discover new forms of humanity in dialogue with others' (2017: 21). Conversation allows for recognition of humanity across diversity and, arguably, is a good way of learning to think, as Arendt was wont to say, without banisters. As her biographer Elisabeth Young-Bruehl suggests, Arendt's moral philosophy is bound up in 'the dialogic, communicative thinking she wished to practice and hoped would be widely practiced in times of crisis' (2004: xxxi–xxxii). In the dark times of the ongoing refugee crisis such a practice is indispensable.

Zygmunt Bauman was also a proponent of the art of dialogue. As he argues: 'Whatever methods or techniques may happen to be applied in the conversation aimed at understanding, need and tend to emerge – as well as to be renegotiated and revised – in the course of that conversation' (2017: 115). This heightened understanding of the outcome of conversation is vital to how we think about the need to activate ethics, aesthetics and the political, broadly under-stood, in the current refugee debate. In this context, we have to reflect on the notion of listening, since there can be no conver-sation without listening. Karina Horsti has taken Tanja Dreher's notion of 'listening across difference' into the arena of the current refugee crisis in a persuasive gesture. Listening across difference signals 'a political process that is potentially difficult, conflictual and aimed at justice which sustains difference' (Dreher, 2009: 448). Such 'political listening' needs 'openness and receptivity' based on a 'shared responsibility to maintain connection and engagement' (449). Thus, 'the politics or ethics of "listening"', Dreher posits, 'foregrounds interaction, exchange and interdependence' (450). It is worth noting Horsti's comment that 'ethical listening' demands an awareness in those who listen to, and thus bear witness to the plight of others, of their own 'privileges and complicities' while maintaining an 'openness to recognizing the incompleteness and unsettledness that emerges in encounters across differences' (Horsti, 2019: 126). We are mindful of this as we go forward in an attempt to maintain 'a listening heart' and 'stand up for human solidarity, beyond all seeming borders of nationality and creed', as Jonathan Wittenberg writes in 'The Erased Person's Tale' (Herd and Pincus, 2019: 110).

Finally, in *Refugee Talk* we align ourselves with what Edward Said labels 'amateurism' – 'the desire to be moved [...] by] unquenchable interest in the larger picture, in making connections across lines and barriers, in refusing to be tied down to a speciality, in caring for ideas and values despite the restrictions of a profession' (1994: 57). In order to explore what we talk about when we talk about the refugee crisis we, too, are interested in 'the larger picture' and do not want our approach to be confined to our training as postcolonial literary scholars. As mentioned, we are concerned citizens as well as academics who worry that our profession fails to engage in the refugee crisis in a radically meaningful manner, either because of an embarrassment about privilege or because acting in solidarity is believed to involve an activist rather than academic agenda. Being concerned and worried, however, are strangely passive emotions. Working within the academy at a safe distance from the scenes of the refugee crisis, our engagement would seem of little value to people in crisis unless, that is, we give up on the 'arm's length' principle that seems to hallmark conventional scholarship. And so, we give up on that expectation. Said's amateur is somebody who breaks routine to move forward 'into something much more lively and radical' (62), a person who considers 'that to be a thinking and concerned member of a society one is entitled to raise moral issues at the heart of even the most technical and professionalized activity as it involves one's country, its power, its mode of interacting with its citizens as well as with other societies' (61). We want this book to engage in what Said terms the act of 'break[ing] down the stereotypes and reductive categories that are so limiting to human thought and communication' (x). *Refugee Talk*, then, comes from our combined perspectives of being actively engaged scholars and citizens. In this manner at least, it is the work of amateurs.

# 1
# Humanity – Ontology, Location and Migration

I chose to distinguish myself not as a refugee, like those festering in camps set up for the famished of Biafra or for displaced Palestinians, not like those who, since time immemorial, had escaped war, starvation, or extreme civil conflict. Nor did I want to cast myself in the prototypical role of migrant, the choice my grandparents had made when they craved a better life abroad. Buffeted by historical demons, akin though I might be to millions setting out unwillingly from a land they called their own, I grabbed hold of the one shred of agency I had extracted from the rubble of my existence and the catastrophe of my country, and decided I would henceforth be an exile, a term that, I thought, would preserve my dignity and freedom, and allow me to take my place in a romantic and heroic tradition. (Ariel Dorfman, 2020)

I was born a citizen and a human being. At four years of age I became something less than human, at least in the eyes of those who do not think of refugees as being human. (Viet Thanh Nguyen, 2018: 11)

A migrant is not only a word, not only news, not only a problem for society: a human being is lived behind this word. He has feelings, hopes for the future, and there are some people waiting for him to come back, and a family waiting for good news. (Babak in Godin et al., 2017: 126)

The epigraphs above speak to the complexities of becoming a refugee and of navigating the discursive territory of such a situation. In order to help us illuminate this experiential and relational situation, in this chapter we turn to theoretical interventions into what we call the refugee lexicon. Under the all-encompassing rubric of 'humanity' we propose that reflections on the indeterminate figure of the refugee involve a rethinking of personhood, of border systems and the idea of (fortress) Europe as well as reconsiderations of the centrality of migration to human history. Pursuing these contingent lines of inquiry, we want to think about four interventions as we unpack refugee personhood and what we term a refugee ontology, and as we question bordered Europe and migration broadly understood. Detailing our proposition, we ask to what extent thinkers studying refugees in the context of World War II can still be helpful in the different world of the contemporary refugee crisis? As postcolonial scholars, we also contemplate whether postcolonial criticism of established hegemonic ideas can be put to productive use in these new contexts. We begin by sketching a trajectory in thinking, from Hannah Arendt and Frantz Fanon writing in the 1950s and 1960s, to Zygmunt Bauman, Giorgio Agamben and Judith Butler, writing in the 1990s and early twenty-first century. This trajectory doubles as a history of ideas that seems vital to us considering the fact that the current crisis is flagged as 'humanity's crisis' (Evans and Bauman, 2016). Reading these thinkers together provides us with a theoretical platform to work from and their ideas inform our thinking and stimulate our reflections on the varied cultural responses to the refugee crisis in the subsequent chapters. We supplement our theoretical considerations with insights from literary texts that give life, as it were, to that which may seem abstract and divorced from lived reality, and with observations from participants in the current refugee debate. In this manner, we hope to achieve a nuanced understanding of the continued relevance of ideas about humanity – diachronically and synchronically presented – in order to engage in the ethical climate of our time and unload the vocabularies that undergird current discourses in which the figure of the refugee is both described *and* created.

## CONTEXTUALISING FRAMES:
## PERSONHOOD AND NEW HUMANISM

This section serves several functions. It provides a survey of central insights that characterise current refugee talk, especially amongst intellectuals. It gives us a context, too, for the refugee lexicon we explore throughout the book. The ideas discussed pivot on the notion of personhood – what Hannah Arendt calls 'the very nature of mankind' (2006: 268) – that has become topical again in the ongoing refugee crisis. In *Refugee Tales III*, David Herd outlines 'three kinds of contextualising frames' for an understanding of how the UK's hostile migration environment affects refugees (2019: 187). The first context is connected to Arendt's writing on totalitarianism and its violent effect on personhood. Indeed, to say that 'Arendt is trending' is an understatement (Stonebridge, 2017: 18). The refugee crisis beckons an explanatory framework, and Arendt is helpful in this context, because, in Stonebridge's words, 'Arendt was one of the first to understand that what looked like a refugee crisis in reality was a crisis for the political and moral authority of the European nation state, particularly for its historic claim to be the home of human rights' (2018: 4). Indeed, as Ned Curthoys insists, Arendt is 'a theorist of the present human condition and the ethical and epistemological challenges it poses to customary ways of thinking' (Curthoys in Cox et al., 2020: 39). A stateless refugee herself, Arendt knew what she was talking about. The fact that she wrote from personal experiences yet managed to transpose these into persuasive theoretical and historical tracts in order to think carefully about how events such as those affecting her life could happen is one reason why her writing is still profoundly illuminating. She was a thinker and a doer, an 'activist-intellectual' (Lee, 2011: 97), and like Frantz Fanon, with whom we will engage shortly, she was a believer in the sanctity of words *and* action. Still, according to Paul Mason's 'radical defence of the human being', reading Arendt is not enough (2019: 112) in the contemporary moment, and that is why we need to read her in company with other scholars.

Arendt was a stateless person for 18 years, without any political rights, yet, as her biographer Young-Bruehl writes, at that time she was also 'most active politically' (2004: 113). It is not surprising that her work evinces a preoccupation with the linked role of social, political and human rights. She ponders the experiences of being a stateless, displaced refugee and how such contingent phenomena are inextricably linked to the notion of the nation and the concept of humanity, or the human status. Statelessness, Arendt writes, reveals 'the crisis of the nation-state' (2007: 235), because stateless, disenfranchised and disgraced refugees are 'changing the demographic maps of Europe' (232–3) and 'break[ing] the old trinity of people-state-territory' (233). Refugees 'find themselves – politically, socially, and legally – in a constantly expanding vacuum' (233). In fact, as William Maley reminds us, 'refugees are products of the system of states, rather than threats to it', they are 'symptoms of a system of states that has failed to live up to its responsibilities' (2016: 11–12). Indeed, 'the modern refugee is the negative of the modern citizen', as Stonebridge succinctly puts it (Stonebridge in Cox et al., 2020: 15). Writing in 1944, Arendt claims that while the sheer number of refugees makes the right of asylum or naturalisation problematic, the 'greatest danger' faced by refugees is 'normalization' (2007: 234). And this problem will remain: 'The real obstacle to solving the problem of refugees and statelessness lies in the fact that it is simply unsolvable as long as peoples are organized within the old system of nation-states' (235). Thus, Arendt's insights speak to the ongoing business of rethinking the political.

In *The Origins of Totalitarianism* (1951) Arendt studies the problem of 'homelessness on an unprecedented scale, rootlessness on an unprecedented scale' in an 'unpredictable' future (2017: ix) through a sustained focus on statelessness that is directly relevant to what is going on in the twenty-first century. Statelessness entails a loss of what Arendt called 'the right to have rights' – 'to live in a framework where one is judged by one's action and opinions' (388) and 'the right of every individual to belong to humanity' (390). This is a right that should be guaranteed by the fact of being human. It is a right to a world – having a place in the world and not being rendered worldless – with world understood in the Arendtian sense of a socio-political relational community of fellow human beings. Thus, as Serena Parekh explains, when a refugee 'became stateless, she became "rightless" as well' (Parekh in Oliver et al., 2019: 149). The right to have rights is linked to agency and voice, that is, to the ability to initiate action and to be heard. It is also inextricably linked to dignity, a constitutive quality of what it means to be human for Arendt (see Morton, 2018: 225).

Agency and dignity are inherent in the human body even if this fact is often questioned in the typically hostile debate on refugees and the right to asylum. According to Homi K. Bhabha, even if dignity is a quality of worth qua human, it is also relational in a refugee context: 'dignity depends upon the acceptance of contingent quick changes in decisions about who I am, who I will be, who I might be', and this is definitory of the 'refugee condition' (Bhabha in Schulze-Engler et al., 2018: 711).

**In conversation, Homi K. Bhabha says:** However simple your language is for terms which you want to give a global significance, that language is involved in a complex cultural and linguistic process of translation. Seemingly simple terms, like dignity, are really not simple at all. They are the outcome of complex cultural and political negotiations and of translation, which in itself is a complex technology of meaning-creation. The problem with these simple terms is that they are fine on the page. They are great rallying cries. But in the realm in which they are truly significant, they have very little purchase. People think that there is a self-evident value in talking about human dignity. But is there a universal value here, if you consider the history of the claims made for human dignity on the one hand, and the attacks on human dignity on the other, even by those who understand that term? Dignity in the Universal Declaration of Human Rights is an inherentist value. But is dignity inherent in the human being? Dignity is, after all, a specific value that comes out of a Europeanised discourse. This notion that we are born with dignity is a convenient way of saying something. But I am not so persuaded, practically or philosophically, by this notion of inherent dignity. I understand why the Universal Declaration with its post-Holocaust history had to draft it like that. But I am beginning to think of dignity less as an ontological issue, the thing I am born with, the thing that defines my being, and more as an agential issue. This came to me from reading eyewitness reports on the critical issues of choice and judgment amongst refugees. For example, take a statement such as this one: I will take this boat to cross the Mediterranean although it is overloaded, although we do not have life jackets, although we know that those

17

who are taking us across might abandon us, although we know that somebody may attack this boat, and although I only have a slim hope of arriving at my destination and finding the good life, I will still take the risk. When I read such statements by refugees, I began to think that dignity is an act. It is a choice made under pressure. You show dignity through the choices you make. When you make a choice for the good life in a context where you think you will face death, then we can think of dignity as agency, not ontology. I have become more interested in questions of dignity as they relate to agential actions in critical moments of choice and risk. That does not mean that you have to be continually at risk in order to establish some concept of dignity. Dignity may well lie in the everyday or in a particular performance of duty, responsibility or hospitality. To me the question of dignity lies in a proleptic judgment: my act of dignity is now in the present, but it comes from thinking of the future and then bringing it back into the present. We do not have to get rid of dignity altogether, but perhaps we need to redefine it by moving from universality to temporality, and from embodiedness to actual agency.

Small wonder, then, that Arendt insists that 'rightless people' (2017: 385) experience a profound sense of not belonging, existentially *and* politically. They suffer a series of losses: their home and 'the impossibility of finding a new one' (384), government protection and 'the loss of legal status' (384) and loss of the 'relevance of speech' (388). Consequently, 'the calamity of the rightless' is that 'they do not belong to any community whatsoever' (386–7) – they are worldless. For Arendt, rightlessness and statelessness have 'two dimensions: a legal/political dimension and an ontological one' (Parekh in Oliver et al., 2019: 141) – and since statelessness is existential and political, it 'require[s] new forms of thinking and imagination' (Stonebridge, 2018: 4). Arendt demonstrates that making people placeless, stateless and rightless is how human beings can be rendered superfluous; how they can be expelled 'from humanity altogether' (2017: 388). That is why statelessness can be considered, in Parekh's words, 'a kind of ontological harm' (Parekh in Oliver et al., 2019: 142). The prime example of this is the totalitarian Nazi concentration camps. However, Arendt suggests that in non-totalitarian countries, too, there is a tendency to want to get rid of 'undesirable elements of all sorts' – such as refugees – 'who have become superfluous and bothersome' (2017: 583). Depriving such people of the right to have rights is tantamount to killing the juridical, moral and individual person in them (596) – thus their 'superfluity on an overcrowded earth' (599) is cemented. They become what Flannery O'Connor in the 1955 story 'The Displaced Person' calls 'the extra people in the world' (1971: 226), and thus not even deserving of the label human.

Another intellectual also much read at the moment is Frantz Fanon. Christopher J. Lee suggests that while Arendt addresses racism 'on a systematic scale' in *The Origins of Totalitarianism*, Fanon focuses on 'the individual experience' of racism in *Black Skin, White Masks* (2011: 101). Reading Arendt and Fanon together illuminates the thorny issue of personhood that is thrown into sharp relief in the current refugee crisis. In their 2016 discussion, Brad Evans asks Zygmunt Bauman if 'we perhaps need a new humanism for the 21st century?' (Evans and Bauman, 2016). We will return to this question at the end of this book. For now, suffice to say that although they do not mention Fanon, we want to bring him into the conversation. In *Black Skin, White Masks* Fanon explores what it feels like to be on the receiving end of racism. Being racialised means being reduced to an inferior object under the destructive gaze of the white man as a black body with 'a third-person consciousness' (1986: 110). All Fanon wants is 'to be a man among other men' (112), insisting on a human equality that demands a radical rethinking of personhood in the world of the 1950s, and today, as we see in the urgency of Black Lives Matter. Fanon, then, is encouraging us to address the 'massive psycho-existential complex' (14) of racism, that 'bankruptcy of man' (86), and to move towards an unspecified 'new humanism' (9). Such a new humanism is only possible if there is a 'healthy encounter between black and white' (80) because it relies on 'reciprocal recognition' (218). In a nutshell, we might say with Fanon that a new humanism demands nothing less that 'a restructuring of the world' (82).

**In conversation, Brad Evans says**: Frantz Fanon's *The Wretched of the Earth* is relevant to the world we live in. I want to focus on the idea of the victim. Fanon was trying to recognise the fact that victims exist. But we are in a different moment today. Now we see the over-determination and the over-representation of victims. In *Resilient Life* we argued that narratives of resilience flatten vulnerability, so that everybody is now vulnerable. The term does not have any resonance anymore. We have seen how the victim in recent times has been appropriated by power and used in order to sanction violence. Victims are constantly being overplayed by political regimes of power, especially in the context of the refugee crisis. From Fanon, then, there is this pivotal moment of how we imagine this triangulation between per-petrators, victims, and witnesses of violence.

An example of such radical restructuring Fanon traces in *The Wretched of the Earth*. After the 'cleansing force' (1990: 74) of a violent process of physical and psychological decolonisation, a new and more 'natural' existence is possible, 'introduced by new men, and with it a new language and a new humanity' (28). This is (still) utopian, yet also the kind of decolonisation that Europe is in dire need of, as we will see in Étienne Balibar's thoughts on the term 'Europe' below. Apart from an insistence on the equality of all human beings – 'a "new humanism" devoid of the racism of the colonial past' in Paul Mason's words (2019: 13) – and that such radical rethinking of personhood needs a new language to go with it, what constitutes this new humanism? Edward Said holds that 'Fanon himself scarcely provides his readers with ... a blueprint for the new ways he has in mind; his main purpose, however, is to indict Europe for having reduced human beings into a hierarchy of races ...' (2014: 21). Following Fanon, Mason insists that 'we need to revive our reflexes for utopian thinking' (2019: 250) and argues for what he brands 'a twenty-first century radical humanism' (210) that relies on 'the three-dimensional human being with a belief in restraint, kindness, mutual obligation and democracy; an army of individuals who can think independently and who mean what they say' (17). Mason insists that we need 'a narrative of hope' (262). But what exactly constitutes a narrative of hope? Certainly 'new humanism' sounds promising, but what does it signify? Perhaps the closest we get to an example of a utopian new humanism is Kelly Oliver's proposal for what she calls an 'Earth ethics', based not only on human rights and radical hospitality and responsibility, but also envisioned in obligations that are 'based on our common planetary home rather than on our national or individual homes' (Oliver in Oliver et al., 2019: 128). In fact, Zygmunt Bauman warns that now more than ever do we need to 'face up to the realities of the "one planet, one humanity" challenges of our times' (2017: 18). 'Humanity is in crisis – and there is no exit from that crisis other than the solidarity of humans', he insists (Evans and Bauman, 2016). It is evident, then, that Fanon's ideas about equality and humanism might still be utopian, but they are also inspirational. And they are still needed.

A third figure that features in intellectual responses to the current refugee crisis is Giorgio Agamben. His writing is preoccupied with the in-between: limit concepts, caesuras, lacunas, and aporias. This preoccupation has bearings on his ideas of personhood and human life, too. In *homo sacer*, Agamben modulates what we understand by the term 'life' via two Greek terms, *zoë*, meaning living, or the simple fact of common biological nature that unites all human beings in what he calls 'bare life', and *bios*, a distinct form of living, a culturally qualified socio-political life (1998: 1). Agamben claims that '[t]he fundamental categorical pair of Western politics is … bare life/political existence, *zoë/bios*, exclusion/inclusion' (8), and he zooms in on the limit figure he calls *homo sacer* (sacred man). This figure embodies bare life, or *zoë*, and is, strangely, a figure that cannot be sacrificed but may be killed without the killer being punished: 'the unpunishability of the killing and the exclusion from sacrifice' are the constitutive elements of this figure (81). Such a 'residual' – or surplus – being (100) is in fact a 'living dead man' (131). Agamben draws on Arendt's thoughts on refugees claiming that the refugee is a limit figure that marks a caesura between 'man and citizen, *nativity* and *nationality*' in her writing (131). Indeed, when Arendt talks about losing the right to have rights, she is gesturing towards the radical loss of what Agamben calls *bios*, or socio-political life. If human beings are divided into the politically marked life (*bios*) and the reduced state of bare life (*zoë*), which is excluded from the political, then these two states of being demand different socio-political responses. Agamben suggests that while humanitarianism 'can only grasp human life in the figure of bare or sacred life' and the rights of man (133), politics can only take seriously the rights of the citizen. This is important in connection with the 'concept of the refugee': refugee is a 'limit concept that radically calls into question the fundamental categories of the nation-states, from the birth-nation to the man-citizen link' and that clears the way 'for a long overdue renewal of categories in the service of a politics in which bare life is no longer separated and excepted, either in the state or in the figure of human rights' (134). Indeed, as Nando Sigona mentions, humanitarianism typically resorts to 'a vocabulary of trauma and vulnerability' when describing refugee conditions (Sigona in Fiddian-Qasmiyeh et al., 2014: 372). In Serena Parekh's words, refugees 'become *objects* of humanitarian aid, bodies to be cared for and protected', rather than 'political *subjects*' in their own right (Parekh in Oliver et al., 2019: 144). Here we see how ethics, politics and personhood become knotted together in ontologically harmful ways.

Agamben also explores how discussions of Nazi concentration camps confuse ethical and juridical categories (1999: 18), apparent in the *Muselmann*, or the Muslim, an example of the figure of *zoë/* bare life/*homo sacer*. This discussion has bearings on the current refugee crisis. Agamben quotes from the first study of *Muselmänner* (1987): 'Seeing them [*Muselmänner*] from afar, one had the impression of seeing Arabs praying' (43), and he writes about the *Muselmann's* 'disfigured face, his "Oriental" agony' which leads survivors to 'hesitate to attribute to him even the mere dignity of the living' (70). *Muselmänner* are seen as hollow husks, lost, and inhabiting 'the extreme threshold between life and death, the human and the inhuman' (47). The *Muselmann* is a shadowy phenomenon: a medical figure, an ethical category, a political limit, an anthropological concept, and an 'indefinite being' (48). Invoking Primo Levi, Agamben suggests that there is an 'impossible dialectic between the survivor and the *Muselmann*' or 'the human and the inhuman' (120). In *If This Is a Man*, Levi explains that *Muselmänner* are 'men in decay' (2013: 99), 'the drowned', 'an anonymous mass, continually renewed and always identical, of non-men ... already too empty to really suffer. One hesitates to call them living' (101). For Levi the *Muselmann* becomes 'all the evil of our time in one image' (101). If the *Muselmann* marks the moment when the human becomes inhuman, or subhuman, the figure illustrates what Agamben calls 'biopolitical caesuras' (1999: 84) – such figures are found along a 'biological continuum' that is aligned with human dignity: 'Thus the non-Aryan passes into the Jew, the Jew into the deportee ..., the deportee into the prisoner ..., until biopolitical caesuras reach their final limit in the camp. This limit is the *Muselmann*. ... Beyond the *Muselmann* lies only the gas chamber' (85).

Reading these icy comments in the context of the current refugee crisis is problematic, even if thought-provoking and, possibly, illuminating. They need careful nuancing. Stephen Morton discusses 'the problems with Agamben's universalizing use of the masculine form *homo sacer* to describe all human life' (2018: 226). To Homi K. Bhabha, conflating the refugee and the *Muselmann* disregards refugee agency expressed through action and risk (2018). In connection with 'the modern global refugee crisis', Sabeen Ahmed critiques how Agamben's '*homo sacer* is incapable of typifying the modern refugee – a subject who urgently demands attention but is often overlooked in political theories that take World War II as the exemplary context of refugee analysis' (Ahmed in Oliver et al., 2019: 153–4). Ahmed is critical of how this figure, so connected to 'a particular political and historical moment' (154), is universalised in a way that exposes the 'unacknowledged Eurocentrism undergirding much of contemporary political philosophy' (154). She draws attention to the problematic running together of refugee, *homo sacer* and *Muselmann* and to the use of the *Muselmann* outside of the context of the Holocaust: 'Agamben simply fails to either philosophically or politically distinguish between or associate the *Muselmann* and the refugee; instead, *both* figures, once ontologically elevated over their historico-material contexts, come to characterize *homo sacer*' (159). Such a failure indicates how we Europeans stick with a familiar theoretical framework whose primary 'ethico-political significance [is] placed on *European* bodies' and whose interest in the current crisis only escalated 'after the influx of stateless attempting to migrate to *Europe*' (165). Critical attention to the fact that the bodies now fleeing to Europe are primarily *Black* or *Brown* and Muslim is missing. That is one reason why there is so much talk of a *European* refugee crisis in Europe. Judith Butler's thoughts on grievability also belong in this conversation with thinkers on the broad notion of personhood and the human. In *Precarious Life*, Butler engages with the 'question of the human' and asks 'Who counts as human? Whose lives count as lives? … What makes for a grievable life?' (2006: 20). These are mind-blowing questions. We might ask, together with Butler, how does the term 'human' work, what does it foreclose and what does it open up (89)? Butler points out that 'some lives are grievable, and others are not; the differential allocation of grievability that decides what kind of subject is and must be grieved, and which kind of subject must not, operates to produce and maintain certain exclusionary conceptions of who is normatively human: what counts as a liveable life and a grievable death' (xiv–xv). In *The Force of Nonviolence*, Butler suggests that '[t]o be grievable is to be interpellated in such a way that you know your life matters; that the loss of your life world matters' (2020: 59). If you are not grieved, you are 'socially dead' (59). With specific reference to the current refugee crisis, Butler also takes issue with Agamben's notion of 'bare life'. She writes that refugees 'amassed along the borders of Europe' (193) cannot be understood as 'bare life'. Instead,

> they are … in a terrible situation: improvising forms of sociality, using cell phones, plotting and taking action when it is possible, drawing maps, learning languages, though in so many instances those activities are not always possible. Even as agency is blocked at every turn, there still remains ways of resisting that very blockage. … When they do make demands for papers, for movement, for entry, they are not precisely overcoming their vulnerability – they are *demonstrating it*, and *demonstrating with it*. (2020: 193–4)

These comments are useful in their ability to help unfreeze frozen notions, to use Arendt's poetic vocabulary that we have already referenced. Butler draws attention to the notion of agency in connection with refugees, and to the potential power of social networks. Refugees are not reduceable to 'bare life' deprived of agency, dignity and sense of their own situation in a globalised and interconnected world. If there is one thing the current refugee crisis demonstrates it is precisely the ambivalent on-off recognition of agency that accompanies the movement-stasis or stop-and-start experiences of mobility and the lasting-temporariness of a future paused. Agency is undoubtedly central to personhood, but it is also clear that for some observers, refugees are considered beings without agency, while for others, refugee demands speak directly to an expression of agency. Perhaps agency is central to refugee experiences? Lev Golinkin, who came to the US as a child refugee from Ukraine, indicates the complexity of agency in ways that might help open this idea up for discussion: 'Once you've made the transition from When are we eating? to When are they feeding us? you know you're a refugee' (Golinkin in Nguyen, 2018: 69).

Martin Gottwald unpacks the concepts of 'burden sharing' and 'responsibility sharing' in ways that link humanitarianism to the question of refugee agency. While states that host large numbers of refugees prefer the term 'burden sharing', humanitarian organisations favour 'a more positive image of refugees and a stronger framework for international cooperation, and prefer the term "responsibility sharing"' (Gottwald in Fiddian-Qasmiyeh et al., 2014: 525). The concept 'burden' suggests a dehumanising and objectifying view of refugees that does not fit with an ethically sustainable humanitarian approach to refugees as individual human beings in need. Humanitarianism can be defined as 'the attempt to alleviate the suffering of distant strangers', Michael Barnett writes (Barnett in Fiddian-Qasmiyeh et al., 2014: 243); it is 'dedicated to preserving and protecting human life' (242). Humanitarian action is 'nestled in discourses of compassion, responsibility, and care' and adheres to the belief that any community 'has obligations to its weakest members' (243). In his exploration of 'the intertwined history of the international refugee regime and the international humanitarian order', Barnett has discovered that 'humanitarianism helped to create a global concern for refugees, and refugees helped to create contemporary humanitarianism' (241–2). After World War II, 'humanitarianism and refugees entered into an increasingly co-dependent relationship' (246). Concomitantly, the UNHCR gradually became more involved in politics and took on a more activist role, 'expanding who it wanted to help, how it wanted to help, and where it wanted to help' (249). Forming what Barnett terms 'a mutual aid society', he reaches the thought-provoking conclusion that '[r]efugees have been good for humanitarianism, and humanitarianism has been good for refugees' (251). But this insight still leaves the troubling question of why it is so difficult to get humanitarian action right. Why do humanitarian acts tend to compromise the sense of agency and choice in the person on the receiving end? The charity Choose Love (https://choose.love/), for example, insists that it is all about 'putting love into action.' Yet in Annie Holmes' story 'Paradise,' the refugee Muhib, stuck in the Calais Jungle and exposed to love in action, explains: 'All volunteers go. And you leave us here in the Jungle, thinking about you, missing you. It's painful', he says, 'so please don't love us so much' (Popoola and Holmes, 2016: 85). Muhib is not in a position to choose *not* to be loved. This is the conundrum of humanitarian acts that put love into action. In order to explore such observations, we now want to get to grips with what we call a refugee ontology.

## A REFUGEE ONTOLOGY:
## BEING – OR BECOMING – A REFUGEE

In *The Sympathizer*, Viet Thanh Nguyen sees Vietnamese refugees as a 'mess of humanity', 'a new kind of species': 'It was so unique that Western media had given it a new name, the *boat people.* ... Depending on one's point of view, these boat people were either runaways from home or orphaned by their country' (2015: 151). The definition of refugee is inevitably contextual. The category 'boat people' effectively lumps individuals together in an image that is unforgettable, and also arguably relatable to the current refugee crisis. In *Voices from the 'Jungle'*, Godin et al. explain that '[t]here is no singular refugee experience or journey' but there are 'common tropes' to be found in refugee accounts (2017: 105). The countries left and the routes taken by refugees are so manifold that a singular label such a 'boat people' cannot work. This fact affects a refugee ontology, the stories that refugees tell and the stories told about them. As such an ontology will demonstrate, however, the refugee is a figure that disturbs and upsets established categories of human rights and moral duties, and it does so in different ways. Refugees typically exist in what David Farrier calls a relationship of 'inclusive exclusion' in connection with the host nation (2011). A refugee ontology also entails a reconsideration of dignity and agency, because 'refugees are people faced with impossible choices' (Loescher, 2021: 82). 'One central but often overlooked fact in refugee debates is the degree of agency and control that the migrant has over his journey' (Tinti and Reitano, 2018: 52). As we have already suggested, agency disturbs the cemented idea that the refugee is a passive victim and an object of suffering. In fact, Daniel Trilling holds that 'being a refugee means *not* doing what you're told' (2018a: 259, our italics).

Linked to agency and control are the intertwined notions of *being* or *becoming* a refugee. Is refugee an identity (a matter of being) or is it an attribute of a pluralised identity (a matter of becoming)? The term 'refugee' is typically mobilised as a temporary label. Some participants in the refugee debate explain what it feels like to *become* a refugee, while others are concerned with what it feels like to *be* a refugee. There is also the problem of whether we talk about *what* a refugee is (a *category* of person) or *who* a refugee is (a person, an individual). If 'refugee' is considered a temporary label, then it is enmeshed not only in dignity, agency and choice *but also* in temporality. In Layla AlAmmar's *Silence Is a Sense* (2021), her Syrian refugee protagonist, a trained linguist, muses on the etymology of the term 'refugee', resourcing Latin: '*re-*"back" and *fugere* "flee". ... If *recall* and *recollect* mean to "call" and "collect" again, does *refugee* contain within it, hidden and folded in a dead language, the notion of perpetual feeling?' (2021: 79). The etymological 'haunting' within the term 'refugee' needs to be kept in mind as we continue to ponder on a refugee ontology and on whether one can ever be a former refugee.

In 'The Dancer's Tale' Lisa Appignanesi showcases such intricacy:

Refugees are a multiplicity of individuals, ordinary and extraordinary, wrenched by circumstances from homes that have become uninhabitable, tossed about in the endless paperwork that nation states engender – ever more so in the age of the computer that proliferates quantifiable categories but has little place for the complexities of the human heart. (Herd and Pincus, 2019: 86)

The category of refugee – 'an impossible aporetic subject' (Oliver in Oliver et al., 2019: 117) – is now more complex than ever. Josh Cohen tries to come to grips with the phrase 'destitute asylum seekers', another category of refugee, in 'The Support Worker's Tale' that takes us beyond the obvious material deprivation, because it is really about:

> the destitution of the whole self. It means being *in* but not *of* the world. ... If no one sells you a pint of milk, or nods good morning or smiles or banters or flirts or asks you directions or if you want to come for a drink, who are you? ... Try to imagine it. You'd wonder if you existed at all. While feeling you exist too much, like there's no space to accommodate the burden of you. (Herd and Pincus, 2017: 74)

The burdensome existential situation of 'being in but not of' a place is also evoked, albeit differently, by the philosopher Simon May. From the unusual position of being 'a hereditary refugee', a person who lives 'as a refugee in the country of [his] birth ... instructed never to arrive anywhere' (2021: 2), May extrapolates on the sacred duty of a refugee:

> never allow yourself to arrive. Contribute everything in your power to your host country, in order to say thank you and to be accepted; be unflinchingly patriotic; support its institutions, and even be pillars of those institutions; but do not succumb to its inner life. Be fully in your new home, but never of it. (2021: 18)

To be physically in the country but spiritually of another speaks to a radical psychic tear. Such a 'sacred duty' sits next to other duties imposed on refugees and the children of refugees, for example, the duty to remember that we will detail in Chapter 4.

Depending on perspective, then, the figure of the refugee is signified in surprisingly different ways. Lawyers define refugees differently from philosophers, literary critics, the person in the street or refugees themselves: 'We are a bunch of ordinary humans locked up simply for seeking refuge', Behrouz Boochani sighs in *No Friend but the Mountains* (2019: 124), indicating, from the experiential position of being confined in a refugee camp, that a refugee is a human being looking for safety but finding that the etymological meaning of refuge as 'shelter' has morphed into that of 'camp' and 'confinement'. Yet, as William Maley observes, refugees, 'especially those in flight, may be almost wholly preoccupied with surviving on a day-to-day basis ... and have little time for voicing their concerns about wider policy' (2016: 148). However, if the question 'What is a refugee?' is one of the pivotal questions of our age, we need a refined answer that eschews lazy closure.

Simon Gikandi posits that for Arendt and Edward Said the central figures of the previous century were 'the figures of the refugee and exile' (2010: 27). Defining refugee and exile from personal perspectives, Arendt and Said tend to use the plural 'we' when diagnosing their condition, and this 'we' can be regarded, Peg Birmingham suggests, as having 'the status of both displacement and place, of both identities and nonidentities' (Birmingham in Oliver et al., 2019: 111). That 'we' of course also 'registers the difficulty of speaking, as a refugee, on behalf of refugees' (Rose in Cox et al., 2020: 52), alerting us to the ethics and politics of representation. Arendt claims that with 'us', Jewish refugees of World War II, the meaning of the term has undergone a profound change. To her, refugees are 'those of us who have been so unfortunate as to arrive in a new country without means and have to be helped by Refugee Committees' (1994: 110). Refugees are 'the kind [of human beings] that are put in concentration camps by their foes and in internment camps by their friends' (111), whose defining experience of being a refugee is loss. In *The Origins of Totalitarianism* (1951) Arendt adds another loss to those of home, occupation and language, namely, 'the loss of government protection' which implies 'the loss of legal status' (2017: 384). Rightless people consequently have lost all kinds of community – and this is important, because the 'right to have rights' means 'to live in a framework where one is judged by one's actions and opinions', that one has a right 'to belong to some kind of organised community' (388) and, most importantly, that one has 'the right of every individual to belong to humanity' (388). The defining characteristic of the figure of the refugee, then, is loss – even the loss of privacy: after a 'rupture of our private lives' (1994: 110), Arendt posits, the identity of a refugee changes with such a frequency 'that nobody can find out who we actually are' (116). Refugees are perceived as 'strange beings' (118), met with suspicion and fear.

Edward Said, too, approaches the refugee from an experiential perspective in his reflections on the figure of the exile. Exile is 'an essential sadness', 'a crippling sorrow of estrangement', and a state that marks 'the unhealable rift between ... the self and its true home' (2000: 180). Responding to the notion that the twentieth century is 'the age of the refugee', Said runs together exile, expatriate, émigré, refugee, displaced person and immigrant, even if he gestures towards a problem in doing so: 'Although it is true anyone prevented from returning home is an exile, some distinctions can be made among exiles, refugees, expatriates, and émigrés', arguing that in contrast to how exile 'originated in the age-old practice of banishment', refugees 'are a creation of the twentieth century state' (186). The term refugee has become 'a political one' and it connotes 'large herds of innocent and bewildered people requiring urgent international assistance', in contrast to the term exile, which suggests 'solitude and spirituality' (187).

The idea that the political term 'refugee' conjures up unnamed masses in need of humanitarian assistance and rescue has become a familiar trope in cultural responses to the current refugee crisis, and it is one that Agamben has addressed. His own response to Arendt's essay is also entitled 'We Refugees'. The refugee names 'a mass phenomenon' rather than an individual (1995: 115) and the label 'refugee' must always 'be considered a temporary position that should lead to either naturalisation or to repatriation' (116). Agamben describes how the rightless refugee has become the only 'imaginable figure' in which we can perceive the 'forms and limits of a political community to come' (114), a community that does not centre on the nation and the citizen but rather on refugium for the individual. There is a paradox here: the figure that has embodied human rights more than any other – namely, the refugee – marks 'the radical crisis of the concept' (116). In fact, the refugee is 'a disquieting element' that unhinges 'the old trinity of state/nation/territory' because he or she breaks up 'the identity between man and citizen, between nativity and nationality' – and paradoxically, Agamben writes, such a marginal figure should be seen as 'the central figure of our political history' (117). The refugee is thus a 'border concept' (117). To Lyndsey Stonebridge, refugees open up a space that is simultaneously 'historical, political, and imaginative' 'for thinking and being *between* states' (2018: 19, our italics). This observation takes the idea of the category of refugee as a limit concept literally and rethinks the individual refugee as a person who forces us all to think politically and ethically outside or in-between already established institutions. As Trilling reminds us, we 'do not have to let [our] thinking be limited by the categories that currently exist' (2018a: 260). Because of the paradoxical centrality of the refugee we should, Agamben holds, 'build our political philosophy anew starting from the one and only figure of the refugee' (1995: 90). Indeed, Stonebridge argues that the 'modern' refugee's history 'is also the history of the changing meanings of political and national citizenship' (2018: 2). Small wonder that 'the consequences of what is in reality not a refugee crisis, but a crisis of moral and political citizenship, are dire – for everyone' (viii).

The figure of the refugee, then, is caught up in territory *and* in temporality in knotty ways that have bearings on the situation of non-refugees. Bauman, himself of refugee background, explains that refugees find themselves 'in a double bind', 'expelled by force or frightened into fleeing out of their native countries, but refused entry into any other' (2004: 138). And this expulsion signifies an ontological loss: refugees 'lose place on earth, they are catapulted into a nowhere' (13), such as camps and detention centres. In this way they become 'the epitome of that extraterritoriality where the roots of the present-day *precarité* of the human condition, that foremost of present-day human fears and anxieties, are sunk' (139). In this 'nowhere' refugees find themselves in a 'new "permanently temporary" location' where, paradoxically, they are 'neither settled nor "on the move", neither sedentary nor nomadic' (141). They are stuck in 'a "frozen transience"', in lasting temporariness that consists of waiting and waiting, as if somebody has pressed the pause button on life. Thus, they become zombies whose 'old identities survive mostly as ghosts' (146), Bauman suggests, embodying Jacques Derrida's 'undecidables', suspended in a position where they are untouchable and unthinkable: 'In a world filled to the brim with imagined communities, they are *unimaginables*' (141).

To Bauman, refugees are also seen to embody 'human waste' that has no 'useful function to play in the land of their arrival and temporary stay' (2012: 41). As the embodiment of human waste, refugees lose 'individualities' and 'idiosyncrasies' because 'waste has no need of fine distinctions and subtle nuances' (41). The dreadful category of 'human waste' speaks directly to Butler's questions, already discussed, of what makes lives grievable and to a profound lack of the radical egalitarian imaginary that she calls for. It also indicates a contempt for life, those lives that are seen as not even worthy of the label human. Brad Evans and Henry Giroux explain that we can understand the term 'wasted life' as 'both a provocative intervention and a precise meditation on the scripting of human life by exploitative regimes of contemporary power' (2015: 47). They also see the term as a 'rallying cry both to expand the notion of critique and to recognize the urgency of rethinking politics beyond a neoliberal framework' (47). The category of 'human waste' has become integral to the kind of refugee talk that simultaneously describes *and* critiques current responses to the refugee crisis, even as it is also used as a label attached to a specific part of humanity.

Experiences of waiting are central to being (or becoming) a refugee. As Gil Loescher reminds us: 'The average duration of a refugee situation is now twenty years' (2021: 44). Waiting thus indexes a complex temporality and is defined in strikingly different ways by commentators. Homi K. Bhabha elaborates on what he calls the 'politics of waiting' that he sees 'not as a passive condition' but rather as 'the anxiety of anticipation played out in the living hell of [the dialectic] of natality/fatality' with refugees 'caught in the anticipatory anxiety of waiting: *waiting* to leave, *waiting* to be caught by the police, *waiting* to have their testimony questioned, *waiting* for the legal documentation to come through, *waiting* for acceptance, *waiting* to make a new life' (Bhabha in Schulze-Engler et al., 2018: 710). Waiting is a constitutive element of being a refugee. If, as David Owen suggests, we are currently seeing a shift away from dignity and towards suffering in attitudes to refugees and that this attitude is coupled with the notion that asylum is a favour rather than a right, then the outcome of such a shift is a politics of rescue rather than a politics of dignity (Owen in Oliver et al., 2019: 19). The refugee, on this view, is somebody who *waits to be rescued*. The consequences of a politics of rescue are expectations of gratitude: if we have rescued suffering refugees we expect gratitude in return. 'This demand for gratitude', Owen explains, is a 'demand for and an affirmation of indignity' (24). Furthermore, 'normative assumptions that lie behind the expectation of gratitude', Carolina Moulin argues, 'are based on a supposed tension between two fundamental rights: freedom and protection' (2012: 54). If you want to be free, you cannot be rescued or protected, because this logic presupposes that if you want to be protected you have to give up your freedom. Such a tension names an aporia that is connected to 'the logic of gratitude' – there is a clash between the search for 'freedom and dignity' (58), on the one hand, and the need for rescue and protection, on the other. The logic of gratitude sees protection as a gift (60) – or a favour – offered the refugee for which the giver, or host nation, expects gratitude in return. Obviously, as Moulin writes, the logic of gratitude 'depends on important power relations and social hierarchies' (62). If the refugee insists on the 'right to have rights' and is perceived as an ungrateful subject, then that refugee behaves in a way that problematises contemporary humanitarian responses. While the refugee may see 'freedom and protection' as 'two sides of the same coin' (67), the receiving nation does not. Again, you cannot be free and demand protection at the same time. And protection is bound up in experiences of waiting, and waiting to be rescued.

Waiting, however, is a word that is more complex than a denotative dictionary definition suggests. Iranian-born 'former' refugee Dina Nayeri, for one, unpacks 'waiting' in an unexpected way in *The Ungrateful Refugee*: 'Limbo', she writes, is 'the itch to make life happen' (2019: 117). Thinking back to her own years of waiting, she elaborates on this obsession, as she calls it, considering the expansive connotations of waiting that are possibly personal and

33

idiosyncratic, but nonetheless thought-provokingly relevant for a refugee ontology. Waiting is agony for those who are made to wait, since it feels like an insult (118). Why are you made to wait, to feel powerless, and for how long? Yet while you wait you can keep 'your instinct for joy' (118) and make friends, form communities and maintain hope for a better life. If you decide not to wait or if you rebel against waiting – as her mother does, when they are placed in an Italian refugee camp, by working and exploring the neighbourhood as a tourist would – you commit the sin called ingratitude, because such acts imply choice and agency, which of course suggests that you have the power to initiate action yourself. Your refusal to be a grateful subject who passively waits for rescue or for something to happen to you is seen as a rebellion that not only upsets the logic of gratitude, it also signals the refugee's claim that freedom and protection are indeed two sides of the same coin.

**In conversation, Dina Nayeri says**: What is interesting about waiting is that it feels as though the world around you has come to a halt and it expects you as a complex human being also to stop, but you cannot. You constantly bounce back and forth between feelings of urgency and feelings of life being over, wanting to do something, to create drama, to create stories and then despairing at life altogether. Refugee waiting is a very specific kind of waiting. No one else is asked to put their whole life and identity on hold for a year or two or even longer. In *The Ungrateful Refugee* I wanted to reframe waiting as something universal. I wanted to link the kind of extreme waiting refugees experience to the kind of waiting that we all experience, when we are in someone else's hand. I think it is important to connect this general experience to the refugee experience of waiting so that maybe people can feel some empathy. One positive side effect of the Covid-19 pandemic is that everyone got to experience some small version of what it is like just to wait and not be able to go on with life exactly as it was before. Perhaps people can make a connection now, and begin to understand what a psychological burden it is for refugees who go through that waiting all the time.

HUMANITY – ONTOLOGY, LOCATION AND MIGRATION

The politics of waiting also affects how Hubert Moore addresses waiting with refugees in 'The Visitor's Tale':

> Visiting detainees brings … you face-to-face with waiting. Not waiting to get in for a visit, that's nothing. It's waiting with. If people are in prison, they have a date for release to live for; if they are in detention, they have no date to live for. They're waiting for whenever. And you're sitting, waiting with them. (Herd and Pincus, 2016: 47)

The unnamed protagonist of Valeria Luiselli's autofiction *Lost Children Archive* pinpoints the notion of waiting, too, when she ponders the complexities involved in answering her daughter's innocuous question, 'What does "refugee" mean, Mama?' (2019: 47). In a self-reflective passage, the mother thinks to herself that:

> A refugee is someone who has already arrived somewhere, in a foreign land, but must wait for an infinite time before actually, fully having arrived. Refugees wait in detention centers, shelters or camps … They wait in long lines for lunch … They wait to be let out … They wait … They wait … They wait … They wait for dignity to be restored. … A child refugee is someone who waits. But instead, I tell her that a refugee is someone who has to find a new home. (2019: 47–8)

Later in the novel, when she overhears her children talking about young refugees as 'lost children', she contemplates that refugees are indeed lost children, '[t]hey are children who have lost the right to a childhood' (75), a right often overshadowed by discussions of seemingly more important rights.

Postcolonial critic Robert Young's insights are also helpful in this book's queries into a refugee ontology attuned to twenty-first century experiences. He writes about 'the politics of invisibility and unreadability' (2012: 22) as an example of postcolonialism's 'unfinished business' (21), positing refugees as 'a new subaltern' whose precarious presence in the West speaks directly to the 'fault lines between the visible and the invisible' (23). Such 'invisible migrants', he writes, 'only move into visibility' (26) when they die in spectacular ways or suddenly appear in vast numbers as we saw in the summer of 2015, when refugees trekked north on European motorways towards safety in Sweden. In the novel *Refuge*, Nayeri portrays how the character Mam'mad – a long-term Iranian refugee in Amsterdam with 'no status, no travel documents, no future' (2017: 222) – sets himself on fire: 'I am here! Mam'mad cried out in his final act', 'burning to be seen' (223), attesting to the visible-invisible conundrum of the status of refugees in the imagination of the host nation. Emma Jane Kirby's reluctant hero in *The Optician of Lampedusa* also succinctly illustrates the visible-invisibility of refugees: 'I saw them every day and yet I did not see them. I did not reach out. Not until that day on the sea when I was confronted for the first time in my life with so many people in great need ... did I stretch out my hand' (2016: 115). Finally, Viet Than Nguyen describes the same conundrum: 'The other exists in a contradiction, or perhaps a paradox, being either invisible or hypervisible, but rarely just visible' (2018: 15) – seldom allowed to be just an ordinary human being. Contemporary refugees, Young holds, are still considered 'surplus', 'redundant', and destined for a life 'waiting for a future that may never come' (2012: 27), pointing not only to the ongoing dehumanisation of refugees, but also to the central questions of disrupted temporality and (in)visibility that an investigation into a refugee ontology must be attentive to. Scholars with a personal refugee history, such as Anna Gotlib, tend to foreground the harm caused by the liminal position of refugees. She proposes that this harm:

> might be a part of what it means to be a refugee in that they are 'systematically' rather than accidentally or inadvertently invisible and inaudible. They are no longer citizens or indeed rightful claim makers of the homes they left behind, but neither are they in a position to make rights claims (or, in fact, any claims) against a new location that has not accepted them as asylum seekers. In refugee camps ... refugees remain in the in-between, between two doors that remain, in all the ways that matter, firmly shut. (Gotlib in Oliver et al., 2019: 242)

This sense of exclusion often lingers after entry has been 'granted', since 'in exchange for safe harbour, their identity-constituting stories are forced into the service of the socio-political, economic and normative needs of host societies' (242). In this way, refugees still wait for recognition of their full and equal humanity.

The figure of the refugee is, as demonstrated above, a radically contingent category – it is relational, situational and contextual. A refugee's existence affects how we non-refugees consider our own humanity, too. Arendt's lesson that 'compassionate solidarity can turn thinking into political action' (Stonebridge, 2017: 21) resonates in the world today, in particular when refugees of past crises are moved by 'the courage of the current generations of refugees … in refusing to be a mere canvas for powerful others' (Gotlib in Oliver et al., 2019: 253). Gotlib reaches out in solidarity and recognition of the fact that despite a long passage of time, 'one is never really a "former" refugee' (253).

We see examples of a similar ethical environment of solidarity in the British 'Refugenes' project that celebrates a refugee heritage (playing with the fanciful idea that 'refugenes' are somehow coded in your DNA) by having well-known British people come forward with their families' refugee stories to 'show that refugees of the past have become the fabric of British society today'. Similarly, the contributions to Viet Thanh Nguyen's The Displaced (2018) can be read as acts of refugee solidarity across time and space. Here we can read how Ukrainian Marina Lewycka, born in a refugee camp in Germany, comments on the difference between Britain in the past and now, where 'the rising volume of anti-immigrant anti-refugee rhetoric in the popular press in the twenty-first century' calls for gestures of solidarity (Lewycka in Nguyen, 2018: 123). We can also contemplate how Vietnamese-born Vu Tran, with the onset of the current crisis, has begun to think of himself again as a refugee. For him, the question 'What is a refugee?' is too simple. It must be rephrased 'What is a refugee like – not only to those who see her but to the refugee herself?' (Tran in Nguyen, 2018; 152). In lieu of an answer, Tran provides us with a list· a refugee is like an orphan who has lost homeland and extended family; she is like an actor, since she must perform assimilation possibly in a new language; and she is like a ghost: 'If she is seen, she might very well be seen through, a spectre both present and distant' (154). Indeed, the refugee resides 'in the space between what is real and imaginary' and it is the 'ghost-like contours of a refugee' (155) that Tran notices in the current refugee crisis. Reflecting on a refugee ontology, then, suggests that the defining experience of being or becoming a refugee is traumatic and complex loss, in which hope is twisted together with bouts of uncertain waiting for a future that can start now, tomorrow or perhaps never.

## 'FORTRESS' EUROPE: IDEAS AND IDEALS

So far, we have established that the refugee is a disturbing limit figure that wrests open the trinity of people-state-territory, and that sits uneasily within a framework that relies on nation and national citizenship. Daniel Trilling calls this the 'paradox of the modern world' – 'if certain rights are supposed to be universal, why can they only be guaranteed through membership of a nation state?' (2018a: 237). This observation beckons reflection on the idea of the nation, or perhaps better in the context of the current crisis, Europe and the EU. As Sam Durrant argues, the refugee crisis should be seen as 'an affective phenomenon of Europe' that throws up 'anxieties about national sovereignty in an era of globalisation' (Durrant in Cox et al., 2020: 611). Because the existence of refugees has profound effects on the performance of national belonging and on citizenship, the cementing of physical barriers of who belongs and who does not has become the default national response to the refugee crisis. To Agnes Woolley, the refugee crisis exposes 'the paradoxes of contemporary globalizing trends which liberalize the flow of money media and goods while reinforcing national borders against those experiencing the worst effects of uneven development' (2014: 6). As he travels with refugees through Europe, Patrick Kingsley realises 'the absurdity of dividing the earth into fairly arbitrary parcels of turf. It's a facile point to make, but sometimes the facile seems profound when you're wandering through Europe with people whose futures depend repeatedly on flouting these invisible lines' (2017: 223).

There has been much talk of 'Fortress Europe' recently. According to Jiska Engelbert et al., 'Fortress Europe' names a tension, built as it is 'on the premise of restraining mobility for some in order to enable freedom for others' (2019: 133). They demonstrate that while 'Europe' is typically 'associated with freedom of movement and the disappearance of borders', the term "'fortress" invokes association with historical experiences that Europe has proudly left behind' (134). 'Fortress Europe' speaks to a contradictory logic where Europe has to 'simultaneously manage the opportunities *and* the political risks of openness' (137). Furthermore, and this is relevant in the context of the refugee crisis, the Dublin regulations (of 2003 and 2015) are also contrarily understood: while they were 'initially posited to secure the rights of refugees' they 'are now used to legitimize their rejection' (136). Fortress Europe, or bordered Europe, attests to an inherent instability that puts the understanding of the EU and its associated ideas, ideals and values in crisis, and no more so than in the period since 2015. In the context of the current refugee crisis, Daniel Trilling suggests that this crisis is 'better described as a border crisis' with border understood as 'a system for filtering people that stretches from the edges of territory into its heart' (2018a: x–xi). Trilling alerts us to the fact that 'as borders have come down within Europe … its external frontier has become increasingly militarized' (viii). Indeed, he argues that 'we are constantly engaged in drawing and redrawing lines of threat and safety: ally and enemy, who belongs and who doesn't' (171). If what we are dealing with is 'Europe's border crisis' (xi), with 'border defence' and not 'protection of life' as 'Europe's priority' (255), then we have to think about the notion of 'border', since this is part of an ethico-political consideration of the current refugee crisis *and* central in refugee talk vocabularies. Trilling has more to say about the 'border crisis' as it unfolds in 2020:

> It would be easy to dismiss what happens at other countries' borders as a matter for them alone, but the pattern is international, and the erosion of rights it represents should concern us all. When states opt for extreme measures to push refugees away from their territory, it threatens to undermine the entire system that exists to protect them. (2020)

Considering the refugee crisis as a border crisis forces us to think not only nationally but also internationally, and to heed how the local and the global are interconnected. Yet the need to stem this inevitable interconnection is made visible in the reliance on borders to keep that which is seen as unwanted within outside. Lyndsey Stonebridge comments on what may be termed a 'border-fetish':

> The nation no longer binds us into an imaginary community, hence our panicked devotion to images of fences and ditches, barbed wire and concrete. Borders are a means of defensively reasserting integrity where there is little, in fact, to bind us together. The larger and more fantastic the wall, the bigger the anxiety. Small wonder we now prefer to see the stateless in terms of their powerlessness and not our own. (2018: 171)

A border crisis suggests a crisis within and between nations that comes acutely to the fore at the time of writing, the pandemic years of 2020–21. Bound up in power relations, borders include and exclude simultaneously. Borders, Randall Hansen writes, 'are basic to the construction and creation of refugee movements in both historical and contemporary contexts' (Hansen in Fiddan-Qasmiyeh et al., 2014: 255) and the production of refugee movements continues to be bound up in 'the maintenance of those boundaries' (257). Borders are embodiments of political attitudes and ethical values, too, and in a globalised world, borders are both national and international. In the current refugee crisis, borders are typically locations of brutality and violence for those who attempt to cross: 'What happened? Why are you here? These are the questions people in the "Jungle" [in Calais] are forced to answer over and over again at each border crossing. ... What is the right answer, the answer each one of these interrogators wishes to hear about the past, and why they came?' (Godin et al., 2017: 22). This state of affairs has an effect on the notion of citizenship and on the status and reception of refugees. A citizen (in contrast to a refugee) is a person 'who enjoys the full panoply of rights – civil, social, economic, and political – accorded by a nation state' (Hansen in Fiddan-Qasmiyeh et al., 2014: 253). The term citizenship thus also includes and excludes: as a two-sided concept it guarantees rights for some people and excludes rights for other people. If we want to rid ourselves of 'the inequality of the global border regime', Reece Jones argues (2017: 179), we need to move 'towards a world of equality of movement and access to resources and opportunities' (170). This call to action is another example of how the current ethico-political climate of ideas is affected by refugees' intrepid border-crossing movement in search of refuge, with refuge understood as *both* a state and a place of safety.

**In conversation, Brad Evans says:** When we talk about borders, we do not talk about walls or fences. We talk about the body. I think the body itself is the border. This is what determines whether I can pass or not. The rest is symbolic.

The longing for safety and the desire for access to resources are caught up in the dream of Europe. How is Europe – or the map of Europe – perceived by refugees? Patrick Kingsley explains how migrants and refugees navigate the continent with an ephemeral Facebook *Baedeker* (2017: 188) that renders Europe 'a confusing blur, filled with places and even countries that they've never heard of. ... In the process, the refugees' journeys constitute a reimagining of Europe's geographic space' (240–1). The map of Europe is constantly under negotiation as refugees manoeuvre borders that are open or closed seemingly at random, and sometimes also hastily erected in order to bar the way. Bhabha explains that in his 'thinking of how mobile the "regional" map has become' as a result of civil and international wars he also considers the changing map of Europe, asking this provocative question: 'Has the refugee crisis not made Syria a "neighbour" to Germany if seen from the perspective of global citizenship?' (Bhabha in Schulze-Engler at al., 2018: 713). Indeed, when Angela Merkel opened up the border 'between' Germany and Syria, by offering asylum to fleeing Syrians, she changed the regional map of Europe in ways that force us to rethink the concept of Europe. We see this indexed by Jenny Erpenbeck's protagonist Richard in *Go, Went, Gone* when he reflects on borders after becoming familiar with Berlin's refugees: 'So a border can suddenly ... become visible, it can suddenly appear where a border never used to be: battles fought in recent years on the borders of

Libya, or of Morocco or Niger, are now taking place in the middle of Berlin-Spandau' (2018a: 209).

**In conversation, Homi K. Bhabha says:** Many refugees say that they want to go Germany or Sweden rather than France or Italy. This wish does not come from an idea of Europe as such, but from a very specific idea of countries with a tradition of welfare, hospitality, and policies against racism. Refugees and migrants are frequently seen as pursuing the 'good life' at the expense of other nations and 'foreign' peoples. This is a profoundly parochial and provincial way of thinking about the history of migration, one that is inadvertently encouraged by the hasty use of the categories of economic and political migrants, useful though these categories are. It changes our perspective on the right to migration if we see migrants and refugees making value-based choices deeply rooted in ethical imperatives and political principles of the global welfare-state. The legal instruments of human rights, policies committed to economic redistribution, the initiatives of global health and global justice, the environmentalist agenda – these principles and beliefs that distinguish the modern world as a place of civility, rationality and hospitality are the values that migrants and refugees seek in their endeavour to find a home. What do refugees want? They want security and civility and the right to hospitality. Just like you and me. However, European countries try to make their borders as impenetrable as they can, not only because they do not want an influx of migrants, but also because their own histories and policies have often created the migrant flows in the first place. What we are witnessing now is a conceptual and ethical remapping of the world.

What work do the signifiers 'Europe' and 'EU' do in a refugee context? To many people outside of the EU, Europe embodies 'the beacon of freedom, democracy and human rights it had aspired to be when it emerged from the wreckage of the Second World War', Charlotte McDonald-Gibson writes (2017: 85). Hassan Blasim's poem 'A Refugee in the Paradise That Is Europe' (2018) picks up this idea in a deeply ironic way. The poem stages an epic refugee journey bracketed by death – escaping death at home, and eventually dying in Europe, after having 'produced children for their paradise' (2018). This Europe is not a paradise; it is a parasite on the refugee body: 'Academics get new grant money to research your body and your soul' all the while expecting 'to come across their own humanity through your tragedy' (2018). Ali Smith's *Spring* castigates Europe's attitudes to refugees, too: 'Any time at all. Here, take it. Take my face. I'm not surprised you want my face. It's the face of now' (2020: 125). Thus, an unnamed and disembodied refugee voice interrupts the narrative, thrusting 'itself' into the story in a defamiliarising manner, a literary gesture we will return to in Chapter 4. It is obvious that a query into what Europe signifies entails reflection on territory or location, on borders, on values, traditions and ideals, and on history and identity. Reporters such as Trilling and Kingsley indict Europe for not living up to its history of tolerance and freedom. To Kingsley, Europe's response to the refugee crisis is nothing less than a 'moral lapse' and 'an abdication of decency' (2017: 293, 265), where 'the identity of post-war Europe is at stake' (293). Recollecting his own grandmother's refugee story at the end of *Lights in the Distance*, Trilling considers how the post-World War II declaration of 'Never Again' 'hits a raw nerve' (2018a: 243) in view of Europe's mishandling of today's refugee crisis. He suggests that the resolving of the 'population upheavals of the twentieth century' provides 'a moral lesson for Europe today', but one that it has failed to live up to (243). Europe is riven by opposing ethical responses to those who are perceived as different: put simply and reductively, by the ideological schism between intolerance and tolerance.

**In conversation, Daniel Trilling says:** The language of humanity, of human rights and civilisation, presents Europe as a beacon to the rest of the world. It is the official narrative of the EU, even the founding myth of European unity. It promotes a different course for post-war Europe with the aim of protecting people's rights. But humanitarian duties quickly run into political difficulties, and practical acts of solidarity and the language surrounding it can become devalued. The EU has failed to live up to that language of humanity in reality. Yet refugees still want to come to

Europe. Many of the people I met felt a strong sense of connection to Europe, and that Europe has a collective responsibility for refugees. Sometimes the reasons for this dream of Europe are quite straightforward: there is no war in most parts of Europe and it can give people protection and refuge. Or perhaps refugees already know somebody in their own situation in Europe. This is, in fact, an under-recognised aspect of why people make decisions about where they want to go: someone might want to go to the UK, for instance, because they have a sister or a cousin there. Of course, there are also much deeper historical and cultural connections. Some people I met considered Britain, say, or France or Italy, relatively familiar places because they were former colonial powers. These connections show that refugees' ideas about Europe are not quite the fantasy, or 'dream,' they are often made out to be. And the connections work both ways: regardless of whether Britain is a member of the EU or not, what happens at its border is intimately connected to what happens at the Greek border, the Syrian border or in the Saharan desert. The refugee crisis was more than a European crisis. It was a global crisis that illustrated how things are connected. Yet many aspects of the ongoing story of migration are still covered almost exclusively as a national issue.

**In conversation, Gulwali Passarlay says:** In Europe today, we have lost our sense of the value of human beings. Where is our humanity and our decency? Europe is in many ways responsible for my presence in Britain – I would not be here if it was not for the war in Afghanistan. In Britain, we put people in detention indefinitely. It is almost worse than a prison, because if you go to prison, at least you know how long you will be there. There is something wrong with the system.

I understand that Europe cannot accept everyone and give all asylum. But if you cannot help, do it with humanity, with compassion, and show solidarity. We need to have an honest conversation involving policy and decision makers and immigration officials. If we cannot offer people asylum, then we need to find a humane way of dealing with that situation.

Many failed asylum seekers become destitute. They crack out of the system and people exploit it. We need to stop the harsh rhetoric, hatred and fear. It is so unnecessary. Most people do not want to be known only as a refugee. I have experienced refugee charities that talk about 'our refugee people.' But it is not your refugee people. I know you have good intentions, but do not dehumanise people; you should call them by their name. Give them some decency. Give them the right to be known by who they are, rather than resort to labels and definition of their status. Of course, people have good intentions, but they always see us just as victims who need help and support.

Bhabha considers the nationalist responses refugees are met with on the borders of Europe as attitudes that question refugees' dignity and humanity. They face a combination of discrimination and dishonour that works differently, but in tandem. While discrimination is 'institutional and systemic' and associated with a violation of human rights, dishonour 'is a different kind of language of social and cultural misrecognition' (2019: 404). In this context, Bhabha outlines how discrimination and dishonour rely on two interlinked biopolitics: while discrimination relies on a 'biopolitics of calculation' trafficking in quotas and statistics, dishonour is a 'biopolitics of affect' relying on emotions such as anxiety and fear (404). These two biopolitical reactions illustrate a European border system in action, and how Europe struggles with the disturbing figure of the refugee. 'Europe' is a sedimented term and, as we have seen, in trouble when defined alongside the current refugee crisis. In this context, is it true that '[t]he system of nation-states virtually guarantees universal national selfishness', as Michael Dummett suggests (2001: 48)? Or can nations also be unselfish and accommodate those who do not fit? As a self-declared 'citizen of everywhere', and with a family history of German Jewish refugees, Peter Gumbel suffers from the 'family demon' of not quite fitting in (2020: 5). To Gumbel, Germany has replaced Britain as 'the hope-bearer in Europe' (19) – symbolised in Angela Merkel's controversial 2015 decision to welcome Syrian refugees, a decision that spoke to the qualities of 'decency, tolerance, and respect that characterise Germany today' (19), flagging the same qualities that tend to be ridiculed and interpreted as signs of weakness by large swathes of public media. The climate of ideas that affect the cultural responses to the refugee crisis seems to be bifurcating, with one track proposing that migration is a natural fact of life and arguing for a borderless world, while the other track cements the idea of the nation-state and sees borders as a natural way of protecting the nation from migrating hordes. Such debates pivot on the problematic presence of borders, on the connotations of the idea of 'Europe', on what Lyndsey Stonebridge terms the 'rights-rich' (2018: 19), and, inevitably, on the figure of the refugee.

**In conversation, Mohsin Hamid says**: I think that the idea of ridiculing solidarity and humanity is part of a larger problem that we face. This problem is that certain values, beliefs and ideas – that all human beings are equal, that we should be able to choose our future collectively and individually – underpin, in theory, Western democracy in, for example countries like America or Denmark. In reality, the truth is that these ideas were always very contingent. They existed at the same time as giant empires were built, slaves were kept, apartheid-like systems were established, and all kinds of inequalities were enforced. So, a long tradition of paying lip service to solidarity and humanity accompanied atrocities of every kind. When we see people asking for democracy, humanity and solidarity now, what is being revealed is an underlying hypocrisy and that many people do not actually believe in these things. They do not believe that people are equal. They do not believe that people should be entitled to participate in democracy and in the selection of politics and leaders. Therefore, what we are seeing ridiculed are values that were formerly held up, but were at least partly hypocritical. We see that people did not fully believe in or espoused these values: much of the time, they behaved completely the opposite, especially in foreign countries and with people who were born in foreign countries. What we are seeing when the idea of helping others is ridiculed is the inner, secret hypocrisy that existed in all societies, and that has now come to the fore because it is possible to hide it no longer.

In his thoughts on 'the very meaning we attach to the name "Europe"', Étienne Balibar and Frank Collins highlight the notion of borders, too, suggesting that there are two contradictory meanings associated with borders, or frontiers, in today's Europe: 'frontiers' and 'confines/outer reaches' (2003: 36), with frontiers suggesting border as an act of closing and excluding and confines/outer reaches suggesting border as open and including. Borders thus have both geopolitical and epistemological functions. The presence of refugees troubles these border functions: 'globalization tends to knock down frontiers with respect to goods and capital while at the same time erecting a whole system of barriers against the influx of a workforce and "right to flight" that migrants exercise' (37). Within Europe, borders operate as 'a statutory *line of partition* separating citizens and noncitizens' (40). Furthermore, Balibar describes how 'borders are vacillating', in the sense that 'they do not work in the same way for "things" and for "people" – not to speak of what is neither a thing nor person: viruses, information, ideas'; nor do they work 'in the same way, "equally," for all people, and notably not for those who come from different parts of the world' (1998: 219). This situation is linked to Europe's history. Balibar argues that even though Europe is postcolonial, having been created by a colonialism that is over, we should now think of Europe as neo-colonial, still reluctantly tethered to a colonial history that it will not come to terms with. This resistance is evidenced in entrenched racism, Balibar and Collins hold, and in its problematic attitude to displaced people, migrants and refugees. These people enact a freedom of movement that should be considered 'a basic claim that must be incorporated within the citizenry of *all people*' (2003: 42).

This basic claim creates problems for Europe's border system. It also suggests that displaced people come with basic demands and expressions of agency and dignity. Balibar writes: 'migrants demand to be able to move about between different parts of the world, between different "worlds," in the sense both of departing and returning, contributing both at home and abroad to a real "decolonization," to the creation of a citizenry *that is not at all based upon a racist anthropology*' (42). We are reminded of Balibar's comment when we read what a Malian refugee tells Trilling in *Lights in the Distance*: 'Because I value my dignity I do not want to be a burden ... on Europe, no. I want to *contribute to the evolution of Europe*, do my bit, even if it's as small as a grain of sand, bring at least my share of the contribution' (2018a: 156, our italics). But is this at all possible, though, considering Europe's colonial history and its current reluctance to accept the repercussions of this history as evidenced in Black Lives Matter and the tearing down of national statues? Will refugees ever be allowed to contribute to the evolution of Europe? This is a question that is profoundly ethical *and* political. In common with thinkers such as Fanon and Butler, Balibar and Collins, too, put forward a possible utopic solution to the discrimination that bars refugees from doing their bit. They insist that while 'frontiers, a system of "external" and "internal" frontiers, ... are radically antidemocratic' (2003: 43), if we desire 'the construction of a democratic Europe', 'a Europe *plain and simple*', frontiers must be 'democratized and segregation and deportation must be resisted' (43). This, however, demands that Europe begins 'to engage in the enterprise of *decolonization at home*' (44). For this decolonising process to succeed we need to rethink how borders work and what effect they have on both citizens and refugees. We need to consider how we want Europe to develop in the twenty-first century. Perhaps this attitudinal decolonising of our understanding of Europe and Europeans is one way of embarking on the road towards the realisation of a Fanonian new humanism and a revitalised political imagination?

**In conversation, Homi K. Bhabha says:** When I talk about the poetic, I am not talking only about poetry, but about the languages of humanistic thinking. I am saying that the notion of the poetic or what I call the poetics or the aesthetic is about introducing into the discourse of policy the language of metaphor and figuration.

**In conversation, Brad Evans says:** For me, the political has always been aligned with an affirmative concept of life. The political means to affirm life in a creative and poetic under-standing of the term. An affirmative concept of the political is not grounded in structures of friends and enemies. If we do away with such structures, we we can impose a universal dogmatism on the world that does not weigh us down or force us into continuous self-regulation. An affirmative concept of the political is open to the future. It is not afraid to speak truth to power or even to speak its own truth. I think we are ushering in a new age of politics right now, which is post-liberal. That is why we need to have a serious conversation about what that politics looks like, because in a post-liberal age, it is looking remarkably undemocratic in terms of the changing configuration of power, where the nation state provides the policing architecture. The emergence of the refugee as a problem and the ongoing crisis of the global pandemic have revealed that liberalism is dead. What is coming in its aftermath is arguably even more policing.

Still, in spite of this call for a dismantling of borders, borders proliferate. According to Shada Islam, the refugee crisis is not really about the number of refugees arriving in Europe, but about ingrained European prejudice: 'Europe's relentless arguments over border controls, asylum claims and mandatory or voluntary "solidarity" hide a darker discussion and deeper divide' (2020), entangled as they are in racism and the legacy of colonialism. In her study of human migration, Sonia Shah explains that 2015 saw 'an unprecedented surge in construction of new border walls' and that '[m]ore borders are fortified by walls and fences today than at any time in history' (2020: 290). Europe's border thinking affects attitudes to refugees, even if, as Shah suggests, the 'border between natives and migrants can be nebulous' (306). Yet border thinking needs difference in order to survive. Refugees, on this view, are *different* from those of us who belong. Jeremy Harding claims that Europe's thinking about refugees is bound up in 'the imputation of a double criminality: not only do [refugees] flout national boundaries, but they consort with criminal smuggling gangs to do so' (2012: 7). Furthermore, their presence in Europe affects how we think about rights, duties and values. Harding proposes a rethinking exercise in this connection: 'Perhaps we should agree to think of rights and values as limited resources, and admit that Europe is now caught in a bitter struggle over who can or can't access them?' (86). Shah proposes a different thought experiment: 'If we were to accept migration as integral to life on a dynamic planet with shifting and unevenly distributed resources, there are any number of ways we could proceed' (2020: 316). 'We can', she suggests, 'turn migration from a crisis into its opposite: a solution' (316). Inspired by such observations, perhaps a rethinking of the centrality of migration to an understanding of humanity is a way forward to a more equitable world where resources, broadly understood, are more evenly distributed in a way that secures refuge – a state *and* a place of safety – for all humans?

## MIGRATION, ASSIMILATION – AND GRATITUDE

Migration is, obviously, central to refugee talk – yet typically problematically so, because, as Paul Collier reminds us, not only is migration highly emotive, it 'has also been politicized before it has been analyzed' (2013: 12). Migration is caught up in ideas of refuge. According to Betts and Collier, refuge 'is about fulfilling a duty of rescue. Born out of our common humanity, it is based on the simple recognition that we have shared obligations towards our fellow human beings' (2018: 6). However, refuge, they argue, 'has become bound up with a broader, and distracting, discussion about the right to migrate' (6). This problem is especially true in connection with the ongoing refugee crisis. Bauman discusses 'humanity on the move': 'millions of migrants wandering the routes once trodden by the "surplus population" discarded by the greenhouses of modernity' (2012: 35). Such refugees are 'the products of globalization and the fullest epitome and incarnation of its frontier-land spirit' (37–8). They are the flip side of the travelling elite (48) restlessly migrating from place to place, suggesting how ingrained movement is to humanity. Indeed, as the editors of *Refugee Imaginaries* suggest: 'We have become accustomed to calling this type of existence precarious, but this does not always do justice to how deeply mass migration has transformed ideas about political and ethical belonging and responsibility, not just for the displaced, but for everybody' (Cox et al., 2020: 2). Migration and asylum seeking have, not surprisingly, been entangled in the securitisation debate. In her discussion of how the securitisation discourse impacts on refugees, Anne Hammerstad explains how security language both creates and reinforces 'divisions between "us" and "them", using the enemy "other" on the outside as a tool for strengthening the community bonds between insiders' (Hammerstad in Fiddian-Qasmiyeh et al., 2014: 268). She refers to pull motives 'of voluntary migrants' and push motives of 'forced migrants', or refugees, and to how the fact that both use 'the same migration channels' has led the UNHCR to employ the unfortunate term 'mixed flows' (270). This term 'suits a securitizing discourse well' because it highlights the 'worrying term "flow"' rather than 'the ambiguous term "mixed"' (270). From a security perspective, refugees are 'criminalized and securitized' for the act of seeking asylum because of the illegal routes they are forced to take and because their arrival is 'considered threatening' since it is constructed as a 'flood' (271).

To continue such lines of inquiry, in her book about the 'centrality of migration in our biology and history' (2020: 11), and how 'migration is encoded in our bodies' (271), Sonia Shah asks a thought-provoking question in relation to the notion of (mass) migration: Where does the idea that species are from, and thus belong in, *one* place and not another originate? 'The idea that certain people and species belong in certain fixed places has had a long history in Western culture. Under its logic, migration is by necessity a catastrophe, because it violates that natural order' (62). The logic it relies on can be summed up in this border-couplet: 'We belong here. *They belong there*' (62). It also relies on the privileging of differences over similarities in (cultural) encounters between people. And it is firmly rooted in 'a sedentarist notion' that sees migration 'as a problem or an exception from the norm' (271). These ideas make up what she terms 'the myth of a sedentary past' (304) that relies on a perception of mobility and migration as the exception, 'while being sedentary, anchored within and attached to nation state is the norm that defines international migratory politics', this time in Claire Gallien's words (2018b: 739).

This myth of a sedentary past is embroiled in a fixed notion of territory that relates to the current refugee crisis in interesting ways. Certainly, the refugee is a migrating figure that brings the very notion of a secure home and a concomitant sense of belonging in disarray. Homi K. Bhabha and Simon Gikandi shed light on this conundrum. Both approach the figure of the refugee from their positions as cosmopolitan members of the postcolonial elites. Their reflections attest, albeit in different ways, to Sam Durrant's argument that 'the unfreedom of the refugee is the melancholy shadow at the heart of cosmopolitan freedom' and that 'the cosmopolitan world-view is reliant on structures of global privilege that function to occlude the refugee's experience of destitution' (Durrant in Cox et al., 2020: 608). Bhabha sees the refugee as a 'vernacular cosmopolitan' who from an interstitial situation translates between cultures and renegotiates traditions 'from a position where "locality" insists on its own terms, while entering into larger national and societal conversations' (2000: 139). In dialogue with Appiah, Bhabha elaborates on the concept 'vernacular cosmopolitanism' as a term that he owes 'to the lifeworld of migration, where to be a diasporic "citizen of the world" is an activity driven by survival' (Appiah and Bhabha, 2018: 188). Vernacular – connoting domestic, quotidian, ordinary – signals to Bhabha 'a subaltern agency of translation' (189) and vernacular cosmopolitans are cosmopolitans 'of necessity' (189), not choice. Appiah calls such vernacular cosmopolitans 'convergent peoples' (189) who are 'picking up on things from places that they didn't start out from and doing things with them' (189), also drawing attention to (a possibly overlooked) expression of creative agency that is typically not attached to this figure. In *Voices from the 'Jungle'*, the Syrian refugee Muhammad comes across as a convergent person when he explains how the 'Jungle' is a school for him: 'I think I deserve a graduation. My life here gave me new views and visions and ways' (Godin et al., 2017: 207). Migration seems to have made a vernacular cosmopolitan out of the young Gulwali Passarlay, too, when he comments on the effect it has on his developing sense of self:

The little rural and conservative boy from Afghanistan had seen and heard so much. The journey, as awful as it was, was certainly opening my eyes and my mind to the world. ... I was no longer the baby fundamentalist I once was. ... I began to think differently. I began to see that my views were borne of a different culture, a culture I still loved and believed passionately in, but that was not how people lived here. I respected that. And I got it. (2019: 180, 346–7)

The notion of locality, however, troubles Gikandi is his reflections on the figure of the refugee. Gikandi evinces what Durrant terms an 'auto-critical account of the vexed relation between cosmopolitanism and refugee life' (Durrant in Cox et al., 2020: 609). To understand how the refugee can be seen as 'signs of a dislocated locality' (Gikandi, 2010: 23) one has to consider the routes – the nature of the journey – taken, and the roots – or *ethne* – remembered. Refugees, Gikandi explains, threaten his 'identity as a cosmopolitan' (23) who crosses borders without a second thought; as 'rejects of failed states' they are not yet cosmopolitan since 'journeys across boundaries and encounters with others do not necessarily lead to a cosmopolitan attitude' (24). Instead, and this is what surprises Gikandi, such journeys may lead to 'a radical attachment to older cultural forms which seem to mock the politics of postcolonial identity' (25). Thus, the refugee is 'the Other of the cosmopolitan; rootless by compulsion, this figure is forced to develop an alternative narrative of global cultural flows, … producing and reproducing localities in the centres of metropolitan culture itself' (26). That is why 'the refugee's presence in the heart of the metropolis challenges the redemptive narrative of postcolonial arrival' (28). Gikandi asks us to consider the role of the local in the ideology and experience of globalisation via the figure of the refugee and to note how 'locality itself has been globalized' (32) in the sense that the language and the structure of nation and the *ethne* haunt contemporary cosmopolitanism and globalisation. This disturbance is embodied, at least for the postcolonial elite, in the figure of the refugee. The refugee as a 'dislocated locality' is illustrated in a *Guardian* article about Somali Bantu families who after years in refugee camps in Kenya and the US, are now settled as farmers in Maine, where they tell Audrea Lim, '[w]e're always trying to recreate the lives that we had back home' (Lim, 2021).

**In correspondence, Simon Gikandi writes:** My article 'Between Roots and Routes' (2010) was written as an indirect response to the work of my colleague Kwame Anthony Appiah and his celebration of cosmopolitanism. I was concerned that the figure of elites circulating in a globalised world was obscuring the real struggle of refugees – people who had been forced out of their countries and had suddenly found themselves homeless and stateless. When I was writing the article at the beginning of the century, there seemed to be a general consensus that refugees constituted a special class of people, worthy of protection by states under international law. Many countries had committed themselves to hosting this class of people who were distinct from other migrants because they were not under protection by their own governments, and were indeed often threatened by the people intended to defend them.

I think I could have complicated my argument by reminding readers that there were other categories of people closing borders besides refugees and cosmopolitans. I could, for example, have called attention to the existence of classes of people who are allowed into the United States under different visa schemes: students, specialised workers, and 'Green Card' holders. All these classes are allowed to work and settle in the country, to send their children to school, and to benefit from social services. Like cosmopolitan elites, they are able to move across boundaries and to maintain ties with their home countries. Another class of migrants are the undocumented – millions of people who have entered other countries and live and work there without rights or the protection of the law. Unless they have claimed and have been granted refugee status, these people remain under the radar of institutions and hence do not recreate their localities as visibly as refugees. I cannot speak with some authority on the European crisis but I suspect these classes exist under different labels in Europe, too.

Are all refugees signs of 'a dislocated locality'? One cannot say that this situation applies to all refugees, but what has struck me as an observer of all the classes I have described above is that the localities left behind seem to have increasing value among the groups that find themselves (a) clustered in particular areas of the new country and (b) closed off from the general population by language, race, class, and religion. In the US, the government has a policy of settling refugees in particular areas (Somalis in Maine, for example), but refugees also tend to find their way to places where people like them have settled (Ethiopians in Washington DC). I think what I should have added is that the same situation applies to migrants of a certain class and the undocumented. They seek refuge in communities that recreate the localities they left behind. Cosmopolitans (and one should include middle-class and upper middle-class migrants like Indian computer specialists in Silicon Valley or Nigerian doctors in the Mid-Atlantic states) do not have the compulsion to maintain strong local ties with the old localities because they are easily incorporated into the new culture through professional and other associations. When refugees are elites (Ethiopian aristocrats exiled after the revolution, African writers in exile, Chinese political activists), they tend to be able to be incorporated into the world of local elites without any discernible problems. So, class is significant. Syrian doctors who seek refuge in Europe are privileged because of their skills; peasants from the same country and even neighbourhood will often languish in camps.

Even if migration is seen as innate to humanity, we want to ask: Does anything mark the *end* of human migration? For a refugee, this, surely, is an important question. Matthew J. Gibney comments that any 'morally defensible account of when return is appropriate' for a refugee must take into consideration the relationship between the refugee and the host country, 'respect for the dignity and autonomy of refugees as agents' and how the refugees will be received by the country once left behind (Gibney in Fiddan-Qasmiyeh et al., 2014: 57). In his exploration of international migration, Khalid Koser numerates three ways that point to migration termination: A migrant can return home to where that person came from (2016: 18), he can become a member of 'transnational communities', living 'in-between nations' (23), coming and going, or he can become a citizen of the host nation (19), and undergo a process of integration and, possibly, even assimilation. For most refugees a return home is impossible since there might not even be a home to return to. Occupying a position in a transnational community is a possibility afforded very few refugees, since it suggests a privileged cosmopolitan situation. This leaves the possibility of becoming a citizen, which, as we have already seen, is a way that is typically barred. Refugees, as we have learned, upset the notion of the nation since they problematise the link between people, state and territory. Still, it is the possibility of becoming a citizen that indicates for many a successful outcome to the journey in search of refuge.

If the refugee is granted asylum, and possibly citizenship, what price is to be paid? We want to bring Nayeri into discussion again, since she has some provocative things to say about the cost involved in becoming a citizen, concomitant with assimilation construed as an act of gratitude. Nayeri explains that expressions of gratitude are profoundly interlaced with perceptions of dignity and humanity, and bound up in a rethinking of the notion of 'assimilation'. Assimilation does not simply mean to adapt and adopt and become alike. Drawing on her own youthful assimilatory project, to her assimilation 'is to please people's senses. It is submission, but also a powerful act of love, unity, brotherhood. It is a complicated and misunderstood metamorphosis' (2019: 341). It is also what is expected of refugees – it is in so many ways a demonstration of gratitude. Indeed, refugees are often 'so broken [that] they beg to be remade into the image of the native. As recipients of magnanimity, they can be pitied' (9). It is this layered refugee experience of suffering, rescue, assimilatory attempts and gratitude that Nayeri draws attention to, asking starkly: 'Why do we ask the desperate to strip off their dignity as the price of help?' (186). If assimilation means to 'become alike' then we can think of it as a grateful attempt on the part of refugees to become less disturbing and to reinscribe themselves into the fabric of humanity. If they are remade 'into the image of the native', surely they are no longer an anxiety-inducing figure that needs to be kept outside the borders of Europe? The fact that gratitude has been part of refugee talk for more than a century makes this question even more pertinent. In his exploration of refugees in modern world history, Peter Gatrell shares a statement made in 1915 by a female Russian refugee:

> Not so long ago, these people [the refugees] lived a full and inde-
> pendent working life. They had the right to be just like us, that
> is, indolent, rude and ungrateful. Now they have lost this pre-
> rogative; their poverty and helplessness oblige them to be meek

and grateful, to smile at people they don't like. (Gatrell in Cox et al., 2020: 31)

This observation is shockingly contemporary and aligns well with Nayeri's intriguing comments. In the search for refuge, assimilation, understood as a demonstration of gratitude, signals the ultimate attempt to shed the refugee status and to become perceived as a part of humanity that has the innate right to have rights. But if the price paid is the defacement of a sense of self that is bound up in a brokering of integrity and personal dignity, then this is indeed the ultimate example of costly radical migration termination.

In this sweeping chapter we have been concerned with how complex the figure of the refugee is in theoretical reflections and in experiential remembering. We have focused on how contingent the refugee is on broader understandings of humanity, on locality and on mobility. Why do we still resort to reductive tropes that simplify rather than illuminate when we talk about refugees? Why is ordinary refugee talk still so unwilling to budge? Why is human migration still vilified and migrants still villainised? How can multiplex theory be translated into everyday language without losing its explanatory traction in, for example, journalistic reportage? In the next chapter we turn to cultural responses to the refugee crisis in media discourses and to acts of reporting responsibly on refugee mobility.

# 2

# Responsibility – News Media and the (Re)framing of Refugees

This chapter is concerned with how the news media have reflected, or shaped, our responses to the refugee crisis and with the crucial role of reporters who document it. And this is, indeed, a discussion that calls on the complicated matter of ethics in representation. According to the Ethical Journalism Network, ethical journalism pays heed to the core principles of responsible journalism that require a reporter to get the facts right and be truthful, fair, impartial and accountable, and always with an awareness of how words and images impact directly or indirectly on the lives of others. As news correspondent Paraic O'Brien suggests, this is part of 'thinking about the mechanics of what we're doing'. In his view, '"ethical reporting" is all about … being aware, being thoughtful, questioning what you're doing and why. It's about involving the audience and, more importantly, the people you are reporting about in the process' (O'Brien, 2020). Such principles are sound, but in reality 'involving the people reported about' is a responsibility that mainstream media has largely neglected in the current refugee crisis. In his sober admittance that when ethically aware reporters document the crisis and assume, for instance, that by exposing unfairness, justice will prevail, Daniel Trilling is aware that this is a naive expectation. Rather, he suggests, ethical journalism distinguishes itself by 'fitting the pieces of a shattered mirror back together, to explain how a person, or a community, has come to find itself at an impasse'. According to Trilling, reporters can thus make their privileged position function in the service of a responsibility that is indeed ethical: '[W]e have the luxury of distance. We can step back from a situation, try to untangle the web of cause and effect that surrounds it, and retell it in a way that makes sense' (Trilling, 2018a: 175). Yet 'making sense', as Trilling would no doubt agree, is ultimately contingent on perspective and it will remain an incomplete gesture as long as the inclusion of refugee voices is evaded in reportage. Mainstream news media can in that sense come to function as a 'digital border' (Chouliaraki and Geogiou in Cox et al., 2020: 184) that bars refugees from active participation in the mediation of the refugee crisis.

Accordingly, in this chapter we pursue two lines of inquiry, set up in a contrast that we hope will be illuminating towards understanding the complex realities involved when refugees are 'storified' in mediated discourses. First, we inquire into the images that mainstream news media set in circulation at the peak of the crisis in 2015 and how these framed, and continue to frame, the dominant narrative about refugees. Such images cluster around two common tropes, that of 'victim' and of 'villain'. Whether benevolent or hostile, dominant images reduce refugees to stereotypes that show little consideration for the full scope of their individual identities and particular biographies. Yet, they have conditioned, if not cemented, our affective responses and made us believe we know who and what refugees are. We next turn to Patrick Kingsley's *The New Odyssey* (2017), Daniel Trilling's *Lights in the Distance* (2018) and Dina Nayeri's *The Ungrateful Refugee* (2019). We employ these book-length works as case studies of how reporters can engage differently with refugees when there is no urgent deadline to meet and when the deliberate intention of the one who reports is to strike up a rapport with those reported about, at close hand and often over extended periods of time. These are works that consciously challenge and reframe the dominant crisis narrative by adding nuance and complexity to the figure of the refugee and by personalising the precarity of being in situations where proper 'arrival' is either pending or denied. We are interested in the different refugee stories that come from Kingsley, Trilling and Nayeri's encounters with refugees, in how they reflect on their role as mediators and the alternative take on responsibility echoed in their books. The proposition we pursue in the course of this chapter takes up Chouliaraki and Stolic's claim that 'at the heart of this "crisis" of humanity ... lies a crisis of responsibility itself' (2017: 1173) and is thus inspired by their insistence that refugees must be granted 'narratability' within mediated communication (1164) as this is an effective means of avoiding stereotyped representations. And this is, we argue, what Kingsley, Trilling and Nayeri accomplish in their extended reportage. We therefore suggest that they rethink the idea of a reporter's responsibility by striving to create a hospitable space for refugee narratability; one that has the effect of 're-humanising' those who are the main protagonists of the refugee crisis. Before we discuss the implications of this redirection in responsible reportage, it is pertinent to trace how mainstream media have framed refugees and the refugee crisis, in and beyond 2015, as Kingsley, Trilling and Nayeri's books work effectively to counter mainstream media frames.

**In conversation, Dina Nayeri says:** One reason why it is difficult for many in the West to see refugees as ordinary human beings is because of the success of the rhetoric 'on the other side' in dehumanising refugees and making them into one faceless mass. When a group of people become nothing but a swarm in your imagination, it is difficult to see their singular achievements and all of the things that we see as unique in ourselves, and that make us curious about our own countrymen and about our own neighbours. We lose that curiosity. It takes an incredible story, a fantastic death or an amazing achievement to make these people individual again. That is really the trick of the other side: they have lumped everyone together into a non-human entity. It is a calculated thing to do. Stories are ultimately what individualises us again, if that is the word, and brings us back to our singular identities. In order to affect this negative rhetoric, we can take responsibility for the genuine curiosity to help bring back the full person of the refugee, to help remake them into who they used to be or into the best version of themselves, the most fulfilled version of themselves. That includes trying not to bring our privileged position into every social interaction.

## VICTIMS OR VILLAINS

Do news media reflect political agendas or do they contribute to the actual shaping of such agendas? This is an open-ended question, but in 2015, when more than 1.3 million people arrived in Europe to seek asylum, there is little doubt that news media impacted forcefully on political responses and public policy, simply because, along with first responders, reporters turned up instantly at the flashpoints to report on the unforeseen vast number of arrivals and the ensuing humanitarian crisis. European nations and the EU were in effect reliant on first-hand reports from the news media in formulating their response and activating interventive measures. And in the immediate period after 2015, reporters continued to provide massive coverage of the impact that refugees had on host nations, in some cases in fact skewing facts and contributing to the crisis (Trilling, 2019) rather than merely reporting on it. This is not necessarily expressive of ill-will but rather a consequence of what may be termed unprepared journalism: 'In ... these situations the news media were able to do their basic job in an emergency situation, which is to communicate what's happening, who's affected, what's needed the most' but '[n]ews media that rush from one crisis point to another are not so good at filling in the gaps, at explaining the obscured systems and long-term failures that might be behind a series of seemingly unconnected events' (Trilling, 2019). This notwithstanding, it is widely recognised that mainstream media have performed, also post-2015, a decisive role in the mediation of Europe's political responses. And, especially important to our inquiry, mainstream media have impacted strongly on public sentiment by engaging audiences in affective responses across an emotional repertoire that spans from sympathy to hostility. As Heidenreich et al. argue: '[t]he complexity and duration of the "crisis" created a climate of uncertainty, which left room for mass media to shape citizens' understanding of what the arrival of these refugees meant for their respective country' (2019: i173), since it is in particular in times of uncertainty that people orient themselves towards mass-media interpretations.

**In conversation, Daniel Trilling says**: There is always an element of the factory production line when you work in the media. This has an effect on your own reporting and the language you use. Language reflects politics to a great extent. Because journalism operates with quite a specialist language that has its own constraints, your ability to deal with the wider context is limited in certain ways. There are good and bad reasons why your language is limited as a journalist. The bad reasons have to do with the fact that you are producing a consumer product that is partly shaped by the demands of the market. This is further distorted by the fact that, certainly in the UK, media ownership is concentrated in the hands of a very few wealthy people and organisations. And it reflects their agenda to a large extent.

This state of affairs affects the way things are framed, written and spoken about. Even if you do not agree with the politics involved, as a journalist, you have to work within that wider framework. Yet when people criticise the media, as a journalist I feel a duty to push back slightly and show that some of the things that can turn out to be constraining are there for very good reasons. In most cases, journalistic language needs to communicate as simply, quickly and directly as possible. It is often about the economy of language. As a journalist you want to be as efficient as possible with your language, so you boil complex concepts down to simple things that can be communicated to a wide, non-specialist audience. Journalism has to work with what people are already familiar with. So even if you might like to reshape people's perceptions, your reporting has to overlap with the language that they are familiar with. Of course, journalism can be manipulated and distorted, but that is not inherently a problem. But it does mean that you have less latitude to push back against the way concepts are framed and defined.

One way that media coverage has sometimes oversimplified the refugee crisis is by making a binary distinction between good, deserving refugees and bad, economic migrants. And again, that reflects current politics because it mirrors a distinction that is implied even in the well-meaning parts of refugee law and immigration policy. The distinction has, of course, also been reinforced by anti-immigration, racist politics. Reporting responsibly should reflect the fuller reality of a situation. I think that the trap that some journalists fall into is that since there is much negative coverage they counter that by treating people like saints or as entirely helpless victims. To avoid this, we need a more democratic form of journalism and media that would enable the fullness of life to be reflected better. Such journalism would reflect the fact that people are part of a society and their role within it cannot be reduced to two-dimensional caricatures.

In a report prepared for the UNHCR on EU press coverage in 2015, Mike Berry et al. state that 'it is impossible to ignore the role of the mass media in influencing public and elite political attitudes towards asylum and migration. The mass media can set agendas and frame debates. They provide the information which citizens use to make sense of the world and their place within it' (2015: 5) and, moreover, '[r]eporting ... does not just reflect the events that are happening and views that are already "out there," it actively contributes to and constructs our understanding of what events mean [... thus shaping] the range of possibilities for understanding what the story *is* on migration and the way we perceive migrants and refugees' (13–14). News frames are therefore hugely consequential. They are not only a journalistic tool or a means of 'presenting relatively complex issues ... in a way that makes them accessible to lay audiences because they play into existing cognitive schemas' (Scheufele and Tewksbury, 2007: 12); they also hold immense power through the vocabularies they make use of and reactivate in their target audiences: 'How migrants are described, categorised and represented matters' (Berry et al., 2015: 13).

**In conversation, Patrick Kingsley says:** To be a good reporter, you have to allow your humanity to drive you and you have to nurture a sense of outrage. But how do we take that sense of outrage that we journalists can stoke by reporting on unhappy things and channel it towards something productive that readers can put their energies towards? You also have to maintain some care and responsibility to the world. I try to be accurate both in my display of a particular fact, but also in the contextual facts that surround it. At the same time, I choose the stories and the themes that I am particularly interested in and passionate about. That is how I think I have remained honest and stayed on the right side of 'truth'.

Part of journalistic responsibility is also opting for the right words and the kinds of framing that keep people engaged in what you write. Journalism is mediation, and when I am mediating the refugee crisis I am writing somebody else's story. Migrants, refugees – whatever we call them at any particular time – are battling for survival and may not have a sense of themselves as being part of the Great Migration today, let alone part of a continuum of human experience that goes back to World War II. This mediation is both inevitable and important. Personally, I try to level with people. I tell them that my reporting is not going to help them in any immediate sense. The only way I can help is by writing their story in a newspaper. And hopefully, eventually, the situation for refugees changes in a particular way or in a general way. So, my reporting might not help the individual refugee. But it may help people in such positions in the future.

I have responsibility to my readers, too, so that they believe what I am reporting is true. If I want my readers to know this story is true, the source is going to be named with some detail about where the source is from. But if I am naming a person, he might be in danger. So that is a tension almost immediately within the framework of journalism. And if I represent this person as somebody in need of help, that will clash with the idea that this person is also an individual with his own desires and goals. If I show that refugees are people in need of help and simultaneously and contradictorily also individuals with their own agency and their own background, then that is another clash. You cannot really reflect on that tension in a single news article. You have to meet a deadline. And even if we say that the problem is the way that news is written, can we envisage a form of news, communication or mediation that does not contain compromises? It seems to me that we do not need more journalists, but journalists with better understanding of the complexities of migration policy and its effects, who can turn the refugee journey into stories and articles that captivate people and engage them in the process of developing better migration management. That is hard – and a boring subject. But it is the only thing that is going to create the pressure on European and national institutions to come up with a system that works better.

**In conversation, Daniel Trilling says:** I always try to report objectively. I tend to think of objectivity as something you apply to writing, not as an absolute value. Whatever approach you take to a subject, whether from a personal point of view or dispassionately sifting information, you can be objective about it. In a way, you are either telling the truth or you are not. When I teach journalism I tell my students that it often comes down to this question: Are you being honest or not? Have you distorted the truth in order to make a point? Of course, you can never know all the facts of a situation, but are you making a) an effort to know as much as you can about a situation, b) from what you know, do the facts support what you are trying to show?

The findings of Myria Georgiou and Rafal Zaborowski (2017) in their report to the European Council on media coverage in Europe around the 2015 crisis peak are, unsurprisingly, very similar to those of Berry et al. Even if significant variations in the representation of refugees are observed, ranging from highly polarised hostile press coverage in some nations (in particular the UK during the Brexit campaign) and concerned benevolent coverage in other nations (in particular Germany and Sweden), Georgiou and Zaborowski conclude that across such variations refugees are rarely given the chance to voice their experience in their own words. Their testimonies are mediated through news stories that tend to pay no attention to the specific geopolitical circumstances they have fled – a point that is corroborated by Berry et al. who detect very limited press coverage of the push factors driving migration flows. Georgiou and Zaborowski observe that refugees are represented as silent outsiders and cast as either vulnerable or dangerous. Whether one or the other hinges on three key 2015 events (2017: 8): Hungary's June decision to build a fence at its border with Serbia and the sight of desperate refugee families tearing at barbed-wire fences; the September circulation of the photographs of the dead body of Kurdish-Syrian toddler Alan Kurdi on a Turkish beach; and the November terrorist attacks in Paris in which at least one of the terrorists had allegedly entered Europe on a refugee boat to Greece. Such events received strong media attention, framing refugees as either innocent victims and thus worthy of humanitarian care, or as threats to the security of European nation-states; that is to say, refugees were framed as objects of pity or scorn. This is, in fact, a predominant pattern in news framing that has remained prevalent since 2015 and indeed one that can also be detected in media coverage prior to 2015 when host nations felt that their capacity for humanitarian care had come under pressure (see Kaye, 2001; Buchanan et al., 2003; Van Gorp, 2005; Gross et al., 2007).

Overall, then, the tropes of victim and villain are a dichotomising feature in news coverage. The former draws on sympathetic, emotionalised representations of victims who passively suffer under circumstances beyond their control, in Trilling's words, 'children, women, families; the vulnerable, the sick, the elderly' (2019). Their stories tend to be unspecified but their unfair fate is conveyed in a language that stimulates an audience response of moral concern and compassion. Conversely, the latter invites negatively inclined representations of refugees in the shape of what Trilling terms 'able-bodied [usually young male] nameless and sometimes faceless people massed at fences or gates', sometimes coupled with a focus on 'people from particular countries' that are framed as suspicious and made 'to suit a political agenda' (2019). Such representations buy into hostile audience emotions; although very little can be, or is, known about 'faceless' strangers and their intentions, the idea conveyed is usually that such '[i]ncoming populations are associated with *illegality, terrorism*, and *crime*' (Greussing and Boomgaarden, 2017: 1751). While the former frame stipulates that refugees deserve our care, the latter infers that they are undeserving 'bogus' asylum seekers likely to drain public resources and systems of care that ought to be reserved for citizens of the host society (1751). As Greussing and Boomgaarden point out, a frame shift from compassion to suspicion redirects 'the focus of public attention towards the (il)legitimacy of asylum seekers' claims' (1751). This is a concern that is emphatically stirred in the employment of words like 'flood', 'waves', 'flows', 'swarms' and 'flocks' to describe large numbers of incoming refugees. Such words are, of course, not neutral descriptors; they invoke a sense of a 'natural' disaster advancing on European nations, rather than one of human emergency. The use of these metaphors invariably constitutes refugees as an 'anonymous, even dehumanised' presence in Europe that is potentially 'deviant or alien to the host society, disrupting its cultural identity, language, and values' (1751). Katie Hopkins' 2015 hateful column for *The Sun* is one extremist case in point. Her representation of refugees as 'cockroaches' and a 'plague of feral humans' was widely condemned, yet as Kingsley notes, it was arguably 'just a brasher articulation of ideas promoted in a more genteel manner by government ministers' (2017: 43). As Berry et al. observe, when the duty of rescue and humanitarian care became increasingly secondary to an intensified focus on borders security, 'the distinction drawn between supposedly illegitimate ("bogus", "fake", cheats") and legitimate ("genuine", "deserving", "*bona fide*") asylum seekers became an important way of justifying punitive public policy' (2015: 15).

According to Chouliaraki and Stolic, the refugee is a 'fundamentally ambivalent media figure', marked by 'symbolic instability' in the fluctuation between defenceless victim and malevolent invader; the refugee is thus 'trapped between these two positions' (2017: 1164). Even if the two tropes of victim and villain seem at first hand to be mutually exclusive, they are highly functional because of their substitutability. They should therefore not 'be seen as antithetical to each other. Victimhood and threat are in fact tactically interchangeable moral claims' (1165), one made on behalf of suffering refugees, the other on behalf of anxious host societies. The substitutability of the tropes is, of course, only made possible by the fact that they are both medially constructed figures of representation. Trilling offers an illustrative example of this when he refers to *The Sun*'s 2015 front-page photograph of Alan Kurdi's dead body on a Turkish beach, a supreme image of innocent victimhood that was accompanied by the newspaper's compassionate call for an urgent escalation of military intervention into the war in Syria, yet just a few weeks later *The Sun* cleared the front page again. This time, however, the cover story was about a group of Iraqi refugees rescued from a capsized boat, now headlined as 'illegals' seeking 'a back door' into Europe (2019). The shift in imagery from lone innocent victim to large group of (dark-skinned) people confronting us with their will, not only to survive but to move on into Europe, marks a change in what we may call the economy of audience affect. This is 'not only a matter of emotional distance or proximity but also, importantly, a matter of ethical commitment' (Chouliaraki and Stolic, 2017: 1172) in interchangeable ways. Again, we may ask: responsibility and ethical commitment towards whom? Refugees or their host societies? In their discussion of how public media functions as a digital border, Chouliaraki and Georgiou maintain that news media trade in 'a precarious combination of ethical claims, security and care' and that this is reflective of the 'dual morality' of 'uphold[ing] the humanitarian imperative to care for vulnerable others and, simultaneously, to protect European citizens from potential threats from those same others' (Chouliaraki and Georgiou in Cox et al., 2020: 184). If the victim trope is tied to a discourse of hospitality and the villain trope to a discourse of securitisation, Chouliaraki and Georgiou posit that such discourses intersect; they are both capable of dehumanising refugees and differ mostly in the degrees of 'hospitability' (185) they make available.

**In conversation, Daniel Trilling says:** It is not that the media lack ethics when it comes to representing refugees. It is that sometimes they have got the wrong ethics! Media coverage of refugees and migrants is very often hostile and dehumanising and sometimes overtly racist, but it is still based on a particular ethical framework. I suppose this framework revolves around some fairly conservative, right-wing ideas about the fact that humans – or some humans, at least – should stay within their countries of origin. A commonly expressed attitude in the UK media is that people should not ask for help from the state if they do not deserve it or if they do not play by the rules. In this particular ethical framework, newspapers both try to follow and to shape a version of 'common sense'. This is commercially sustainable, and also what suits the politics of the owners.

Chouliaraki and Stolic draw attention to how the clustering of people into the undifferentiated category of victim defines them 'in terms of their corporeal vulnerability' and 'physical destitution'. This deprives them not only of their individual 'biographical specificity' but also of their capacity to legitimately 'articulate political will or rational argument' (2017: 1164). Bodies in need – conceived, as we discussed in Chapter 1 with reference to Agamben's notion of 'bare life' – are not expected to have or require such possibilities of manoeuvre, their agency is not recognised. This does not apply to the people in the equally undifferentiated category of villain, yet here political will and agency are expected to be malevolent and harmful to host societies: 'Instead of a humanitarian response, their criminalised agency mobilises fear and legitimises the securitisation practices that encamp or deport them' (1165). Accordingly, as Chouliaraki and Stolic argue, 'by relying on the tropes of powerless vulnerability and agentive malevolence' media representations ambivalently cast the refugee as 'either a sufferer or a threat, yet never human' (1165). What we can conclude, then, is that the troped configurations of refugees miss the point that they are neither merely victims (saints) nor villains (evil-doers) but human beings, yet human beings whose equal right to humanity is seriously challenged. It is no exaggeration to say that while refugees are literally kept in custody at the border by Europe's continued reluctance to find solutions to the crisis, they are also at the same time symbolically confined by the digital borders of mainstream media that objectify them at the cost of recognising their shared humanity. This is the outcome when news media traffic in easy binaries. In Chouliaraki and Georgiou's words, refugees are mediated as 'ambivalent subjectivities' rarely granted 'the dignity that people deserve as human beings' (Chouliaraki and Georgiou in Cox et al., 2020: 187). Mainstream news media thereby arguably contribute to a process of 'dehumanisation' in which refugees' 'biopolitical integrity is protected, but symbolic recognition is denied them' (187).

The number of asylum seekers has declined continuously since 2015 and is now at a level that is certainly manageable. Yet the distinction between 'deserving' and 'undeserving' asylum seekers remains pronounced in mainstream news and EU politics alike. The victim-villain tropes are still rigidly upheld and this calls for scrutiny. One explanation for the resilience of these reductive tropes to predetermine our understanding of who refugees are might be found in Chouliaraki and Stolic's suggestion that when 'the refugee emerges as a victim of geo-political conflict in need of protection' in one frame yet appears as 'a threat to the nation-based order' and therefore to be rejected in another, this is tied up with 'a deep-seated orientalism that continues to reproduce historical tropes of colonial imagery in contemporary portrayals of mobile populations' (2017: 1164). Both the empathy-fostering humanitarian frame and the hostility-fostering threat frame create an essentialist 'us and them' divide between native populations and the newly arrived. And this is a divide that makes native populations suspect that cultural differences between 'us' and 'them' are likely to be incommensurable – even if the number of asylum seekers has dropped.

**In conversation, Homi K. Bhabha says**: Refugees who take risks on perilous journeys to apply for asylum do it out of hope and optimism. Perhaps they realise that they will be treated as desperate people who come from nowhere with nothing to offer. This is a stereotypical simplification. There is, of course, a sense of desperation that accompanies the condition of displacement. However, refugees and migrants come bearing the skills of a lifetime, with the education and culture of their lifeworlds. They are world-makers fallen on dark times who seek the very values that define a modern society of success and civility. The tragic economic and political conditions that make them flee their home-lives and livelihoods are not of their making. 'All of Europe was responsible for Kurtz', Joseph Conrad writes in *Heart of Darkness*, his classic novel on the moral contradictions and culpabilities of colonialism. Today, as the global world extends its networks of webbed power – cutting deals, 'shorting' markets, and playing fast and loose with the lives of 'others' – it is time to say, 'Nobody is innocent of the fate of a single refugee anywhere; nobody is free of the misery of any migrant wherever she be.' You have to see that in the choices refugees make and the risks that they take, there is a profound humanity, a profound optimism, and a profound sense of hope. And it is not simply an unrealistic utopian hope.

## MERELY HUMAN

What we can extract from the above, then, is an acute sense that mainstream media have found it difficult to address what we have introduced as refugee 'narratability'. In mainstream media discourses the victim-villain binary can have distorting effects on how refugees are represented and perceived. In her critique of what she terms 'master public narratives' about refugees (Gotlib in Oliver et al., 2019: 239) – and we consider mainstream media to contribute to such narratives – Anna Gotlib is concerned that, whether sympathetic or hostile, they have the power to render refugees structurally 'invisible and inaudible' (242) as agents in their own right. These seemingly 'difficult-to-alter' narratives can be both 'morally and epistemologically damaging' (243) for refugees because when reduced to one stereotype or another, they are simultaneously excluded from the meaning-making processes in the public mediation of 'who they are, what they desire, and their capabilities and intentions, past histories, and possible futures' (239). This silencing of refugee voices 'strips' refugees of agency and the possibility of empowerment through participation (247). Refugees must therefore, Gotlib insists, be given the opportunity 'to tell their own stories regardless of whether these stories reflect the expected, the stereotypical, or the desirable model of the refugee' (240).

**In conversation, Gulwali Passarlay says**: Journalists often ask me if they can speak to somebody who recently arrived on a dinghy from France to England. But such people are traumatised and do not want to talk to the media. Then journalists want to talk to somebody with refugee experiences, like me. And I have done hundreds of interviews and I know that a lot of refugees just want to live and not to be involved in the whole discussion. They do not want to be labelled, they just want to get on with their lives. That is why so few of us are willing to be spokespeople, because it comes with responsibility. It is not easy, but I am happy to be a spokesperson.

I do a lot of activism and campaigning. I see myself as an educator on issues of migration and refugee protection. In my talks and in my writing, I keep mixing the pronouns 'we', 'us' and 'them' because I am mixed myself: I am Afghan, but also British. I have lived here most of my life. I am not a refugee; that is not my name, it is just my legal status. Even though I am not a citizen, I still feel part of this society. Yet even when I get my passport, there will be people who will not see me as a fellow citizen. So, I have a conflict within myself. Since I feel like a part of this community now, I am not speaking as an outsider. But I am also an Afghan; that's my heritage. That mixture is who I am.

I do not want *The Lightless Sky* to be about me. I want it to be about refugees, and about what we can do to help and support them. I have made it my duty to speak out and share our experiences. I do not find pleasure in sharing my story and I wish I did not have to. But it is important that somebody speaks out. My Afghan friends say: 'So, you have written a book; it is not a big deal, we have all made the same journey.' And that is exactly the point! It is not a big deal for us, but it should be a big deal for other people. Our experiences should not be normalised.

The world has changed in many ways since I was on the journey, yet parallels remain. The hardship, the brutality and being treated as a commodity by smugglers are the same. My specific experiences are somewhat different from many refugee experiences today. But at the same time, my story is not extraordinary.

I want my book to be a contribution to public memory. There are a lot of stories of refugees, but many are not recorded. I hope my book becomes a historical record in the archives where people look back at it in the future and reflect on what it is all about. In the book I want readers to be better informed about what refugees go through. I want to give readers the full picture, and show them that I had a life before I became a refugee. I did not become a refugee out of nowhere. Most people do have a life and they want to keep that life. If I had a choice, I would want to be with my loved ones, I would not want to be in the UK. But I remain grateful that Britain took me in and gave me so many opportunities.

I want to explain to readers that we refugees have agency. We are human beings. We should be treated as equals.

Unfortunately, however, we find ourselves born in the wrong place at the wrong time. We find ourselves in a difficult situation where the circumstances are out of our control. Most of all, I just want to explain that we should be treated with the decency and dignity that everyone deserves. We are human beings like everyone else and we have quite interesting stories, perhaps even more interesting stories than most people in Europe.

Gotlib is specifically alert to how stereotyped representations of refugees exclude them from what she calls 'shared moral spaces' (239); when represented as 'angels, demons, or helpless victims' by those who hold narrative power, refugees will invariably be presented to the world without a 'human face' and integrity as moral agents. Pertaining specifically to news media coverage and the role of reporters, Gotlib's critique appears to resonate with Chouliaraki and Stolic who address the need for alternative conceptions of responsible journalism that work deliberately to re-humanise the figure of the refugee without modifying assumptions. News media, they argue, must engage in a rethinking of responsible journalism. In fact, they take the idea of ethical journalism a decisive step further than what we outlined above. Adopting Roger Silverstone's distinction between 'formal responsibility' and 'substantive responsibility', they bring this distinction to bear on the reporter who covers the refugee crisis. While the former, in tune with the principles of ethical journalism, means that reporters are professionally responsible and accountable for their own acts and the representational choices made in the mediation of the refugee crisis, the latter is morally indebted as it involves 'responsibility for the condition of the other' (Silverstone in Chouliaraki and Stolic, 2017: 1173) – the other in this case meaning the refugee. This has far-reaching implications as it not only means involving those reported about, but that those reported about are granted 'narratability' in publicly mediated discourses. To Chouliaraki and Stoic, refugee narratability entails 'the ability to articulate own life histories, trajectories and aspirations as irreducibly human endeavours' (1164) and it has the advantage of curbing the objectification of refugees by bringing them into the realm of conversation as active participants. This is no easy task. Not only must reporters rethink conventional journalistic practices, the task is further complicated by the fact that reporters engage with refugees within 'systemic relationships of power, sovereign and biopolitical' (1174) that work to disable reciprocity in communication. Chouliaraki and Stolic contend, however, that 'we [must] turn these relationships into a site of struggle, where the norms of humanity, agency, and responsibility are constantly at stake' (1174). Substantive responsibility, then, speaks directly to a moral engagement with humanity and even if perhaps an overly hopeful best practice, taking it on holds potential because it offers an alternative way of engaging with refugees from a perspective that combines ethics with moral concern.

Chouliaraki and Stolic are – and so are we – inspired by Hannah Arendt's conception of the public 'space of appearance' in which the 'performance of voice is a world-disclosing practice' (1174) that generates visibility and audibility, in Gotlib's critique precisely what master public narratives erase. The space of appearance comes into existence when 'actors gather together for the purpose of discussing and deliberating about matters of public concern' and 'to undertake some common project' (Passerin d'Entréves, 2001: 77). To Arendt, it is a space of action made up by the 'sharing of words and deeds' (1998: 197), but its existence is fragile, Arendt cautions: 'wherever people gather together, it is potentially there, but only potentially, not necessarily, and not forever' (199). Still, as in Xavier Marquez' reading of Arendt, such a space can facilitate 'horizontal [i.e. reciprocal] relationships [that] enable participants to escape the roles and rules that normalize or even oppress them in other social spaces, to disclose their individuality, and to begin something new' (2012: 7). Following a similar reading of Arendt, Chouliaraki and Stolic tie the relational and contingent condition- ing of substantive responsibility to Arendt's conception of the space of appearance as 'in principle, open to all' (2017: 1174). They are well aware of the imbalance of power and privilege when reporters engage with refugees: 'Substantive responsibility here does not nec- essarily mean that refugees are *de facto* ... equal participants in this space, but rather that the boundaries around "who speaks" in these spaces become permeable and open to be claimed by a plurality of voices that seek social and political recognition' (1174). In the remaining parts of this chapter we explore how the book-length reportages of Patrick Kingsley, Daniel Trilling and Dina Nayeri succeed in reframing the figure of the refugee by opening 'the boundaries around who speaks' in ways that resonate with Chouliaraki and Stolic's call for mediated communication to facilitate 'social and political recognition' of refugees. Kingsley, Trilling and Nayeri may, or indeed may not, subscribe to the idea of substantive responsibility in reporting except, perhaps, as a desirable ideal, but in practical terms their books can, we posit, be read as the outcome of engaging with refugees from the perspectives just outlined.

## WITNESS OR PARTICIPANT

Addressing the ethical challenges of reporting on the refugee crisis, Patrick Kingsley suggests that these are bound up in the vexed relationship between witnessing and participation and complicated by the fact that good journalism must be objective, provide accurate information and reject partisan advocacy (2019). This, however, does not mean that the framing of refugee stories does not have an unequivocal ethical trajectory. As he comments on the work that went into *The New Odyssey*: 'The point of my journalism was to foster compassion for others', there was a 'responsibility to dispel myths about migration, but not with ideological frameworks of my own' (2019). Accordingly, *The New Odyssey* focuses on individual lives – one in particular – and specific journeys as a means of 'shifting the conversation away from the anonymising and alienating discourses of a foreign swarm' towards 'convey[ing] the idea that every boatload arriving on the shores of the northern Mediterranean was full of individuals with their own personalities, and flaws, and dreams and histories' (2019). Daniel Trilling explains the choices he made for *Lights in the Distance* along similar lines:

[T]he starting point should be the migrants themselves. Their experiences are often treated as secondary to the question of what to do with them. On the one hand, you have the weight of anti-immigration propaganda. On the other, you have the messages of humanitarian organizations that want to stress people's vulnerability, or their good nature, or their exceptional achievements. Most though, are neither innocents nor villains, but people trying to retain control over their lives and making complex decisions ... Like the rest of us, they are constantly making and remaking stories that explain their place in the world. (2018a: 262)

Trilling comments that he attempted to (re)present the individual testimonies shared in 'as open and honest a way as possible' and therefore chose to narrate 'our encounters in the first person' because 'I want you to see these people as I did, and not let their harshest experiences overshadow the other aspects of their personalities' (266). Both Kingsley and Trilling deliberately facilitate refugee narratability even if they themselves perform the role of mediator. In *The Ungrateful Refugee*, Dina Nayeri is equally observant of how refugees are in need of being listened to rather than talked, or reported, about. She, however, is a reporting literary writer and a former refugee herself. This shapes an approach that most strongly evokes the idea of substantive responsibility:

A reframing is in order. I want to make sense of the world's reaction ... I feel a duty: I've lived as an American for years ... I've been both Muslim and Christian. There are secrets I can show the native-born that new arrivals don't dare reveal ... I was looking for stories, for whispers of stories hidden by shame or trauma ... I came across dozens of stories; I have chosen a few to follow ... tales all the more harrowing because they are commonplace now and, in the asylum office, often disbelieved. (2019: 13)

I *do* know why I'm here – I've come because the world is turning its back on refugees ... I have a skill born out of my own idle refugee days ... I'm here to make a few stories leap out from the trepid simmer of information and to carry those stories to the West. (2019: 139)

The three books employ the mixed genre of reportage and commentary yet are distinguished by Kingsley's preference for creative non-fiction, Trilling's for unadorned journalistic documentation, and Nayeri's for autobiographically inflected montage. All, however, make use of zoom-in and zoom-out perspectives that in combination provide the complex and nuanced understanding of the refugee situation that mainstream news mediations or master public narratives lack. Kingsley, Trilling and Nayeri are aware that there are few levellers of their privileged position as 'reporting' witnesses to refugees' traumatising experiences, other than their desire to create a space in which individual refugees can tell their stories in ways that reach beyond the confinements of their present lives. And this is precisely what is understood by the public space of appearance. The space of appearance that eventuates in the three books under discussion here is, we argue, centred on the common project of creating awareness of the refugee situation through interaction between reporters and refugees gathered in a space that provides, even if temporarily, an escape from the roles and rules that prescribe communication in other social spaces (Marquez, 2012). Significantly, in the space of appearance refugees escape the stereotypical roles they are assigned in other social spaces and appear, like the reporters they engage with, as individuals with projects and moral agency. And equally significant, reporters cannot maintain a rigid distinction between witnessing and participation. Thus, the public space of appearance involves not only the co-presence of actors convening in pursuit of a common purpose, it is also contingent on the forming of relationships that, despite inequalities in other social spaces, are reciprocal. As Trilling notes: 'I followed my subjects' progress for a long time ... and we needed to trust one another to make it work' (2018a: 265–6). Trust can be troubled by the fact that refugees whose asylum applications are in process are prone to make constant assessments of how, or whether to, engage in conversation, yet when the common goal is to create awareness and, as Kingsley notes, with the aim to 'improve public understanding and perhaps in the process to change the way [the broader audience will] react positively to the reporter's aim to foster empathy' (2019), then trust grows from that shared endeavour. It is not our objective here to offer in-depth analyses of the three books; rather we extract three interrelated ideas that are central in all of them, yet particularly pronounced in one or the other. These are:

empathy, trust and truthfulness. Such words are invested in ethics and belong in the refugee lexicon we pursue in this book.

## EMPATHY

*The New Odyssey* is the result of Patrick Kingsley's 2015 journey to 17 countries across three continents with the aim to 'witness the migration crisis in more breadth and depth' (2017: 12) than media outlets usually make possible. This provides Kingsley with a comprehensive template for 'filling in the gaps' and exploring the push and pull factors and the international political failures that refugees suffer the consequences of (Trilling, 2019). In Kingsley's words, *The New Odyssey* is:

> about why [refugees] keep coming, and how they do it. It's about the smugglers who help them on their way, and the coast-guards who rescue them at the other end. The volunteers that feed them, the hoteliers that house them, and the border agents trying to keep them out. And the politicians looking the other way. (2017: 11)

Such a broad canvas can only lead to a complex telling; one that is crucial to the project of creating a profound awareness of the barriers and obstacles refugees face in their search for refuge. And a complex telling seems a prerequisite for an understanding of the experiences that refugees, once granted narratability, relate. Kingsley interchangeably zooms out to the broader politics of the refugee crisis and zooms in on the consequences such politics have for refugees, thereby making overlooked connections between cause and effect painfully evident. Contrary to the connotations of an unimpeded swarm of refugees directly headed for Europe, Kingsley traces the refugee journey as a process of numerous stops and starts interrupted by agonising periods of waiting for the next possible move or pushback over borders just crossed. To be in flight is a matter of life or death. Refugees know the risks but will push on nevertheless. Risk-taking is 'the least worst option', as Ghanaian Abdo tells Kingsley: 'you know in French we say, "Cabri mort n'a

par peur du couteau." A dead goat doesn't fear the butcher's knife'
(128). Or as a Syrian refugee waiting in Egypt tells him:

> Even if there was a [European] decision to drown the migrant
> boats, there will still be people going by boat because the individ-
> ual considers himself dead already. Right now Syrians consider
> themselves dead. Maybe not physically, but psychologically and
> socially [a Syrian] is a destroyed human being, he's reached the
> point of death. (2017: 129)

Such statements are significant. They are not uttered to invoke
pity; rather, as matter-of-fact statements they register at a deeper
emotional level than that of appeal. Their affect is one of fatalistic withdrawal from the expectation that refugee lives count as
valuable and grievable.

Kingsley maps the affective experiences of refugees in their
passage towards safety as they come into contact with an array of
unreliable negotiators and genuine helpers, ranging from Hajj, the
Libyan smuggler with a law degree who somewhat dubiously 'wants
to be considered a smuggler with ethics' (73) to Hans Breuer, the
Jewish Austrian shepherd who volunteers to help refugees across
the Hungarian-Austrian border and whose ethical commitment, as
the son of a father who was a refugee during World War II, needs
no ratification: 'Jews, Muslims, Christians – it's not important …
We are all humans' (276). Kingsley also comes across the English
Kempson couple who live on Lesbos, busy filling a 'humanitarian vacuum' (179) by setting out to rescue when incoming boats
appear on the horizon, simply because 'you can't do nothing' (181).
And he encounters the Serbian priest Tibor Varga who assists
refugees along their routes. He is 'totally convinced that when
you help the needy, you're helping god with something' (229), but
also responding defiantly to the European fear that 'an influx of
foreigners will erode European values' because 'what values will
there be to uphold if we abandon our duty to protect those less
fortunate than ourselves?' (232). These responses are not driven
by sentimental pity but by a moral obligation to act responsibly
towards fellow human beings in need, even if as helpers they do
not engage personally with the refugees they encounter beyond the

point of rescue or assistance in crossing borders 'illegally'. Indispensable humanitarian work at the hotspots of the crisis rarely extends beyond the emergency of rescue. Still, as a team member on an MSF rescue ship in the Mediterranean explains to Kingsley, it is protocol to welcome those rescued as onboard guests: '[w]e're like the character in Dante's *Inferno* who takes Virgil to the other side of the river Styx. … We are like the parentheses of normality between a very hard situation in Libya, and another one in Europe, a period of safety and rest and dignity in which they are considered human beings' (141–42). Another team member is less poetic and adds that '[t]he smell of humanity … is something that will stick with me the longest. The smell of people who have had fear going through them for a long time – that fear has a smell of its own' (151).

Such is the reality of saving people from drowning as the consequence of inhumane European politics, an urgent enterprise in which, it goes without saying, there is little space to consider refugee narratability. Kingsley's stay onboard the MSF ship calls into question a reporter's ethical challenge of how to balance witnessing and participation. On the crowded ship, this

is a slightly awkward place to report from. There's barely any space to stand, and I find myself interviewing people while squatting over sleeping migrants. The MSF team could do with an extra hand on deck, rather than someone asking endless questions. … I put down my notebook and start behaving like a human being. (2017: 150)

However, as rescued human cargo, as Chouliaraki and Stolic note, refugees appear to the world as an undifferentiated 'mass of unfortunates' within 'a field of representation that reduces their life to corporeal existence and the [bare] needs of the body' (2017: 1167). In an emergency situation, even a hospitable welcome on an MSF ship of course cannot wish away the reality that refugees are at the mercy of the humanitarian benevolence of their hosts and that, reaching port, what they are likely to experience is, at best, 'generalised pity' (Boltanski in Chouliaraki and Stolic, 2017: 1167) rather than recognition of their political rights as refugees. In the context of rescue, refugees are generally perceived as a depersonalised vulnerable presence with no attention to what brought 'the unfortunates' into the situation they need to be rescued from.

However, extensive reportage from the many flashpoints of the refugee crisis provides the contextual framing for Kingsley's in-depth focus in *The New Odyssey* which is to follow the journey of one particular man, 'a Syrian called Hashem al-Souki' (2017: 12), from their first encounter in Egypt to Hashem's final arrival in Sweden, three years after he fled home in Damascus:

> Every other chapter … is about Hashem's quest for safety. His very personal narrative is juxtaposed with the narrative of the wider crisis, allowing us to cycle between the journey of an individual and that of the continent he passes through. Why Hashem in particular? He's no freedom fighter or superhero. He's just an ordinary Syrian. But that's why I want to tell his story. It's the story of an everyman, in whose footsteps any of us could one day tread. (2017: 12–13)

In mainstream news, Hashem, who survived a sinking boat in the Mediterranean in 2015, would have registered merely as part of a 'faceless' group of people rescued from drowning, to be included in the statistical tally. He would be without a name, a face and a story to tell. *The New Odyssey*, however, foregrounds Hashem's story and grants him narratability when the interaction between Kingsley (or rather Patrick) and Hashem brings about the public space of appearance that is so pivotal to the idea of substantive responsibility. Kingsley mediates Hashem's story, but Hashem contributes with his own voice as the relation between the reporter and his source opens up an equitable space of mutual recognition of what each can contribute to the common project of creating awareness about the refugee crisis and those who, like Hashem, struggle against the odds every day of their journey.

The story that Hashem shares with Kingsley is one that takes us beyond stereotypes. Hashem is a victim of circumstance but also comes across as a moral agent who wants the world to listen and understand 'why people like me are risking our lives' (326), thus his acceptance to let Kingsley into his life. His sudden arrest one

REFUGEE TALK: PROPOSITIONS ON ETHICS AND AESTHETICS

evening in 2012 was unexpected because Hashem 'isn't particularly political. He's just a thirty-seven-year-old civil servant at the regional water board' who attempts to stay clear of escalating state and sectarian violence in Syria; '[h]e focuses on the water business and minds his own' (17). But his family life changes dramatically with the random neighbourhood arrests that take him into secret cells and torture rooms. After having been incarcerated for six months and with his neighbourhood now besieged, Hashem escapes with his family to Egypt. The experience of prison and torture is not what Hashem dwells on, it is his responsibility for his family's future that weighs on his mind when Kingsley first meets him. The despair of being suddenly uprooted from his home and not being sure of how to keep his family safe is what drives him:

> Hashem reckons his hopes and dreams are over. But his children's are still worth dying for. 'I'm risking my life for something bigger, for ambitions bigger than this. ... If I fail, I fail alone. But, by risking this, I might achieve a dream for three children: my children – and maybe my grandchildren as well'. (2017: 13)

Hashem leaves behind his family in relative safety in Egypt and with 'a notebook so that he could keep an accurate record of what happened onboard, and a camera to supplement his notetaking' (328), he embarks on the Mediterranean crossing to meet up with Kingsley again. Kingsley then accompanies Hashem on the risky journey by train up through Europe. Here, he observes from a distance, but close enough to witness, the silent drama of Hashem's nervy avoidance of numerous border controls by pretending to be a local dozing behind a constantly shifting selection of national newspapers. Hashem is lucky, he manages the long European train journey from Italy to Sweden without being detected and eventually reaches Sweden. His story, unfortunately, is not extraordinary. Rather, in being the story of an everyman – a man, a husband and a father who is willing to put his own life at stake to save that of his family – it is a story that strikes empathy without pity because it is relatable, dignified and bereft of all the clichés of the public master narratives about refugees and their 'ulterior' motives. Hashem's journey can be made known and named, of course, only because when Kingsley's book is published, he has reached a place of safety where he can await family reunion and 'live in dignity' (306).

Kingsley's witnessing and co-presence on Hashem's journey is an intense experience: '[a]s a human being, it was very hard not to get involved' (329). But, substantive responsibility would not have it any other way. If Kingsley is guided by a moral obligation to strike empathy for those that Europe so readily turns its back against by prioritising securitisation over humanity, then his intimate reportage of Hashem's courageous journey succeeds to expel the idea of the refugee as a distant stranger. This is because Kingsley reports from a position of proximity rather than distance and because Hashem's affect thereby becomes a shared concern. Empathy is more than a professional or rhetorical gesture, it is genuinely the result of their interaction in the public space of appearance where Hashem appears as a particular man and not a particular type of refugee. This impacts on Kingsley's choice of words in representing Hashem. The stale vocabularies associated with refugees and their journeys are exchanged with new ones, or rather, new to the context. In *The New Odyssey*, Hashem and fellow Syrians who share the experience of being expelled from home are not representative of a feared flood of incoming refugees, they are 'voyagers' of the 'The Great Syrian Migration'. What is unusual about Kingsley's portrait of Hashem is its double frame. Kingsley's witnessing of Hashem's determination and capacity for endurance makes him recognise Hashem's journey as 'one of epic heroism – a kind of latterday Homeric Odyssey' (253). As Kingsley reports, '[t]o watch this dignified man limp across an unknown continent … determined to provide his family with a safer future … has been a lesson to me' (305). At journey's end, Hashem is seen by Kingsley to be both a much tried everyday Syrian who, in spite of the odds, has finally reached his destination *and* a bone-weary warrior coming out of battle at long last:

Hashem is exhausted – physically, mentally and emotionally. The past three years have been punctured by constant trauma, and frequent humiliation. The past two weeks have seen him risk arrest, death and starvation to cross a sea and a continent.

He is thirsty, hungry, smelly, sleep-deprived. ... And every step
he walks, he feels a pang from his infected foot. (2017: 253)

This double frame is significant. When his journey is referenced
as a heroic achievement – and not as an illegal transgression into
European territories – Hashem himself is troped outside of the stereotypes of victim and villain. Substituting a stereotyped framing
with an epic one does not seem trite or excessive, although it is not
a framing that Hashem himself has had any say in. It is refresh-
ingly unusual but, judging from the detailed hardships of Hashem's
story, at the same time appropriate.

The collaboration of Kingsley and Hashem, a reporter and his
source, clearly builds on the forging of a human relationship of
reciprocity that grows from unconditional kindness towards the
other. This is rare in journalism where there is usually not enough
time to pursue it. At the end of the book, in 'A message from Hashem
Al-Souki', Hashem explains the situation in Syria that left him and
his family with no other option than to leave and that participating
in Kingsley's book project was 'a chance to speak freely – to use
this right that we in Syria have been deprived of for forty years. I
want our voice to reach the world' (326). Despite all the suffering
endured, Hashem points to the many things learned on the way
about how 'life has many cultures and ways of thinking' (326) but
irrespective of that there are 'many people who will always give you
the hope and determination to plough through the darkness' (326).
And in this process, 'Patrick has become part of my family – he is
not just a journalist or a friend, but an important part of my life'
(326). Conversely, in 'Acknowledgments', Kingsley thanks Hashem
for 'letting [him] into his life' and for the lessons learned from
him 'about love, resilience, dedication, parenthood and dignity'
(330). This we read as the strongest possible outcome of Arendt's
insistence on the potential and 'world-disclosing' capacity of the
public space of appearance. The working relationship between
Hashem and Kingsley (that would bit by bit become a friendship)
is one in which Kingsley is at pains to stick to the journalistic
role of being a witness to Hashem's journey without stepping into
the role of participant. While that is 'literally true', as Kingsley
recognises in retrospect, he was perhaps 'indirectly participating

all along' (2019). Yet this does not compromise Kingsley's integrity as a reporter; rather it points to how a working relationship that pursues a common purpose must rely on trust and all participants must 'be seen and heard as ... equal' (Arendt, 1998: 50). This invariably calls on witnessing as well as participation.

**In conversation, Patrick Kingsley says:** Even if I did not actively seek out to show the complexity of individual refugees, I feel strongly that it is important to humanise refugees in news reporting. That does not mean that you have to portray refugees as angels, which of course they are not. Neither are we – we are just people and so are they. There are dangers involved in the act of humanising a complex phenomenon through one person, as I in part do in *The New Odyssey*. Hashem is presented almost as an everyman, in the sense that his ordinariness is empha-sised in the narrative. So, I run the risk of objectifying him and he becomes an emblem or a symbol. In the process of mediating the story of his attempt to regain agency, I also somehow remove his agency. There is always a tension and a compromise in what I am doing. In the course of the book, Hashem and I move from subject and observer to two friends who have had a very interesting experience together. When the family reach Sweden, I go with them, not as an observer, but as their friend. During the act of reporting his journey, for professional reasons it was important that I attempted, as far as possible, to observe rather than to participate in his journey. But still my mediation of this journey made me a participant, whether I like it or not. At the end of the book, I hope that I manage to strike a balance that is acceptable.

## TRUST

In *The New Odyssey* Kingsley notes that 'it's sometimes hard to get people to trust me on the trail. How do they know I won't misrep-resent them? ... My conversation-starters in Arabic help to build a rapport, but some people naturally don't want to take the risk of talking.' This is particularly the case with women, he adds, 'which is why [his] book doesn't contain so many female voices' (2017: 220).

The question of the gendered refugee is an important concern, one that Georgiou and Zaborowski (2017) draw attention to in their report to the European Council. They note that news media have a disproportionately low coverage rate on female refugees (2017: 3). This is, however, not likely to be deliberately overlooked by reporters but a consequence of the fact that female refugees are less likely to share their stories than male refugees. They often feel vulnerable and insecure in their interactions with reporters and potentially also within refugee communities if they travel unaccompanied by husbands or male family members.

**In conversation, Daniel Trilling says**: *Lights in the Distance* is mainly narrated in the first person, although it is not at all confessional. An early draft was written in the third person and from an omniscient narrator's perspective. I thought that I would just be the equivalent of a fly-on-the-wall documentary maker. I ditched this idea because it did not work narratively. I did not feel that I was telling the truth about the situation, because it was important to show how I was able to build up relationships with people, or the different ways in which they and I were able to negotiate particular spaces. I also decided to follow a number of different stories rather than focusing on a symbolic individual narrative. I explored different situations that focused on individuals trying to retain control over their situation with varying degrees of success.

In *Lights in the Distance* Daniel Trilling tells the stories of eight individual refugees, three of whom are women, and their initial reluctance to talk to a journalist confirms Kingsley's observation. 'We keep having journalists visit, and they want to hear our stories, but, tell me, what can you do? Nothing changes' (2018a: 174) exclaims a frustrated Hakima from Afghanistan who is stranded with her family in migrant-hostile Athens when Trilling meets her. Trilling falls short of an answer but 'mumble[s] something that [he] thought would sound encouraging about … members of [his] own family [who] had been refugees once, and they had got through it – but [his] words fell on stony ground' (174). He also tells the story of Zainab, 'a quiet thirty-year-old with a cautious demeanour' (38) who escaped Iraq and ISIS with her three children after her father was killed and her husband disappeared. In such a situation, a story 'mediated through a translator' is made difficult by the fact that the setup can feel like 'a formal inquiry' (39), with the journalist having stepped into a place where less sympathetic interviewers had previously sat. As Trilling relates:

> Our conversation lapsed into silence, partly because of the language barrier, but also because we didn't yet know what to make of one another. Perhaps she was uneasy talking to a man, or I was more hesitant to ask questions of a woman. I felt like Zainab wasn't sure whether I was someone who would help her or exploit her; this was a weighing-up process she must have been through more than once on her journey. I wanted, as far as possible, to hear Zainab's story the way she wanted to tell it. So I suggested that I leave my Dictaphone with her and she record her story in Arabic. I would then get a friend to translate it. (2018a: 39)

The above examples show how difficult it is to bring about a space of appearance in which (female) refugees feel secure enough to participate without being apprehensive about the presence of a (male) reporter. However, the third woman that Trilling gets in contact with is Fatima from Nigeria. She is naturally outgoing and interested in conversation even if she says that '[w]e get in trouble if we talk to journalists' (121) and Trilling notes her initial doubts about 'whether or not to trust journalists' (119). Fatima is a 35-year-old 'pragmatic, sometimes brusque woman' (116) whose story captivates Trilling because of its atypical trajectory. Anna Gotlib comments that 'non-essentialist conceptions of refugees' are urgently needed to counter the 'toxic' assumptions about 'dependence and victimhood' so prevalent in master public narratives (Gotlib in Oliver et al., 2019: 249). The victim narrative, as Gotlib argues, is 'yet another way to silence [… and] make small' (247). Fatima, however, certainly steps into the vacant place in reportage of the resourceful female refugee who defies all stereotypes about the silent victim. She is vocal and initially agrees to talk to Trilling merely in her capacity of being a refugee activist with an agenda and busy schedule. A relationship of reciprocity forms during their meetings helped along by Trilling's willingness to function as Fatima's chauffeur on her many errands. This give-and-take arrangement eventually makes Fatima trust Trilling enough to disclose her story (including her experiences in Nigeria and Libya and escape from both countries); not as a sequence of events, but bit by bit: 'As I drove, with Fatima sat behind, rather than facing me, interview style, she was more forthcoming' (2018a: 121).

Fatima's claim for asylum is based on a complex story. She crossed the Sahara twice to live in Libya, the first time as an economic migrant, the last time as a refugee upon receiving a death threat after her participation in organised protests against the corruption of the Nigerian government. She intended to stay in Libya, worked hard to sustain a fair living but also advocated women's rights. With political conflicts escalating in Libya, it became risky for Black Africans to live there, with public assaults and random killings, and Fatima resolved in 2015 to pay smugglers to bring her to Europe: 'Let me live', she thought on boarding the dinghy 'and I will make it my mission to help people who come through Libya, to raise alarm about what is happening, especially to women and children' (116). Fatima is not prone to sentimentalising her story and she chooses not to abide by the expectation that an asylum seeker stays in place and waits until further notice. Fatima is confident enough to stand up at a conference in Sicily on the migrant crisis and address the audience upfront: 'don't just come and ask me questions and sell my story or sell my voice; we need a change' (137). Moreover, she spends her 'pocket money' from the reception centre on buying food for rejected migrants who live in cave-like conditions on the outskirts of town. She documents their plight and shares her recordings with Trilling. Drawing on her inside knowledge of sex-trafficking of young Nigerian women, she has set up a Facebook group to 'tell the truth' (135) about refugees' lives, and she functions as a 'cultural mediator' (140) in the local hospital. She is clearly entrepreneurial. She wants to make a charity that helps women split from the abusive 'accidental husbands' (119) they married en route to make their journey safer – and she dreams of setting up an African theatre group (140) and an 'African kitchen' (160) in Sicily. Her story is compelling because by performing as a moral agent in the midst of a refugee crisis that she herself is part of, she nevertheless assumes responsibility for unfortunate others that the humanitarian setup in Sicily fails to extend to refugees, Fatima included. When Trilling asks her why she has 'taken to wearing a crucifix around her neck' and 'sharing Christian, as well as Muslim memes on Facebook', her pragmatic response is telling: 'I am Muslim. But I don't want to be more on the side of one religion than the other. Because I want to help people and I want them to be able to come to me' (158). Fatima is self-made, unapologetic, and perhaps seen to lack the gratitude with which to win recognition from her host society. As Trilling notes: 'Fatima was kicking hard against the current, trying to give her life some shape. It was as if, by declaring herself a woman's rights activist, or a social entrepreneur, or a theatre producer, she was trying to will one of these roles into existence' (143). This notwithstanding, Fatima's voice registers loud and clear in Trilling's narrative of the refugee crisis, and it is one to be reckoned with because it debunks the stereotype of the gendered refugee as a mere victim.

Like Kingsley, Trilling travelled extensively while researching his book, to 'places where the fault lines in Europe's asylum system were most evident' (265) and interviewed 'scores of people' (266). The selection of individual stories aim to give 'a fairly representative – although not comprehensive – picture of the people who have come to Europe in search of asylum' (265). And like Kingsley, Trilling provides a comprehensive layout of the facts, myths and public sentiments that surround the refugee crisis and this works to contextualise the individual refugee stories that he zooms in on. In her advocacy of non-essentialist representations of refugees that do not lump refugees into a faceless mass of unfortunates, Anna Gotlib quotes Lara Zahabi-Bekdash for pointing out that undifferentiated representations 'strip them from the only thing they still own; their stories, relationships and experiences as human beings. We forget that there are as many refugee stories, experiences, and identities as there are refugees. We forget how complex identities are' (Gotlib in Oliver et al., 2019: 248). *Lights in the Distance*, however, is attentive both to the diversity of refugee stories and to the complexity of identities, especially as the refugees Trilling engages in conversation with speak both as individuals with personal biographies and as refugees deadlocked because of host societies' neglect of human rights and misconception of moral duties. What transpires from such conversations, however, is that being a refugee is to live in a state of emergency or uncertainty where one is rarely granted the narratability that can alert listeners to how complex *and* individual identities are. It is of course an obstacle to bringing this out that refugees who engage with reporters are aware that the lack of anonymity and the disclosure of too much information might put them at risk. It is therefore crucially important to establish a relationship of trust between the reporter and his source. The public performance of voice, to rehearse Arendt again, relies on exchange within a space of reciprocity and, at least situational, equality, a space in which participants trust each other enough to know that stories are shared in pursuit of a common purpose. This is again bound up in ethics because trust travels with ethics. Indeed, they are mutually reinforcing. In *Lights in the Distance* we come across two stories in particular that showcase this as a prerequisite for Trilling's effort to endow his sources with narratability and thus move beyond commonplace stereotypes.

The first is Jamal's story. Trilling meets Jamal in the Jungle in Calais in 2014 'where he had emerged from a tent pitched underneath a canal bridge, into the drizzle' (2018a: 3); a 'skinny, shivering young man' who told him in 'lively, American-inflected English' (3) that he had already spent five years 'illegally' within the EU since his flight as a teenager from Sudan. So far he had been unsuccessful in his efforts to move on. Contact details were swapped, Jamal disappeared, but months later contacted Trilling online from a 'northern European country' where he had been granted asylum and was now ready to meet up again: 'He said he'd explain everything: how he ended up in Calais, what had gone wrong there; how he'd left. I said I wanted to know a lot, and that it might take several days of interviews. He was fine with that' (4). There is nothing unusual about the short interview and Jamal's brief sketch of a long journey at their first encounter in Calais – in the short format of mainstream media news this would qualify as an ethical commitment to including those reported about – but the circumstances of their second encounter alter their interaction in significant ways. First of all, it is Jamal who contacts Trilling again – they meet in Jamal's apartment for newly arrived refugees somewhere in northern Europe. Here, Jamal is the host and Trilling the guest. Crucially, however, within this space of relative safety, Jamal can trust Trilling to witness his story in its fullness and report on it without putting him in danger. 'As we ate' (4) Trilling writes, 'Jamal told me about his childhood in … Khartoum and about his parents – pious, working-class people who saw the Iraqi dictator Saddam Hussein as a hero because "he stood up to the West"' (4–5) – and about his teenage favourite pastime of watching American crime series (thus his American accent) and his mundane life experiences. Well into their talk that spans three days, Jamal discloses the events that led up to his arrest by the Sudanese government, his dream of 'a better life' (7) in Europe, his escape and experience of being smuggled across borders. His journey, too, is one of stops and starts without a proper sense of direction or destination. After years of squatting in Patras in a disused factory occupied by a Sudanese migrant community, Jamal eventually made it to the Jungle in Calais where he became entangled in violent ethnic conflicts within the camp, but also built up quite a reputation as 'king of skipping' (50) for those, like himself, hunting for an illegal lorry passage to England.

Jamal's story is full of pain. Occasionally, he does not 'feel secure enough in his new home' to 'go into details' (64) but agrees to tell 'just enough' (64) to flesh out his story of 'the messy reality of life' (64). At the end of the last day, 'waiting for the stew to finish cooking' (67), Jamal explains to Trilling in uncanny detail the procedure of how men in Calais would burn off their fingerprints to avoid registration in the Eurodac police database: '"Like this," he said, gripping my hand and pressing it into the handle of the fridge door. He pushed my index finger into the metal and ran it downwards, firmly, two or three times' (67). Leading up to this moment that quite physically draws Trilling into Jamal's affect, Trilling asks '[w]hy did he trust me, and why did I trust him back?' (67). He does not provide an answer, but a likely explanation is that trust has grown from the humane environment of their conversations, where Trilling has listened over days to a much fuller story of Jamal's life than Jamal could possibly have shared with Trilling in the harsh setting of the Jungle in Calais that quite simply offers no context for proper human connectivity between a reporter and a refugee. Clearly, connectivity builds trust and trust requires participation and involvement in one form or another. It is, significantly, in the country of refuge where Jamal expects his first ever 'real' passport and so no longer needs to 'be afraid of everything in my head' (67) that the relationship of reciprocity between Trilling and Jamal makes it possible for Jamal to restore himself as an individual with a biography in excess of the refugee tag.

**In conversation, Daniel Trilling says**: *Lights in the Distance* is about my encounters with people seeking asylum. In the book I write about Jamal, a young man originally from Sudan, and reflect on why I trusted him and why he trusted me back. I did trust him, and I sat with him for three days while he told me his long story. He could have made it all up. But I was sure he had not. What was it about him that made me trust him? I think it was the way we interacted. He was open about things and willing to make a direct connection with me. I would not say that ours was an equal relationship because there was the obvious power imbalance between us. Of course, I was in a much more privileged position as a journalist. But Jamal was not sharing information with me in the expectation of some kind of short-term reward. The people I met were in desperate situations and needed immediate forms of help that I was unable to provide because I thought, ethically, it is not appropriate for me to be intervening in that way and to be a journalist at the same time. I had to develop a way of dealing with that situation that I could be comfortable with. I tried to be quite clear about what I was doing. I told people I met that I was writing a book about the way in which people in their situation are being treated so that readers in Europe get a better under-standing of what is happening, and, hopefully in the future they can get their governments to make better decisions. But it will probably not help you in your situation right now. That is something I said to people quite openly.

The other story in which trust is pivotal is Caesar's story and what is noteworthy here is the fact that Caesar insists from the very beginning to enter into conversation with Trilling as a moral agent. As we have seen, the idea of refugee agency is almost expected to be oxymoronic in mainstream news coverage. To recognise this would be to disturb the cemented idea that refugees are passive victims without capacity or interest in engaging in the politics of the dismal situation they are entangled in. This is not the case with Caesar. Trilling had known Caesar (a name he adopted to veil his identity) online for two months before they meet up in Sicily in 2015. Until then, he had been 'a username, a blurry avatar that didn't show his face, and a deep voice with rolled *rs* and stuttered out *ts*' (105). It is significant that their relationship begins at Caesar's initiative through an online friend request. Upon Trilling's acceptance, Caesar initiates it by asking the first of many later questions directed at the politics of the refugee crisis: 'What do you think of the situation for refugees in Italy?' (99). This role reversal in the journalistic questioning routine comes to define many of their talks in Sicily. Reluctant to disclose the most hurtful details of his experience as a refugee, usually wrapped up in the repeated phrase '*C'est tres ... tres compliqué*' (106), Caesar is hesitant when Trilling asks for a lengthy interview and replies that 'I want some time to think about *mes paramètres* first' which Trilling takes to mean that he needs 'to think about what he was prepared to reveal and what he wasn't' (145).

As it turns out, having left his wife and son behind in Mali is not a story that can be readily shared. It is too painful and so are the emotions related to the memories of flight where Caesar often tells 'only the briefest of details before switching subjects' (109). Trilling therefore treads a delicate ethical line in subsequent talks as 'short bursts of detail about the journey to Europe were like watching objects break the surface of a lake' (130). Caesar, one of the 'ringleaders' (146) in political protests back in Mali, had his home ransacked by soldiers who killed his mother, beat up and kidnapped Caesar and his younger brother, and dropped them off far into the desert to die. They barely survived, but rescued by shepherds, they eventually made it to Libya, only to be imprisoned, tortured, and, Caesar implies without relating personal experiences, abused because the prison guards 'had sexual appetites' (149). Once released, the two brothers worked under slave-like conditions for a Libyan farmer until they had 'earned' their passage to Europe, where after desperate days of drifting, they were 'plucked from the sea' (155) by the Italian coast guard. Observing the ethical limits of responsible journalism, Trilling asks Caesar 'to stop his story there' (155). From what Caesar shares, and the implications of what he does not, Trilling understands why Caesar would rather forget than memorise and why he now needs his two years of waiting to end, determined as he is 'to disappear into everyday life' (133–4).

Spending time together, however, builds up a connection between Caesar and Trilling that grows into a relationship of trust in the sense that Caesar complies with Trilling's request for a story, but also quite naturally expects Trilling to comply with his request for assistance. When Caesar is keen to know the outcome of European Council meetings, Trilling provides the updates, when he hears about an EU project for asylum seekers and refugees that he might be eligible for, Trilling finds out the details. And when Caesar becomes 'fixated on a new destination' (128), he insists on Trilling's help: 'I need you to find out some information for me. … How does Norway treat Malian refugees? Does it do Dublin returns to Italy? And what categories are exempt? How can you get regular papers in Norway? And can you travel there if you've been given refugee status in Italy?' (129). In tune with the nature of their 'working' relationship, Trilling lists the questions and promises to make enquires. In that sense, their cooperation appears to rest on mutuality and this helps to 'equalise' the unspoken tension between a reporter and his source that often makes it impossible to create a space of appearance in which refugee agency is recognised. Like Jamal's and Fatima's stories, Caesar's story is unique and like them, Caesar resists the victim position in his interactions with Trilling. As he says, 'I value my dignity' (156).

Dignity is the operative word when Caesar shares his thoughts on the refugee crisis. He is politically well informed and 'convinced of Europe's moral responsibility towards migrants from Africa' (134). Europe, he says 'sowed chaos in African countries and if it wasn't for that we wouldn't have to flee for our lives' (100). Caesar is an unapologetic and aspiring refugee, a moral agent who knows that rescue and protection is a right and should not be considered a favour. That he wants this to be recognised is central on his agenda in his conversation with Trilling: 'You can't reverse the situation now; we've become part of the landscape' (108). The dustjacket of *Lights in the Distance* commends Trilling for '[c]ombining forensic enquiry with moral passion' in the exploration of 'the vast human tragedy behind newspaper headlines about refugees'. If considered with reference to the public space of appearance, this can also be seen as part and parcel of the common project around which reporter and refugees gather, but notably in a context where the roles of both parties are renegotiable. It is timely here to rehearse Marquez' point that in such a context, or rather space, participants may circumvent the roles and rules that determine their interactions in other social spaces, just as we recall Chouliaraki and Stolic's point that in that space 'a plurality of voices that seek social and political recognition' (2017: 1174) can be heard and recognised. Trilling's responsibility as reporter is enacted through his book's contribution to the common project of moving beyond the trope of passive victimhood. This, then, also becomes a project of promoting diverse and non-essentialist conceptions of refugees.

## TRUTHFULNESS

The many encounters with refugees that went into *Lights in the Distance* make Trilling aware that '[b]eing a refugee ... you continue bending the rules, telling untruths, concealing yourself, even after you've left immediate danger, because that's the way you negotiate a hostile system' (2018a: 257–8). This is a fact that looms large in Dina Nayeri's *The Ungrateful Refugee*. As she points out, this is not because refugees do not have truthful testimonies to present but because they are aware that an asylum officer is very likely not 'listening for the truth. He's looking for a single lie' (2019: 247) that can rationalise rejection. Yet 'truth', as Nayeri reminds us, is not synonymous with fact: 'Truth is hard work ... you can lie with sloppy facts. And you can tell the truth with well-crafted fiction' (277) because '[a] fact, given disproportionate context and attention, can lie about a life' just as an adjusted story 'can be true when it throws a light on the unseen, those unclaimed spectacles that ... shame and trauma keep hidden from view' (262).

Assuming substantive responsibility in her reportage of the current refugee crisis is not a challenge Nayeri must take up. It is implicit in her approach. As a former child refugee who fled Iran in 1988 with her mother and brother, Nayeri has personal experience of what is means to be encamped, to be (dis)believed, to be made to wait without any promise of when and how life can begin again. Perhaps this is the reason why she can dig deeper into how refugees 'negotiate a hostile system' than non-refugees can or dare and why she is keen to emphasise that in evaluating refugee testimonies it is truthfulness rather than a shallow conception of truth as merely factual that must take priority. Nayeri is 'peeking in different corners than the authorities' – as she readily admits:

> I wasn't looking for discrepancies. I abhor cynical traps that …
> catch out trauma victims for their memory lapses. I don't have
> accent-verifying software. I saw the truth of these stories in
> corroborating scars … I saw truth in grieving, fearful eyes, in
> shaking hands, in the anxiety of children and the sorrow of the
> elderly. (2019: 14)

But this kind of experiential truth may not lend itself to language. Many refugees have been severely traumatised by their experiences to an extent where traumatic memory cannot be turned into a straightforward narrative memory that can be shared with others. As Agnes Woolley observes, there may be a limit as to 'how far the experiences of refugees and asylum seekers are communicable at all' (2014: 3). Nayeri's book abounds with examples where this is the case: 'When you lift your babies into a dinghy, you show your truth. Shame, trauma and fear may strike you mute, but that act is enough' (2019: 279).

*The Ungrateful Refugee* braids Nayeri's own refugee story and 'chameleon life' (119) with the reportage of the current crisis and is therefore also an impassioned account of the lives of those who currently wait. As a former refugee, her interest in 'the feared "swarms"' speaks to what that phrase obscures: 'stories of uprooting and transformation without guarantees, of remaking the face and the body, those first murderous refugee steps – the annihilation of the self, then an ascent from the grave' (14). Thus, her book engages primarily with the affective experience of being or becoming a refugee that we explored in Chapter 1, though here from a double perspective where Nayeri both remembers her own story and witnesses those of others.

**In conversation, Dina Nayeri says:** In the writing of *The Ungrateful Refugee*, I was bound up in constant contradictions and constant terror. I had to tell myself that I was there for a good reason, and that I was taking these stories out in the world – and that it was important that I did so. Even though in the moment the people I met might look at me with great disappointment when they saw that I could not do anything for their particular case, in a bigger sense, I was doing something that I had to do. I also did not want to cause pain to the people I talked to. Even if you do share the language and the culture and you spend time with them, you are inevitably going to put your finger in the wound. The trauma is there. You cannot spend much time with people without forming attachments and without stirring up hope. That is how it was.

I am not a journalist, I am a storyteller. Journalism provides us with a true state of the world, with facts, with eyes and ears in places where we cannot be with accountability, I suppose. As a storyteller I want readers to lose themselves in a story and to forget the world. That is not the aim of journalists. I am trying to create a world inside the mind. These are the kinds of stories that we remember. These are the kinds of stories that bind themselves to us with our own psychology, with our own hearts, with our own stories and experiences. And as a result, they stay and cause us to act. It is not accountability that makes us adhere to a cause and inspire us to affect the world. It is these individual stories, and how we have been lost in them and found ourselves in them. When you get to know something that is familiar about the human experience, that makes us act. And I am trying to get people to act.

*The Ungrateful Refugee* 'recalibrates the conversation around the refugee experience', as suggested on the book's dustjacket. This recalibration is fuelled not only by the fact that Nayeri is a former refugee but also by the fact that she is a literary writer. The combination of her sense of 'duty' (13) and her 'skill' (139) means that the refugees she encounters do not have to be granted narratability in their conversation with her as the 'reporter', rather narratability is the immediate outcome of a public space of appearance in which all participants, including Nayeri, can draw on the same experience of knowing well what it takes to 'hang on to life [... and] to rescue that life from the fiction pile' (14), that is to say, the rejection pile of disbelieving authorities. Nayeri's book offers many insights into the past and present lives of individual refugees, but here we want to focus specifically on her mediation of two 'post-escape' experiences that are particularly soul draining: endless waiting in the 'permanently temporary' location of camps (Bauman's term) and the simultaneous burden of having to prepare a testimony that will fit into the asylum authorities' repertoire of credible stories, aware that this is more a matter of luck than justice.

When Nayeri visits the Katsikas camp in Greece, she presents herself as a collector of stories (169), 'an Iranian lady looking for other Iranians' (157) and is immediately made to feel welcome as she walks the rows of 'Isoboxes', the container lodgings of refugees who are literally, in Nöelle McAfee's disturbingly precise phrase, 'warehoused in perpetuity' (McAfee in Oliver et al., 2019: 33): 'Come over! Come to ours ... Come to my house, lady' (2019: 161). Iranian Majid and Farzaneh greet her with a well-known Farsi expression: 'Come in, come in, sit with us ... We'll tell you stories that will make you grow horns' (157). This is not how a visiting journalist would be approached. Trust does not have to be built up, it is there right away because Nayeri once went through what the people in the camp are now going through. And their stories do make her grow horns although not in the convivial storytelling way suggested by the proverb. They are accompanied by 'mobile videos' and they resonate with 'scenes from a nightmare' as do all the stories Nayeri listens to 'in every Isobox' (169). Her meeting with the Afghan couple Valid and Taraa and their children overwhelms Nayeri. They 'launch into [the horrors of their] story without fanfare' (179) yet it makes her feel that her 'duty' and 'skill' can seem irrelevant to people who are desperate for more practical interventions: 'Is it cruel for a person who's come unstuck to return to another's purgatory?' (181). Nayeri asks herself this question when a camp friend of Valid and Taraa urges her to take their youngest son with her back to England.: 'He's nine ... still has a chance to make a life, to bring his family later ... If you don't want him, drop him off in a camp in England' (180), 'They will take unaccompanied minors ... [t]he state will raise him. He will have ... human rights' (181). Nayeri is lost for words at the thought that Valid and Taraa would be prepared to give their son away. In retrospect, she resorts to Roland Barthes' philosophical proposition in *A Lover's Discourse* that the one who is kept in prolonged waiting will become erratic: 'Did they truly offer me their son, or is this Barthes's loss of proportion – the desire to cut the waiting into pieces, to manage it?' (181). Barthes helps to explain but this does not soothe Nayeri's discomfort about revisiting 'this strange waiting place, this limbo that shaped [her], that is now shaping thousands of others' (187). Waiting, as Barthes explores, is 'both delirium and subjection. Illness and torture' (128). To be made to wait is 'the ultimate indignity' and 'power is to impose it' (118). Yet transferred to a refugee camp where constant waiting not only 'amplifies your responses' (145) but affects your mental state of mind in more disturbing ways, this can be consequential to your chances for a future:

> When you are waiting for life to begin, you're prone to spectacle, to theatre and, as any asylum seeker who has looked into the cold eyes of an immigration officer knows, no one believes melodrama. In life and in fiction, hysteria is the ultimate lie and the waiting are most prone to it. (Nayeri, 2019: 145)

Nayeri's witnessing of how the refugees she meets in camps around Europe are at risk of losing their sanity from endless futile waiting exemplifies with real stories of real lives the effects of what Kelly Oliver (2017) has termed a 'carceral humanitarianism' that robs refugees of their entitlement to dignity. As Nayeri observes:

> with each passing day, the refugee behaves less like an honest petitioner, ... he becomes intense, unattractive. What irony for the asylum seeker to know that every hour in limbo makes his

story less believable ... and salvation less likely. He grows frantic, a risk to a new country. Meanwhile ... the insidious nativist rhetoric shouted down from safe perches, doesn't sound like a lie at all – it sounds clever, rational, calm. (2019: 280)

Asylum seekers wait for an asylum interview and this takes, of course, the psychosomatic symptoms and the entire 'scenography' of waiting to a different level. The most daring way in which Nayeri assumes substantive responsibility for refugees waiting in limbo is by uncovering how asylum procedures, when they criminalise petitioners from the outset, are cynical and inhumane, if not guilty of further traumatising those questioned beyond repair. She reports on many questioning routines that result in what David Owen calls 'testimonial indignity' (Owen in Oliver et al., 2019: 22), cases where, for instance, women will rather falsely claim to need protection because of their sexual orientation than relive the trauma of repeated war rapes:

'I'm a lesbian from Ethiopia. I will be killed.' *How do you have sex with a woman? Describe it to me.*

How is one to present the truth to such a listener? When he accepts only one danger when there are hundreds. When he has no empathy for the daily threat of unchecked violence, when the soldiers, who may not have been targeting you specifically, shattered your psyche, nonetheless. How do you make your *true* story the 'right' kind of true? If your listener already has far greater lies embedded into their worldview, then the only way to sneak the truth into their mind is covertly. (Nayeri, 2019: 277)

Nayeri is aware that refugee testimonies are 'complex and muddled' (9), but they always spring from '[a] tortured mind, terror of a wasted future' and that this is what brings people to abandon home and dare 'stepping into a dinghy' or 'braving militarised mountains' (9). She notes that reasons for escape 'always include a fear *and* a tangible hope. It's a reinvention that grows out of your nightmares, but also your drive and your agency' (9–10).

In her sharply executed dissection of the dangers of hitting the wrong key when refugees present their story in an asylum interview, Nayeri recollects her training as a literary writer and the two pivotal questions a writer must consider: what makes a story true and what makes it worth telling? 'Orphan details' that are 'specific' yet 'strange and [that] seem not to belong' (239) bring a story to life as 'true', in the sense of truthful, and defining 'moments of undoing' where 'someone's world tilts on its axis and they are forever changed' make it worth telling, causing the reader to 'imagine *everything that came before and everything after*' (240). For this to work, 'you must slice out a "wedge" from the arc of a life. The wedge is that life's most vital story' because '[t]he consequence of choosing the wrong wedge is that your story strikes false' (240). Transferred into the asylum interview room, the consequences of slicing the wrong wedge, because the truest one is full of shame or unspeakable trauma, invariably leads to rejection. Nayeri reports on many such examples, such as the story of Houshiar from Iran whom she meets in the Netherlands for a long conversation. He has left wife and son behind and his claim, based on the threat of persecution after his conversion to Christianity, has been rejected: 'They said, I didn't explain my apostasy from Islam well enough' (254), he tells Nayeri. As a fellow Iranian listening intently to his story, Nayeri thinks: 'The more he speaks, the more I crave the real story – it isn't that I don't believe the one he is offering. I just know he has a better, more fundamental one' (254); he had picked the 'wrong wedge' (253). Acknowledging that you 'can't just tell a closeted, married, Iranian man that he needs to face his sexuality' (259) – and that this must be suggested 'without violating Iranian social rules' and therefore 'cloaked' in 'a second meaning'(258) – Nayeri sees that 'the missing part of Houshiar's story' hides an 'essential truth' (261), yet one that fear and shame prevent him from including in his testimony: 'his life in Iran would [have been] entirely in the shadows until … he crosses paths with the wrong person and … might be hanged. The truest thing is that he needs and deserves asylum' (261). But so far, Houshiar has had no luck.

Interspersed throughout the chapters of *The Ungrateful Refugee*, Nayeri turns the stories of two unconnected Iranian men, Kaweh and Kambiz, into a refugee parable about luck. A few years apart and prior to the current crisis, both fled imminent danger in Iran, one because of Kurdish political activism, the other because of an alleged adulterous affair for which the religious police might 'hang him from a crane' (66). After their dangerous journeys across continents, both arrived 'illegally' by lorry in Britain and the Netherlands, respectively, both were entrepreneurial and now 'harbouring big dreams' (55). Nayeri is 'drawn to the place where their stories diverge, the vital hinge where one man is believed and the other is not' (55). Kaweh claimed asylum en route in Turkey with the UNHCR, eventually made it and within little more than a decade gained fame as 'one of the most accomplished young asylum lawyers in London' (235) and one of Nayeri's consultants for the writing of her book. Kambiz, however, claimed asylum in the Netherlands, was repeatedly rejected and put in detention. Worn out by a decade of futile waiting, he made the news on 6 April 2011 when he set fire to himself on Dam Square in Amsterdam. As his lawyer tells Nayeri: 'Living without perspective, like a worm. Waiting for Godot. Who can live like this? Humans need meaning. Kambiz broke because he needed purpose and family and progress' (228). This makes Nayeri ask: 'Why was one believed and the other sent away? How did each tell his story?' (238). They both presented truthful claims. Kaweh's battle to be believed was rewarded, Kambiz' did not fit into the narrow conceptions of truth that the asylum regime works by. So precarious is the boundary between life and death.

Throughout her book, Nayeri enacts what this chapter has pursued as substantive responsibility for those who wait in or outside camps around Europe. Her witnessing of the 'dignitary harm' (Owen's phrase) that refugees are made to endure prompts her to speak truth to power and indict those who believe that moral decency is a contingent matter:

For centuries, the civilised world has respected 'the right of asylum.' It is an ancient juridical concept recognising the right of the imperilled to sanctuary. Historically, whatever criticisms arise, every Western government has respected and understood this principle – until now. In this new century, this simple, foundational belief is in question among the world's freest, most comfortable populations. When they do internalise the obligation to make room, they do so grudgingly, or with arguments about the supplication and usefulness of immigrants. Most, still, call them liars, opportunists, a scourge. (2019: 276)

As her engagement with refugees of the current crisis unveils, truth and politics rarely 'stand on common ground'; they are 'not on good terms' to borrow the words of Samantha Rose Hill (2020) for Arendt's exploration of the politics of truth. Proposing that we engage with asylum seekers in good faith and attentive to the truth-fulness that lie inherent in testimonies that appear to be untidy and incoherent, Nayeri gestures towards the change of attitude and procedure that can redeem Europe's moral reputation. Her writerly skill is particularly sharp when presenting the stories that come out of her many encounters with refugees. She confronts her reader upfront:

Consume these lives as entertainment, or education or threats to your person. It is your choice how to hear their voices. Use all that you know to spot every false stroke of the brush. Be the asylum officer. Or, if you prefer, read as you would a box of letters from a ruin, dispatches from another time that we dust off and readily believe, because the dead want nothing from us. (2019: 15)

As we have explored in this chapter, the main 'protagonists' of the refugee crisis have been objectified and storifed in such reductive ways by mainstream media that this can be said to have contributed in problematic ways to master public narratives about refugees that construe them to be merely a problem that host societies must deal with. Yet, as we have also explored, a different approach to mediated representations of the refugee crisis is brought about by reporters who facilitate refugee narratability and engage with refugees within the public space of appearance, theorised by Arendt and practised by Kingsley, Trilling and Nayeri in their contributions to a more nuanced discussion of how the political context of the crisis affects refugees in inhumane ways. In their reportage of the crisis, we find no stereotypical victims and villains, only people with multifaceted stories to tell and with complex identities that cannot be reduced to the standard conceptions that European politicians and media regularly resort to in their responses to the crisis. Kingsley, Trilling and Nayeri stress the importance of co-presence and interaction in their engagements with refugees. But are there other forms of mediation that can activate refugee narratability differently with a view to promoting more immediate forms of agency and self-representation? This is the focus of the next chapter where we turn to the collaborative efforts of art and activism as an ethical and aesthetic response to the call for solidarity with refugees.

# 3

# Solidarity – Storytelling as Activism

In the EU political arena, solidarity is a word that has taken a decisive turn in post-2015 refugee talk. Former German Chancellor Angela Merkel's 2015 'Wir schaffen das' declaration was admirable because it was an unconditional gesture of solidarity with refugees, but it soon lost momentum as it prompted a nationalist backlash and has since been replaced by, for example, French President Macron's different 2019 conception of the term: 'The European Union hasn't shown enough solidarity with countries handling first arrivals' (Deutsche Welle, 2019). Solidarity, in Macron's adaptation, entails a commitment within the EU to share the 'unfair' burden carried by member states at the external borders. In 2020, the European Council sought to rectify this imbalance with the proposed 'Pact on Migration and Asylum' soon to be critiqued for its 'à-la-carte' model of solidarity with a choice of responsibilities principally designed to filter speedily migrants who are to be rejected and less explicit concerning the politics of resettlement. This signals a reduced focus on securing that the claims of asylum seekers, whatever the outcome, are deemed worthy of recognition and a primary concern with consolidating a unified EU response, borrowing Mladjo Ivanovic's words, to 'manage populations that are seen as posing risks' (Ivanovic in Oliver et al., 2019: 47). This turns asylum seekers into 'a product of negotiation' (48) which again impinges on the effect of humanitarian efforts to alleviate, or perhaps manage, human suffering. As Ivanovic argues: 'questions of solidarity with those who seek refuge … cannot be examined separately from the organizational structure that dominates our present moral discourse' in which 'different dimensions of the moral, economic, and political intersect with and determine one another in various ways that come to define what humanism and solidarity are' (45). In view of the stalemate such intersections can result in, we posit that solidarity is a term in crisis and contend that the ethically robust values it connotes must again take centre stage. For argument's sake, we take the economic dimension out of the equation, leave nation-state politics to politicians and turn instead towards the rehabilitation of solidarity as it is enacted in collaborations between people, that is to say, between concerned citizens and refugees.

In this chapter we propose that, ethically speaking and in a very basic sense, solidarity is what you show people in need and not an economic negotiation between nations about what is (not) affordable. Solidarity with refugees must be based on human rights as shared rights and not weakened by the assumption that showing compassion for vulnerable others is a sufficient gesture. As Ivanovic points out, it is precisely in assuming this that humanitarianism fails: 'by invoking human vulnerability and suffering as the moral cornerstones of solidarity, humanitarianism collapses important political questions of responsibility and justice with moralizing discourses around which the Western public is called to organize a charitable action toward the misfortune of refugees' whereby 'compassion cultivates a flawed disposition of solidarity that often ignores the historical injustices and contemporary inequalities sustained by a dehumanizing logic of ... neoliberalism' (56). And such a political logic, as David Owen observes, informs a humanitarian 'ideology' in which 'obligations to refugees are pictured in terms of humanitarian aid as moral obligations that we should fulfil, as long as the costs of doing so are low, rather than as obligations of justice' (Owen in Oliver et al., 2019: 18–19). As this critique brings out, protection and care are no guarantee against injustice – far from it. Solidarity proper, however, requires action in the service of justice.

To highlight this, we will explore how activism and art go hand in hand in the endeavour to advocate and activate solidarity in ways that stir, and possibly change, our cultural responses to fellow human beings in need. After considering solidarity as an ethical idea and taking an overall point of departure in the human power carried by telling and sharing stories, this chapter branches out into case studies of textual or visual art work that call attention to the centrality of solidarity in the encounter between citizens and refugees. The critique of European humanitarianism looms large in all this work. First, we discuss the continuous *Refugee Tales* project (2016–) of 'walking in solidarity with people who have been indefinitely detained' (refugeetales.org) which has so far resulted in four collections of refugee stories that grant asylum seekers visibility and audibility as participatory agents in the narrative of the current crisis. Next we address the inherent critique of 'carceral humanitarianism' (Kelly Oliver's term) emerging from Kate Evans' 2017 graphic novel *Threads from the Refugee Crisis* and the 'Perilous Journey' digital cartoons about three Syrian refugees, published in the *Guardian* in 2015. Finally, we explore Richard Mosse's 2017 documentary art installation *Incoming* along with Hassan Akkad's en route documentation of his journey to Europe featured in the 2016 BBC series *Exodus: Our Journey to Europe*. Here, we are particularly alert to how unfamiliar points of view and means of representation in the two documentaries prompt cognitive responses in viewers that push for deep thinking about Europe's handling of the refugee crisis as the documentaries urge viewers not only to feel compassion, but to act on that feeling. In all of this, solidarity comes with a vocabulary that is closely linked, as in all chapters of this book, to empathy and dignity. Under the rubric of responsibility, we focused in the previous chapter on the importance of forming reciprocal relations between reporters and their sources. In this chapter we take such relations for granted in our exploration of the solidarity that exists between citizens and refugees in the context of art and activism. But we add equally important ideas like sharing, caring and kinship. These are all terms that become prominent when people create ties in pursuit of justice. Because we now set out to consider artistic approaches to solidarity, the link between politics, ethics and aesthetics will be especially pronounced. Our proposition for this chapter, then, is that solidarity, when lifted from state politics into more immediate relations between people, is imbued with the radical potential to challenge dominant political discourses that mute, marginalise and metamorphose refugees into distant strangers whose needs exceed our resources. Once returned to its basic grounding in rights and justice, solidarity cannot be bended and mended as an instrument of crisis management – and the moral compass must be adjusted accordingly.

**In conversation, Patrick Kingsley says**: In recent years we have had a number of crises within Europe – the financial crisis and austerity, the crisis of Western democracy, the climate crisis and so on. Consequently, our lives in Europe have become more vexed than they used to be. So, when we are asked to care about the refugee crisis on top of all this, and to show kindness and solidarity to refugees who come from places outside Europe, it seems like an exhausting project for many Europeans. For some people, then, there is a tension or a clash between the care and solidarity that we show each other within, for example, Britain, and the care and solidarity we are asked to show refugees and migrants outside or coming into the nation. In fact, we need to reflect on our understanding of hospitality and solidarity in this context. Perhaps the truest form of hospitality is when you offer somebody sanctuary and tell them to act normally, as you might at home, and we will treat you as a citizen or resident. We should think about what it tells us about ourselves when we expect refugees to be perfect angels. Are we acting like this because we still see the world in black and white? Why do we find it so hard to appreciate, and feel solidarity with, humanity in all its complexity?

**In conversation, Dina Nayeri says**: Part of the reason why humanitarian responses to the refugee crisis are hard to get right is because of people's motives. The powerful, the native born have the power to redirect things like resources, to demand that the rules at the border be different, and so on. So, the powerful people become the audience; they are the ones to whom everything is directed. And when they are the audience, what they want becomes ingrained in the narrative. And if they want to feel good, then the way that they can feel good is to have gratitude signalled to them. That is how expectations of gratitude become embedded in humanitarian stories. The fact that people try to make economic arguments for refugees complicates matters. Why are we making an economic argument for refugees when it is a humanitarian question? Even when we defend refugees by saying that they add to our economies it does not actually make sense. Defending refugees has nothing to do with what value they add. Yet it seems to speak to a deeper kind of embedded need for us to try to feel as though we are good people who are doing good, and we are making our own country better off by allowing refugees in. It is a simplistic message that does not allow for much complexity. A lot of charities have to speak to people in a way that is effective and with their motivations in mind in order to achieve some short-term success. They want to do good.

Irene Ludji suggests that '[t]o be human means to be in solidarity with others. The implementation of human rights is only possible through the practice of solidarity as a moral obligation' (2018: 434). While we agree with this shorthand insistence on the link between solidarity and a rights-based moral commitment, it is also true that the concept of solidarity is 'complex' and 'multi-dimensional' (Bauder and Juffs, 2020). It can therefore be advocated in different ways to suit specific political agendas, as we indicated with reference to the EU's current preoccupation with solidarity as a burden-sharing obligation between member states. In concrete ways, citizens' resolve to act in solidarity with refugees is therefore often made difficult by the antagonistic procedures of receiving nation-states. As David Hollenbach observes, '[r]efugees are people who have fallen through the cracks of the nation-state system' (2019: 32) and therefore their needs will not be met '[i]f solidarity extends only as far as national or cultural borders' (33). Moreover, as Melina Duarte points out, we witnessed in 2015 and beyond a 'criminalization of solidarity' (2019: 29) when the '[d]uty to help was made illegal [… and] types of assistance normally understood as humanitarian by the EU become, for political reasons, classified as subversive, insurgent and criminal at the state and supra-state levels' (30). This is testified in the Danish documentary *Humanity on Trial* (2019) about Danish Salam Aldeen, a former refugee who felt it was his duty to travel to Greece in 2015 to help save refugees of the current moment from drowning at sea. He was eventually intercepted by the Greek coast guard and charged with human trafficking, an offence for which he risked a life sentence.

**In conversation, Patrick Kingsley says:** The activists I met on my journeys in connection with writing *The New Odyssey* all felt a moral responsibility to help. They reacted because of religious persuasion or from a sense of duty to their own personal migration histories or because it would be morally repugnant to ignore people in need who are literally at your front door. The activists were not particularly interested in the Middle East, the Syrian war or the Afghan conflict. And they did not have time to engage with the people they were helping. In fact, they were not interested in the individual backstories of the refugees. Instead, they typically responded to them as emblems and symbols of something. They were helping for symbolic reasons, and I do not say that to undermine what they do. I just feel it is worth noting that even when you are doing something for good reasons, it is hard to respond to people as individuals rather than as emblems. The activists I talked to did not have time to respond to the people they helped as individuals.

Unlike human rights, solidarity is not a matter of legislation but of a moral sentiment that is contingent and contextual. The concept of solidarity, as Bauder and Juffs observe, thus 'escapes a single definition' and in the context of, for example, humanitarian care this 'creates the problem that the ontological and normative complexities of the concept … often remain unclear [which …] may result in the fragmentation and inconsistent application of "solidarity"' (2020: 47). In her discussion of the ethics of solidarity and human rights, Ludji, however, proposes a workable combination of Richard Rorty's and Anselm Min's philosophical ideas, borrowing from Rorty the idea that solidarity is contingent on 'the ability to expand the concept of "us"'(430) and 'enlarging the circle of the "we"' (434) by including vulnerable others into our midst, and from Min, the idea that in a global world we are all connected and affected by the 'twofold dialectic' of 'differentiation' and 'interdependence' (436) and thus '[e]ngagement between those who are other to each other must take place in the spirit of respect and openness' (437). Rorty argues that solidarity is an effect of human reason, Min believes it is intrinsic to 'the sociality of human nature' (436), but in both conceptions, solidarity is considered an 'ethical task' (436) that involves the promotion of justice. In that sense solidarity is, as Lilie Chouliaraki sums up, 'a fundamentally political project' (2017: 59). We add that more concretely it is a social act unfolding in a particular time and place from people, with people and for people. This notwithstanding, Chouliaraki detects a current depoliticisation of solidarity that is worrying. In her view, 'there is something distinct about the ways in which the [spectator's] self figures in contemporary humanitarianism' (49). This indicates 'the retreat of an other-oriented morality, where doing good to others is about our common humanity and asks nothing back ... and the emergence of a self-oriented morality where doing good to others is about "how I feel" and must, therefore, be rewarded by minor gratifications to the self' (50). This 'new emotionality' (50) is highly affective but also, in a political sense, impotent. Chouliaraki thus calls for a new ethics or 'alternative imaginations of solidarity' (58) with refugees that are neither overreliant on spectators' emotions nor on their self-reflexive responses, but one that acts on the shared value of 'justice as a minimum "common pursuit"' in recognition of 'what it means to be a human being' (59). Referring to 'the culture of sympathy' (59), Chouliaraki posits that such imaginations should 'aim at fulfilling two communicative requirements'. First, they should include what Chouliaraki terms the 'distant other' 'so that they can be seen, heard and recognised; and second, they should address the question of why it is important that we act on their vulnerability – a question that makes the critique of power and the pursuit of justice a part of our public practice of solidarity' (58–9). It is from this perspective that we pursue the concept of solidarity when we zoom in on art as a form of activism that pursues the ethics of solidarity, yet from perspectives that are also attentive to the aesthetic dimensions of this endeavour.

**In conversation, Brad Evans says**: Solidarity does not impose conditions. I think the problem with solidarity today is, first of all, the performativity of it. Solidarity has become a digital performativity with people showing how much solidarity they are in with others. And they use the term solidarity, but it is empty of substance and ethics. Perhaps the best solidarity is the one that is not uttered, in the same way that the best humanitarian actions do not come with public recognition. The better acts of humanitarianism and solidarity go unnoticed, rather than becoming a spectacle and a media performance. Perhaps the biggest fracture I see in solidarity today is less ideological, but rather based on a certain intolerance of ideas that seems generational to me. Considering the fact that the most vulnerable of the refugee populations are overwhelmingly young children and the elderly we also have to be mindful of the generational fracturing within solidarity today.

As Marguerite Nguyen and Catherine Fung problematise, however, there can be 'a tension between the ethics and aesthetics of making refugee experience visible' (2016: 2). Refugee aesthetics, they argue, 'whether produced by or about refugees' are objects of humanitarian concern and '[t]his frame of reference casts refugees as abject victims and downplays the particularities of refugee situations, including nation-state accountability and specific refugee histories and politics' (2). And this can have distorting effects. Nowhere is this tension, we find, more strongly pronounced than in the gross appropriation of toddler Alan Kurdi's washed-ashore body on a Turkish beach in 2015. The photographic images went viral and stirred loud, short-term moral outrage about the loss of an innocent life, but the public exposure failed to draw attention to the wider context of how, morally and ethically, Europe is accountable for the loss of thousands of lives, including Alan Kurdi's, as a consequence of its failure to provide safe passage for people in flight. The compassionate response to this tragic story eventually withered away and gave rise instead to Alan Kurdi's afterlife as a reconfigured icon of suffering in a host of artistic memes on social media and a proliferation of academic essays on the necro-aesthetics of the spectacularised image of 'the boy on the beach'. In effect, Alan Kurdi has become a stolen identity exhibiting the tension between ethics and aesthetic at the same time as it constitutes what we regard as an utterly inappropriate example of 'body snatching'. This violates the memory of Alan Kurdi. In Homi K. Bhabha's memorable phrase: 'Even the dead have human rights' (Bhabha in Schulze-Engler et al., 2018: 702). In his miniature painting, 'Aftermath (Alan Kurdi)' (2020), Shorsh Saleh deliberately avoids abstracting Alan Kurdi's story and pays homage instead to his all too short life. Stripped down to the simple use of natural pigments on handmade paper, Alan Kurdi's small body is shown to have fallen off the grid of moral compassion, lying outside the frame image of an ominously swirling dark sea upon which floats a fatally coloured red paper ship. Here ethics and aesthetics combine as the emotion called forth is one of pure and profound sorrow. This image resonates strongly with us as a call to let Alan Kurdi rest in peace, free of further appropriation.

Concerning the aesthetics of solidarity more generally, Jeremy Gilbert is interested in the ability of what he calls 'potent collectivities' to effect change in the current political climate of the world where nativist backlashes against democratic culture are becoming increasingly common. As he puts it: 'An urgent question [...is] what forms of meaningful solidarity can be produced in this context, on any imaginable scale .... In particular, a question worth considering here is what role ... aesthetic practice might play in the production of relations, experiences and affects of solidarity?' (2020). These are crucial questions. As we will now explore, meaningful solidarity is indeed produced when citizens and refugees enter into relationships of collaboration, or 'allyship' (Brooks, 2020), where citizens' moral obligation to care intersects with refugees' push for subjectivity in representation. As art is an aesthetic practice for citizens and refugees alike, we are interested in how collaborative activist art contributes to a refugee aesthetics. First, however, we must pay attention to the necessary dialectic of telling and listening to stories that such artistic collaborations depend on.

## STORYTELLING AND STORYLISTENING

In a passage from *The Ungrateful Refugee*, Dina Nayeri highlights the centrality of storytelling and storylistening to the traumatic experience of becoming a refugee:

In a refugee camp, stories are everything. Everyone has one, having just slipped out from the grip of a nightmare ... . It wasn't just a pastime. Our stories were drumming with power ... . We had created our life's great story; next would come the waiting time, camp, where we would tell it. Then the struggle for asylum, when we would craft it. Then assimilation into new lives, when we would perform it for the entertainment of the native-born. ... Our story was a sacred thread woven into my identity. (2019: 6–7)

For refugees, stories can be felt like a matter of life or death. Your story is connected to your sense of self as an integral, almost sacred, part of your identity. Storytelling 'is simultaneously individual and collective, positional and situated, rooted in the past as well as in the present and future', Nando Sigona writes (Sigona in Fiddian-Qas-miyeh et al., 2014: 370). According to Jonathan Wittenberg, the story is 'an ancient and profoundly eloquent form of protest' – 'a countercultural act of validation' (2019), connected to recognition and acknowledgement between teller and listener. In *The Human Condition*, Hannah Arendt even suggests that storytelling is intimately bound up in being recognised as a human being. She holds that when we tell other people our story something happens: 'The presence of others who see what we see and hear what we hear assures us of the reality of the world and ourselves' (1998: 50), with world understood as interrelation among mankind. 'The world' is 'the thing that arises between people and in which everything that individuals carry with them innately can become visible and audible', she teaches us (1970: 10). Thus, stories come to life in the twinned acts of telling *and* listening, where the teller is, ideally, seen and heard, recognised and acknowledged. In this way, stories are the ties that bind us together as fellow human beings.

**In conversation, Dina Nayeri says**: When we listen to someone's story in solidarity, it does not mean that we necessarily agree with every political thing embedded in the story. It simply means that we listen as a human, with the desire for a person to come out of trauma, to be saved, and to regain something of themselves. To regain a life is how you listen in solidarity. Along the way, refugees encounter so many people who are not listening like that and that is a tragedy, on top of the original tragedies of a refugee life. The way we listen to stories differs according to the kind of stories that we listen to. When we listen to stories from people who we are naturally empathetic toward, we listen with our whole heart, we listen to empathise, we listen to understand. When, for instance, we read fiction, we open our hearts and are looking for a moving experience. And we are given a moving experience because we are open to it. The way asylum officers listen to stories is with a checklist, just hoping to catch out one detail that will help them reject. That is not how you honestly listen to stories, that is not listening in solidarity. In my writing I invite readers to put aside their own motivation and their own distrust, and not think about all the ways that these stories might harm them, because individually they do not, and even collectively they do not. We read with our own motivations. And I think that this is not just a disservice. It is a violence to people who are vulnerable, and for whom it is already hard to share those stories. It takes so much to bring up those stories when you have gone through trauma. Can you imagine the added violence of having your refugee stories listened to with suspicion and with some other motivating force at play?

Stories, storytelling and storylistening are a central component of any refugee talk. Stories are, in so many ways, refugees' only portable property, seen in a literal sense in Jackie Kay's 'The Smuggled Person's Tale' when the refugee arrives at her house, 'with his story in his rucksack' (Herd and Pincus, 2017: 105). But this is also often property that host nations attempt to wrest away from refugees. That is why refugees need *multiple* stories in order to manoeuvre their perilous journeys to safety, or multiple versions of the same story. The narrator of Hassan Blasim's 'The Reality and the Record' pinpoints the multi-layered aspect of stories and the contingency on *who* is listening and *how*:

Everyone staying at the refugee reception centre has two stories
– the real and the one for the record. The stories for the record

REFUGEE TALK: PROPOSITIONS ON ETHICS AND AESTHETICS

are the ones the new refugees tell to obtain the right to humanitarian asylum, written down in the immigration department and preserved in their private files. The real stories remain locked in the hearts of the refugees, for them to mull over in complete secrecy. That's not to say it's easy to tell the two stories apart. They merge and it becomes impossible to distinguish them. (2016: 1)

What Blasim's narrator describes is a subtle demonstration of agency in the face of a hostile environment that is unwilling to acknowledge this. Indeed, as Daniel Trilling writes: 'All too often, the voices of refugees … are reduced to pure testimony, which is then interpreted and contextualised on their behalf … . Any meaningful response to this has to address the question of who gets to tell stories, as well as what kinds of stories are told' (2019). And, we add, who listens to the stories told. It is not enough to insist on the importance of telling your story. For this to be a meaningful process, there has to be a listener. In his memoir *The Lightless Sky*, Gulwali Passarlay tells of the 'impersonal' and 'strange' UK asylum process in which the telling of his life story is 'utterly at odds with [his] culture' (2019: 331). He has to tell his story 'to a bunch of strangers sitting around a table' in a situation far removed from what he needs as a frightened 13-year old boy: 'I needed to feel safe and secure to be able to talk. This process was the opposite of that' (331). As David Constantine writes in 'The Orphan's Tale': 'Every storyteller wants to be believed. Belief persuades. Every storyteller wants to be persuasive' (Herd and Pincus, 2019: 11). For mutual trust and respectful listening to happen, though, Anna Gotlib proposes that 'we have to learn to do less damage with words' (2017: E-82). This is vital in a storytelling context because 'stories create (and destroy) identities' (Gotlib in Oliver et al., 2019: 239). In the words of Dadaab-born Asad Hussein: 'When you are not the one telling the story, it's a lot harder to come across as an equal, because your voice is stifled and only the storyteller's is heard' (2020).

One undercurrent in this book is the vexed issue of representation. Since many of the stories we explore are *about* refugees we have to be alert to how we quickly can become, again in Gotlib's words, 'ventriloquists for refugees, and strip them from the only things they still own; their stories, relationships and experiences as human beings' (Gotlib in Oliver et al., 2019: 248). Indeed, we might want to learn from photographer Giles Duley's insistence that 'I don't see myself as "giving people a voice." They already have a voice; I want to amplify their voice' (2018: 4). Or, as the artist Sophie Herxheimer says, '[i]t's an obvious thing to say, but when we share the stories, we *share* the stories' (2018: 60). These are important comments that speak to that vital intertwined act of telling and listening, which is, of course, a profound gesture of sharing. Inevitably, that collaborative motion is highly critical of the one-sided representation that is deaf to other voices than your own. The typical stories about refugees told in the media, as we have seen, bifurcate into master narratives about the extraordinary, individual refugee and the many grateful victims that are objects of our pity or the masses of ungrateful and unwanted villains who bring disease and destruction. In other words, we cannot help but 'inhabit a realm of stereotype created by news images', as Lisa Appignanesi puts it in 'The Dancer's Tale' (Herd and Pincus, 2019: 85). Gotlib suggests that there are three versions of a refugee seen from the host nation's perspective: 'heroic strivers', 'dangerous and threatening' people, and 'passive victims' (Gotlib in Oliver et al., 2019: 245). In such a reductive scenario refugees become 'narratively erased and their stories made to reflect the socioeconomic and political needs of host societies' (240). Storytelling is, in a refugee context, thus contingent on ethical, political and aesthetic considerations. The act of telling your own story in your own way, and in your own words is a profound demonstration of agency and awareness of the power of language and this can be upsetting and disturbing for host societies who traffic in already-established stereotypical narratives about the perceived other. When refugees tell their own stories, even if they are not those that the host society wants to hear, that act, or that protest, is a cathartic way to 'reclaim themselves as bearers of complex, multicultural identities that resist the master narrative's insistence on xenophobic ... versions of who they are that only serve to exotify and trivialize their difficult, contested lives', Gotlib claims (240). Refugee agency expressed through storytelling is a way of contesting what Gotlib calls the 'silent archetypes of "the refugee" ... a silent cultural canvas' (242).

Sometimes this 'narrative erasure' happens 'in exchange for safe harbor' (242). Refugees have to perform their gratitude again and again through total assimilation even if it costs them their sense of self. To be sure, Gotlib elaborates, if '[n]arrative equals control, and control equals power' (246), then this is true both for the host nation's reductive master narrative *and* for the refugee's complex counter-narrative.

In a refugee context, we argue, story(telling) is aligned with the language of dignity and the distribution of luck, both bad luck and good luck. According to David Owen, 'moral dignity is now identified as a single status of basic equality ascribed to all human beings and given clear legal expression as universal human rights' (Owen in Oliver et al., 2019: 15). A 'dignity-based framework' (17) can help to understand how refugees are simultaneously cast as people of exceptional status (as refugees in search of safety and with legitimate claims to protection and rights) and as (just) people; they have 'the dignity *of* one's person as a bearer of equal status expressed in human or civic rights' and they have 'dignity *in* one's person' that entitles the refugee to equal status as human being (16). In this framework, the 'narrative erasure' that silences refugees' voices and refuses to listen to their stories can be regarded as an example of what Owen calls 'epistemic dignitary harm' (22). Such dignitary harm is an act of violence that affects the refugee's sense of self. 'More and more as I write these pages, I am confident that, though refuge is undeniably today's battle, dignity is tomorrow's' (186), Nayeri explains, pointing towards the centrality of dignity and storytelling control in what it means to be (seen and heard as) human, to have a place in the world and your story taken seriously. Listening to the stories of fellow human beings is part of this battle. The intertwined acts of telling stories and listening to stories help to world, in the Arendtian sense, to make people visible and audible and thus secure a place among mankind. This is the manner in which stories world: they help in 'enlarging the circle of the we'.

The worlding that storytelling makes possible is not only attached to a mutual recognition of dignity. It is also, again in a refugee context, inextricably infiltrated with luck. Existential and socio-political homelessness 'robs refugees not only of a sense of physical and psychological security, but of a sense of themselves as persons' (2017: E-67). For Gotlib, refugees' loss of home is equal to the loss of 'their story' (E-68), or, more precisely, the rupture of their story when a refugee becomes homeless in what Gotlib calls 'a state of permanent non-belonging' (E-68). From an Arendtian perspective, refugees are thus disowned both by their nation-state and by the global community (E-69). This is a refugee's bad luck. Again, we are reminded that what we termed a refugee ontology in Chapter 1 pivots on an impossible state of liminality, of complex temporal, social and geographical in-betweenness.

Gotlib also explores how a set of circumstances – luck – makes a difference to how we are perceived and how we perceive and evaluate our actions. She argues that how refugees are seen and how their agency is construed have a lot to do with moral luck – and that how refugees see themselves as persons in an existential and socio-political context is predominantly a matter of good or bad luck. She explains that 'refugee systemic luck traps refugees in a two-tiered system of oppression: While an unpredictable and uncontrollable bad-luck force acts on an already-oppressed people by making their flight existentially necessary, a more systematically and deliberately enacted luck-making takes over once they are homeless and stranded between an impossible home and an uncertain future' (E-70). Concomitant with this system is a two-step way of understanding refugee systemic luck: 'First, the refugees are thrown into historical, geopolitical circumstances not of their own choosing. Second, they must contend with the actions and the powerful master narratives of those who may, or may not, offer them asylum' (E-71). This systemic luck consequently stories refugees in different ways: some refugees are storied by the host nation as underserving and unwanted (bad luck) and other refugees are storied as wanted and deserving (good luck).

**In conversation, Dina Nayeri says**: What are you born into? That is the biggest piece of good or bad luck that we are all subject to. But then there are other kinds of luck along the way. There is your education and your background in understanding refugee law and refugee matters. If you arrive in a new country and you know nothing about the Geneva Convention and the specific legal definitions of refugee, you are already lost. If you do not have the luck of being offered a lawyer, then you are probably going to say things that will invalidate your case. A refugee according to the Geneva Convention is not what most refugees think. So, running into the right charity or getting the right legal help is a huge element of luck that determines whether or not the asylum application is successful. And after that it is the kind of luck that the poor have to hope for all the time: you depend on other people's charity, the right policies in the country that you live in, and the circumstances that will allow you to thrive. When you have a certain amount of money, you can make your own luck. You can create safety nets for yourself. And then you can have the kind of children that have safety nets below their safety nets.

As Gulwali Passarlay writes when he is finally offered asylum, after experiencing both bad and good luck on his epic journey from Afghanistan to the UK: 'I know that, being able to stay here, I am one of the lucky ones. Many have gone back to uncertain futures' (2019: 376). Storytelling is thus central to refugee debates in two contradictory yet inextricably linked ways: the stories told about refugees that are bound up in reductive stereotypes and unimaginative master tropes of deserving and undeserving, or grateful and ungrateful, and the refugees' own stories that are as varied and complex as the people who tell them. These stories can be discredited, misconstrued and disregarded in epistemically harmful ways that produce psychic dents to the storyteller's dignity and agency, and to their sense of self. Or they can be listened to with openness, empathy and curiosity in ways that are mindful of the trust and faith such shared moments attest to. This is the point of departure of the *Refugee Tales* project to which we now turn.

## WALKING AND TALKING IN SOLIDARITY

In *The Ungrateful Refugee*, Dina Nayeri draws attention to the often insidious effects of language: 'And here is the biggest lie in the refugee crisis. It isn't the faulty individual stories. It is the language of disaster often used to describe incoming refugees –

*deluge* or *flood* or *swarm*. These words are lies' (2019: 279). Such 'flawed terminologies', to use Tinti and Reitano's phrase, urgently need to be exposed and debunked as a central part of any attempt to 'elevate the discourse' (2018: 275, 279). The *Refugee Tales* project and books (Herd and Pincus, 2016, 2017, 2019, 2021) represent one way in which the discourse surrounding the refugee crisis can be elevated. The shared effort of walking and talking with refugees and migrants in detention in the UK is at the heart of the project. By walking 'in solidarity with refugees' the project aims to 'call attention to the fact, to call out the fact' of the UK's policy of indefinite detention and 'call for that practice to end' (2019: 183). The project's use of the verb 'to call' deliberately reminds us that 'to call' *also* means to shout, announce, rouse, request, demand and summon action. But since it is not enough to elevate the discourse, the project evinces a profound, possibly utopic, belief that a discursive call to action can have material and socio-political effect. It is, as Siobhan Brownlie puts it, 'an advocacy and protest project' that intertwines political activism with 'the worlds of literature, theatre and history' (2020: 141). Helen Barr posits that the project 'engages minds, body, creativity and political will' (2019: 79) since it is 'text and action' (79) revolving around stories 'heard on the move' and 'read in a book' (80), while the project's explicit political agenda 'is to make audible and mobile persons locked out of due process and indefinitely detained' (84). The fact that the project's combined walking and storytelling sessions have been successfully repeated since the first walk in 2015 showcases public interest even if the aim of ending indefinite detention has not been achieved (yet). As Shami Chakrabarti writes on the dustjacket to the first *Refugee Tales*: 'Readers will surely be moved to move their leaders to action' (2016). In the project, art and activism, and ethics and aesthetics clearly operate in tandem.

In the prologue to *Refugee Tales*, David Herd sets the stage for a celebratory 'spectacle of welcome' (2016: vii): the book(s) are 'a declaration ... Of solidarity' accompanied by a walk 'In solidarity' (v). That double act of solidarity leads to a rethinking of language: as we listen to the stories told we engage in 'a whole new language/ Of travel and assembly and curiosity/And welcome' (viii) and as we do so, we 'call for/ ... an end/To this inhuman discourse' that characterises the current hostile refugee talk (x). The *Refugee Tales* use Geoffrey Chaucer's *The Canterbury Tales* as inspirational template, and this is a propitious choice. As Herd explains: 'Drawing, structurally, on *The Canterbury Tales,* the project thus had three fundamental elements: a culturally charged sense of space, the visible fact of human movement, and an exchange of information through the act of telling stories' (133). Brownlie's discussion of *Refugee Tales* draws on Michael Rothberg's notion of 'multidirectional memory' that 'binds together individual spatial, temporal and cultural sites through highlighting similarities, and thus has a human bonding effect, solidarity across difference' (2020: 154–5). There is also a political function of multidirectional memory in that it 'involves an "ethic of comparison in which the past and present maintain a hold on each other that can be translated into a political network with a practical program"' (2020: 155). The impression we get when reading the refugee stories in tandem with Chaucer's tales is this creative inclusiveness that opens up for new insights and, possibly, new action. Helen Barr explains that 'Chaucerian geography situates Englishness within an international arena' (2019: 85) and this is seen in *The Canterbury Tales*, which, according to biographer Peter Ackroyd, 'is an experiment in diversity, a poem devoted to the celebration of variety and change' (2005: 157). The diversity that the tales celebrate is also evident in their linguistic registers. Ackroyd explains that Chaucer was writing the stories in a period when the English language 'was at its most flexible and unpredictable. … It was rich and unfixed, altering with each generation of speakers' (88). In the words of Astrid Erll: 'Chaucer shows what the English language can do, the *Refugee Tales* show what the English language should do' (2020). These comments on Chaucer's tales affect a discussion of the *Refuge Tales*. They, too, can be said to be an experiment in and celebration of diversity, in language and linguistic registers, in form and genres, and in the sheer number of stories urgently shared between teller and listener, within and outside of the books. As Barr maintains: 'While the texts of the tales chart a harsh geography, the tales as action and as a collection of shared voices change the terms of a debate about migrancy that criminalises human movement' (2019: 91). The stories are, so to speak, an aesthetic experiment, wrapping traumatic stories in the language and forms of poetry and prose that are emotionally affective and creative, as these lines from refugee A's 'The Foster Child's Tale' so efficaciously illustrate: 'Detention is the chapter that keeps on going./No full-stops' (Herd and Pincus, 2019: 30).

The walk in the 'ancient pathways' (Herd and Pincus, 2016: 138) is an effective way of making the invisible – refugees and migrants in detention – visible and part of the world, in an Arendtian sense. Together walkers in solidarity assert 'their place in the landscape' (134) as a way of 're-making' space (138), with space understood as 'a sense of cultural and political environment' (134), 'outside the hostile environment' instigated by then Home Secretary Theresa May in 2012 (2019: 184) where stories 'can be told and heard in a respectful manner' (2017: 115). As Barr contends, '[i]n the exchange and the listening of tales, England has no borders. It affords textual hospitality to nations and persons from across the sea' (2019: 86). Herd draws on Arendt's notion of 'space of appearance' to explain how lack of recognition before the law is an attempt to 'prevent the person from making an appearance', which is exactly what detention does – it 'separates people out so that, in a literal sense, they are not recognised' (2017: 122). The space that *Refugee Tales* secures, then, 'is a space of recognition' where the stories can be 'safely heard' (122). '[M]utuality of recognition' is key, because such recognition is 'rooted in the proper hearing of stories' (123).

The prologue to *Refugee Tales II* speaks to the importance of a safe storytelling space; it ironically echoes the American Declaration of Independence and its statement of human rights by situating it in a refugee context: 'Listen, Friend/We hold this truth/To be self-evident/That a person/Who has a story/Requires space' (2017: 1). The plural truths of the original Declaration have been crystallised into *one* pivotal truth: the right to tell a story in a cultural and political environment that is willing to listen with respect and interest is 'A basic entitlement' (1). The walk, Herd explains, 'enables ... the circulation of stories', the kind of human circulation 'that UK immigration legislation appears determined to prevent' (114–15). In fact, the hearing that takes place 'might shape/A polity' (2), indicating how art and activism literally wander hand in hand, explicitly demonstrating a 'call to change' (2019: 1). To Barr:

> [t]he collective efforts of the Project in walking and talking and in writing and publication are to create exactly such a polity, a space of appearance that is counter to the hostile environment of immigration law in the UK. … In creating a space of appearance, and a polity out of the structural model of Chaucer's *Canterbury Tales*, *The Refugee Tales* project reads back into Chaucer's work a community of fellowship and common purpose. (2019: 101, 103)

That space of appearance was manifested in the 2019 walk intending to construct 'a politics capable of thinking beyond borders' (Herd and Pincus, 2019: 185) suggesting that the stories told in *Refugee Tales III* propound the ethical demand that as we listen to the stories we also need to demand an end to the violence enacted on refugees under cover of the hostile environment. We need to realise how 'personhood itself is systematically attacked' (187) and that violence breaches human rights in a way that renders refugees 'outside the provision of […] an] ethical framework' (189). From a literary perspective Astrid Erll zooms in on what she calls the *Refugee Tales* project's 'literary activism' that forces us to recognise this harm enacted on personhood. Literary activism is bound up in communicative memory, relational remembering and empathetic listening (Erll, 2020). The project's ethical agenda is expressed through collective action with walking as a key strategy of memory activism (Erll, 2020), arguing that walking in solidarity with refugees creates the kind of collectivity that leads to responsibility. Jana Wiggenhauser speaks in a more sceptical manner to the project's profound belief in the efficacy of storytelling: 'Ultimately, one might question if storytelling can in fact lead to a meaningful change of perspective or inspire political activism. Audiences might be emotionally touched by the stories, yet their estrangement from the narrated experiences might foreclose any real-world actions' (2018). Perhaps this is hinted at in Ali Smith's 'The Detainee's Tale' which ends on a chilling note, with the detainee voicing his frustration: 'But when I came to this place, when I came to your country, you say. I sit forward. I'm listening. You shake your head. I thought you would help me, you say' (Herd and Pincus, 2016: 62). Obviously, the act of listening is not enough in and of itself.

Reading the books back-to-back, we notice the move towards more and more self-representation in *Refuge Tales III*. In the first book, Herd shares the project's thoughts on mediation and the vexed issue of representation, and why the detainees themselves did not tell their own unmediated stories. He points out that traumatised individuals cannot be expected to speak about their experiences in front of an audience, and, furthermore, because of their precarious legal status, they need to remain anonymous for their own protection. As he recounts to Brownlie, the need for anonymity is important because 'the Home Office holds an account of their story and that any discrepancy with another account could be detrimental to their case' (Brownlie, 2020: 160). There cannot be any discrepancy between the 'real' story and the story 'for the record', to echo Blasim's narrator, even if the story for the record might in fact never actually be recorded. Hence, 'the narrative dynamic' of the books, based on the collaborative and supportive effort of telling and listening to stories: 'to tell another person's tale one has to listen at length and very closely' (Herd and Pincus, 2016: 141). The story is thus 'passed on' and the fact that 'other people acknowledge the experience that constitutes the story' signals that 'they register responsibility' (142). In *Refugee Tales III*, Herd further elaborates on the project's 'collaborative model of storytelling' (2019: 192) which began as an exchange 'between the person whose story it is and the writer with whom they were in conversation' pointing out how significant it is that 'the stories presented in this volume have at least been shared' (2017: 123). Collaboration and sharing are clearly the operative words. Indeed, as Herd writes in the Afterword to *Refugee Tales III*, since there is such hostility to a person's story, this suggests that 'the story itself is powerful, that where it is told and heard in its entirety it will have an altering effect. To tell and to hear a story … is to establish an intimate connection' (2019: 191). This is compellingly suggested in a piece of dialogue from Jonathan Wittenberg's 'The Erased Person's Tale':

So, I ask him, why does he want me, or anyone else, to tell his story? Wouldn't it be more powerful coming directly from him? His response is that he needs someone else to hear, a person outside the immediate experience, to *acknowledge* and *record* what happened to him and to those whose sufferings he saw and *shared*. He wants me to be his *witness*, not because his narrative requires verification, but because of the *fact of hearing* itself; because it signifies that in a world which often seeks to deny and disbelieve such accounts, his story has been *absorbed by a listening heart*. ... I become a *partner in testament* to the ongoing reality of cruelty and suffering. This is an *obligation* to which I am deeply committed. ... Researching the fate of my family taught me the importance of being a *vigilant witness* against evil and heartlessness and to stand up for *human solidarity*, beyond all seeming borders of nationality and creed. ... S needs me, us, to be *allies*. (Herd and Pincus, 2019: 110, our italics)

The words in italics suggest a lexicon of ethical exchange, of supportive allyship in the intimate team of teller and listener-writer. They are in solidarity with each other as partners and witnesses – and stronger together. It seems to us that this quotation sums up the ethical heart of the *Refugee Tales* project.

Aesthetics is also an integral part of the collaborative exchange of stories, from the focus on language to the reflection on structure and genre and how to make the most effective and affective story that will impact on the listeners' emotions. There is an 'inherent teachability' in the *Refugee Tales*, Erll argues (2020), that is the result of their literariness, or what we experience as the aesthetic pleasure involved in reading and teaching them. Exposing 'the lexicon of suspension' (Herd and Pincus, 2016: 135) with its associated vocabulary of 'detention', 'stasis', 'pending' and 'removal', the *Refugee Tales* project is engaged in a discursive ethico-political undertaking bound up in 'the proposal that the language of national space be re-read, that we read back through to find the expression that gestures outwards' (139). The return to Chaucer's world and words is one track in this effort. The space that such a return opens up is where 'new forms of language and solidarity can emerge' (Herd and Pincus, 2017: 115). And there is urgent need for a reinvigorated language that opens up and includes rather than fends off and excludes. In the stories shared, the project demonstrates how asylum seekers are 'locked out of the language' as they experience the host nation's many efforts to 'thwart, disrupt, or discredit their accounts' (119). What Barr calls 'the linguistic imprisonment of the refugees' (2019: 95) is illustrated in the tales where 'refugees are tripped up and lost, especially in language' (94). In that sense, the *Refugee Tales* project is a powerful critique of what Emma Parsons calls 'EDL (English as a Detention Language) ... the esoteric words and exhausting syntax that will determine your life' in 'The Teacher's Tale' (Herd and Pincus, 2019: 141). Small wonder, then, that Herd insists '[w]hatever else, the language needs to change' (2016: 143). Because 'the language itself is hostile' (Herd and Pincus, 2019: 191) we suggest that the change begins by repacking the language and by taking control of your story, so that you disrupt the host nation's master narratives. In this way, refugees can traverse the 'border' of language (120) and open up a space for new stories that are real, and not just for the record.

## EXPOSING INHUMANITY

As inherent in Kelly Oliver's phrase 'carceral humanitarianism', Europe has responded to the current refugee crisis by turning 'refugees into criminals and charity cases simultaneously' which has resulted in 'the troubling justification for locking them up or locking them in' inside detention centres or makeshift camps of 'sorely inadequate conditions' (Oliver in Oliver et al., 2019: 120–1). This is made evident in Kate Evans' graphic novel *Threads* (2017). Evans is an activist artist and *Threads* introduces yet another unusual genre for acting in solidarity with refugees, one that is particularly suited to representing precarious lives; as Evans argues: 'Comics are an excellent way of telling stories of migration and displacement, as they can be humanising and nuanced, yet preserve anonymity. No-one is illegal' (Cartoon Kate, *Facebook*). *Threads* documents Evans' visits to the Jungle in Calais in 2015–16, including short trips to a neighbouring camp in Dunkirk. In Calais, she worked as a volunteer in support of refugees living in deplorable conditions in 'a microcosmic Disunited Nations' (2017: 8) where the hostility of state authorities and the goodwill of volunteers are the two contrasting points of contact refugees have with the surrounding world. *Threads* is, quite literally, framed by delicate lacework. The opening image is one of early nineteenth-century lace-making women producing 'Meters high' and 'Miles long' (7) ribbons of white lace that form the twenty-first-century semitransparent motorway partitions that lead past the Jungle towards the harbour of Calais. In the ending image, the women stack their craftwork as building blocks for the UK government's construction of a '£2 million four-metre-high wall around the port of Calais' (176). The visual trope of lace sets off Evans' story of the Jungle as political from beginning to end as the irony of Calais' fame as a French lacemaking city is not lost on Evans. The flourishing lace industry was founded in 1816 by migrant British lace-makers who after decades of war with France saw Calais as an entry point to the Continent and the possibility of a new start in life. In subsequent decades, their particular skill boosted the city's economy and cultural renown. Ironically, then, lace was once a craft that opened borders for migrants, but in *Threads* it is employed as a metaphor for sealed borders that exclude migrants, caught up between France and England and between the city itself and the refugee camp at its outskirts, as Evans makes clear by having lace rather than the cartoon device of gutters separate panels and sketches. This defamiliarisation of an exquisite cultural design and tradition effectively brings home the political point that what contemporary refugees might have to offer their host communities is left 'in the gutter'. They are caged in, hidden from public view, and left to fend for themselves in squalor, 'quite literally, the pits' (61).

**In conversation, Kate Evans says**: Comics are a great way of getting ideas across because my job as a comics artist is to make things simple. I do lots of non-fiction comics about complicated subjects where I break them down and get them across in simple ways so that people do not feel lectured to. What I do in *Threads* is graphic reportage. It is a niche thing and it makes you a participant in events. Because refugees have to be anonymous under the terms of the Dublin conventions, you cannot make an identifiable representation of a refugee in Calais. I make refugees into people in *Threads*. At one point in the story, I get out my pen and say, would you like me to draw a picture of you? It was really nice to be able to give something that is essentially useless but that recognises a refugee as a person. I think my comics work well because through my depictions you can see that people are just people. In the book I make myself look really stupid. The character that is me makes naive comments or tries to do naive things. I did not necessarily do that in real life. Part of the reason why I made myself so stupid is because the whole situation is stupid and so inadequate that I decided to embody that. I do not care about turning myself into a clown. We are all clowns. But it feeds into a comment about comics and activism, which is if you can make someone laugh, then you are halfway to changing their mind. One reason why I called the story *Threads* is that it is just a tiny, insignificant thread in an enormous tapestry of millions of displaced people, of the people they are in touch with and the people whose lives interweave. One thing I am annoyed about, though, is that I used the term 'refugee crisis' in the title. I have really regretted that, because if you use the word crisis it implies a short period of time and that it can be solved. I should have called it *Threads from the Ongoing, Unfolding Humanitarian Emergency That Nobody's Talking about and Everyone's Pretending Doesn't Exist*.

As Frances Newman sums up, *Threads* 'weaves together personal testimonies, political rhetoric, media reportage, tweets and aid agency statistics, underpinned by a common humanity of desperate people coming into contact with others trying to help; there is soul searching, frustration and hard lessons to be learnt' (2017). Evans' graphic reportage, we argue, resonates with Chouliaraki's call, as previously referenced, for 'the critique of power and the pursuit of justice [to become] a part of our public practice of solidarity' (2017: 59). The critique of power looms large in *Threads*, in multiple ways. Notably, in otherwise colourful panels, Evans' critique of Europe's complicity in aggravating the current humanitarian crisis is predominantly sketched in bleak grey, brown and black pencil strokes against a background of obscured light. Power shows off when, for instance, a US fighter plane bombs a hospital in Afghanistan (17), power speaks when mean-faced Marine Le Pen yells of 'bravely battling the Muslim invasion' (10) or when the repulsed demeanour of Theresa May warns against welcoming refugees because 'We will CRACK DOWN' (18). Power prohibits human dignity and its brutal physical force is felt when thugs attack refugees with iron bars in the streets of Calais (28–31), when the police in full combat gear storm into the shed of a pregnant single mother and assault her (127–31) or when cross-armed British border police suddenly apprehend a refugee at the harbour and subject him to an unnecessarily violent arrest (136–9). Such is the reality of life if you are a refugee hidden from view in makeshift camps where refugee rights are not observed and teargas and bulldozers are instruments of power. In *Threads*, we do not read about it, we see it happening.

The sum of large- and small-scale events where power is inhumanely employed makes the 'pursuit of justice' as 'a part of the public practise of solidarity' an urgent task, as evidenced also by the host of scornful text messages that Evans receives and that criminalise her efforts to help: 'It's people like YOU that invite all those people here' (72), 'You are the locks that do no good' (24), 'We need to purge this scum with fire there's no other choice' (152), 'These cute refugee babies grow into vile adults who want to destroy our country and all that's in it' (32). While the insertion of such messages is 'a great narrative device – technology as a hostile chorus', as Erica Smith points out (2017), it also testifies to the public rhetoric of heated antagonism as an accomplice of power. This all seriously discredits 'Europe's brand of humanity' (Mukherjee, 2019). And it compromises the effect of humanitarian relief work. As the increasingly frustrated author-narrator of her graphic novel, Evans 'thinks aloud' about the impasse of humanitarian concern in the face of scrupulous power. The questions are pressing: 'What are we doing, swanning about Calais, congratulating ourselves on our fabulous relief effort?' (2017: 55) when refugees' lack of right to have rights keeps blocking their access to justice. Distributing oranges to refugees where the police obstruct the provision of dry bedding for needy children in a damp camp, Evans sighs in exasperation at the ineffective provisions of 'bleeding heart liberals' (144): 'What are we fucking doing? We can't solve this with oranges!' (64). As Evans impels her readers to understand, relief work must exchange humanitarian pity with politically voiced anger about Europe's indifferent attitude to human suffering. Only this can pave the way to justice. Mladjo Ivanovic argues that humanitarian language 'offers a seductive simplification of our reality without real commitment to action' (Ivanovic in Oliver at al., 2019: 46) which can make 'affective dispositions' of solidarity 'collapse either into self-absorption or voyeurism' (58). Pertaining to the question of the ethics of solidarity, he asks: 'what are the consequences when we mobilize compassion rather than challenge underlying injustices?' (48). Based on her experiences in the camps, Evans raises the same question by inferring that as long as the overarching question of injustice remains unaddressed, relief workers should not 'be satisfied with only distributing oranges and feel good about their charitable disposition' (Mukherjee, 2019).

**In conversation, Kate Evans says:** The situation in the Jungle of Calais exacerbates underlying inequalities that mirror global inequalities, where a certain number of nations are hoarding all of the resources. The real problem is this creation of a microcosm of inequality that mirrors a macrocosm of inequality. When I was a volunteer, I was a provider of goods. You have food and sleeping bags and the people you are giving these to are your charitable recipients. It sets up a weird dynamic where the people who are desperate for everything in life can only be given a certain amount, and I ended up like a border-guard or a police-officer having to hold the line against people. I found that strange and compromising. Volunteering as a middle-class white woman from England is also feeding into an apolitical historical tradition in England where the wife of the wealthy landowner distributes gifts to the poor. What we were doing in Calais was a bit like that. Everyone can absolve their conscience by sending someone a sleeping bag, but this is not going to mean that the EU will give refugees actual homes. Still, I love grassroots political action, particularly when it creates autonomous spaces where people come together. So, I came back to Calais and participated in more relief work.

The fact remains that charity organisations intersect uneasily with radical action to change society. The only real point in us going to Calais would have been if we had had someone in the back of our car and driven them to the UK. But it was not a place where you could create actual political activism. For me, the overriding political message from Calais was that refugees are the people who do not have rights. I have the privilege of a platform and pen.

Ultimately, being in solidarity with refugees involves more than practical support. In Reshmi Mukherjee's view, it requires a critical thinking exercise of 'learning to learn by unlearning' (2019), for instance, the fixed assumptions and ideas that lie inherent in European humanitarianism. Evans' personal encounters with individual refugees who share their stories with her inform, we find, such an 'exercise' as it unlearns pity-based empathy and becomes an instructive lesson on the irreducible value of human dignity. In her analysis of *Threads*, Mukherjee resources postcolonial thinkers Ranajit Guha and Gayatri Spivak and argues that *Threads* serves as an important 'archive' of the refugee experience as Evans successfully draws '"history from below" and makes marginal voices visible in places where it has been stopped from historicization' (2019) and been replaced by the well-known (colonial) narrative of Europe as the benevolent saviour of unfortunate others. It is, however, in her capacity of being an artist that Evans' efforts to act in solidarity with refugees make a real difference. Art is a broker that transcends 'linguistic and cultural boundaries' (Evans, 2017: 35). As she ponders, 'what can I give someone who has very little and is about to lose even that? I can give them a piece of paper with their portrait on' (75). As refugees queue up to pose for Evans, the volunteer-refugee relationship changes into a collaborative artistic project of quite literally documenting the human face of the refugee. This is a mutual activity of giving and receiving in return – Evans draws and refugees share details of their lives. Drawing a portrait is a slow process and, as Evans muses, becomes 'an intimate thing' when you 'sit and study every feature of a face' (106) to craft a visual image that also touches upon what the artist senses to be the 'essence' of the person depicted. To be seen and recognised as an individual is a rare thing in the context of a camp and, as Erica Smith observes, drawing a portrait is thus a 'powerful action' as '[e]yes meet and a connection is made' (2017).

It is, of course, significant that in all her portraits and sketches depicting refugees, Evans 'draws against' the common tropes of victims and villains as seen, for example, in the 'Good Chance Dome' community centre where we encounter 'grown men, hunched over, colouring in with felt-tip pens' (2017: 35) art work of their own, in defiance of the commonplace expectation that such men should pose a threat to Europe. Similarly, when the aforementioned pregnant mother is physically assaulted, Evans has her transcend the role of mere passive victim. As she explains, she sticks to the facts but 'I use every trick in the book' that will 'intensify that representation. I use full page frames, I use intense colour ... . I make the woman stare back defiantly into the eyes of the policeman who is assaulting her. I give her agency. I give her a moment of resistance' (Evans in Davies, 2017: 6–7). As the camp residents are evicted and new camps will continue to pop up elsewhere, a man who 'can't draw' walks into the Good Chance Dome to add his presence by stencilling his hand because '[n]ow more than ever, he needs to make a mark, [t]o know he still exists' (2017: 161). In a final effort at collaborative creative art work, refugee children draw the outlines of their bodies as paper shapes that are 'Hung out to Dry on Red Tape between Power Lines' (164), drawn by Evans as red lace, where the colour red, of course, is a double reference to Europe's bloody assault on humanity and to compassion in the hearts of those who care. *Threads* makes sure that refugees, to repeat Chouliaraki's call, are 'seen, heard, and recognised' although it still remains for the wider European public that clings to hostile nationalist agendas to do the same.

**In conversation, Kate Evans says:** Humanitarian action is hard to get right, but we do not have to get it right. We can do what we can do and then we can recognise, analyse and talk about the difficulties. It is not that we should not have been in the Jungle of Calais and that we should not have given out stuff. We could have done it better. We should have done it better. But you have to do things wrong in order to get them right. I did not expect the Jungle to be like it was. I did not expect there to be such an incredible scale of humanitarian need that deservedly needs to be addressed. I do not want my critical comments to sound like what we were doing there was irrelevant because it was not. People would have starved and frozen if we had not done what we did. I think sometimes on the left we can be very hamstrung by the narcissism of small differences. I do not think that we should go into a difficult, unfair and impossible situation with the idea that we can solve it. I think we can witness it and that is good enough.

'A Perilous Journey' (2015) also has an activist agenda that draws attention to why we must care about and be in solidarity with refugees, but it brings this out slightly differently from *Threads*. It is produced by PositiveNegatives, a non-profit organisation that crafts 'co-creative' material on human rights and humanitarian issues, by 'adapting personal stories into art, education and advocacy material' in close collaboration with those whose stories are told (PositiveNegatives). PositiveNegatives stories are 'simple' narratives drawn in black or grey on white with brief emotive captions which, we argue, work towards direct unadorned communication wherein the reader's transformation into 'viewer' and participant becomes central. The three separate stories in 'A Perilous Journey' are first-person narratives as told to the PositiveNegatives collective by Khalid, Hasko and Mohammad; three Syrian men who embark on the same dangerous journey towards Europe, yet whose respective backgrounds as student, artist and manual worker are very different. As their distinct individualities are brought to the fore, they, too, contradict the fatigued media trope of predatory young Middle-Eastern men who pose a security threat. The protagonists only introduce themselves by their first names as the veiling of ID details is pivotal to most refugees, yet the photographs inserted at the end of each cartoon authenticate the actual stories they narrate. As Johannes Schmid observes, however, Mohammad is only 'shown as a headless upper body with his hands folded in a pleading motion with the caption underneath telling us that he is still waiting for the decision whether he'd be granted asylum' which also 'serve[s] to drive home the moral immediacy through the affective potential of photography' (2019: 82).

As we see in *Threads*, visual storytelling has a specific appeal; in Kathy Burrell and Kathrin Hörschelmann's words, it bridges '"witnessing" and imagination' (2019: 50). Quoting John Berger's point that 'seeing comes before words' (47), the 'lines of sight' (51) can shift perception in ways that promote empathetic responses in the viewer. This is particularly true of 'A Perilous Journey' as 'narrative strips have to be read spatially' whereby the viewer must fill in 'gaps between frames' (50) by way of imagination. In their view, this means that '[t]he consumption of the story is not passive …, an interaction, an element of reciprocity, is created' (50). This adds an aesthetic value to visual storytelling that is unique. Graphic narratives, they point out, accentuate this 'through the use of very specific modalities such as carefully drawn facial expressions, as well as a direct line into the inner lives and thought of the narrators' (51) or indeed through the affectivity of touch as communicated through body language in response to, for example, harrowing experiences of torture or intense longing for family. While this is a crucial point in itself, we are specifically interested in pursuing the link between storytelling, aesthetics and solidarity and argue that this comes into full vision if we view the three stories together as a 'refugee triptych', that is to say, as side-by-side individual 'panels' that complement each other by presenting variant expressions of refugee affectivity. With Khalid, Hasko and Mohammad's faces mostly turned towards the viewer, the possibility of an intimate connection that enhances communication is established just as the 'thoughtful, humanising graphic strips' (Burrell and Hörschelmann, 2019: 47) centre stage how these three Syrian men 'see' their situation and, most importantly, as in the Hasko centre panel, how they see us 'seeing' them. As Europeans acting in solidarity with refugees are nowhere to be found in the strips, save the token sympathetic but complacent asylum-centre staff, the cartoons rely on establishing an empathetic connection with viewers that will make them step into this vacant place. As Burrell and Hörschelmann observe, the emotions of the three protagonists 'are not just confined to their bodies but are working relationally and in tension with the wider structures and contexts of their positions as refugees' (53), yet we suggest that this works in tandem with how their experiences literally *and* metaphorically visualise the vocabulary of refugee talk.

In Khalid's story, loss of freedom and the sense of entrapment are sketched in the graphic details that frame his life – from his ordinary days as a young, contented 'Western lifestyle' university student that come to an end when civil war turns Damascus into a 'gilded cage' to his days of endless waiting in limbo in the Norwegian asylum centre where he is reprimanded for not observing curfew hours. Khalid is seen as caged in, still imprisoned by his graphic memories of being tortured and kept in detention in the notorious 'Building 215' of the secret police and by the memory of his anxious mother who, had she known about his political activities, he tells us, would have 'locked me up' at home to keep him safe. As pensive Khalid looks out into the world outside his window in the centre or talks to us sitting on a stairstep inside it, the visuality of window frame and staircase railings makes us see these as the redrawn prison bars that still keep Khalid in custody. Mohammad also speaks to us from a Norwegian asylum centre about his past life in Syria where he was a hardworking labourer whose income was necessary for his family's survival. He had 'backed the protesters', been visited twice by Assad's security forces before he fled to Iraqi Kurdistan where he worked to send money home until the arrival of ISIS propelled him to risk the perilous journey through 'Fortress Europe' in search of a hospitable place of refuge that will allow him to work in support of his impoverished family in Syria. Kept in a position of indeterminate waiting and mental stasis, Mohammad is heartbroken, weighed down by a feeling of having betrayed his father who had to resort to a loan shark to make his son's 'illegal' passage to Europe possible. We see that Mohammad frequently avoids direct eye contact. The visuality of his always bent-over body posture and protective gesture in showing photos of the family he has not seen for three years affect the viewer and make Khalid's grief palpable and relatable without the use of words. Again, this highlights that storytelling also has a strong visual component that may lie beyond spoken language.

**In conversation, Brad Evans says:** Privilege takes many different forms. I teach political violence and I talk about the conditions of refugees. I begin with Warsan Shire's poem 'Home'. It is a phenomenal way of getting students into thinking about the problem of privilege. What does it mean to have a home? Who is actually speaking? How might people with certain privileges step back from the debate? How might other voices have an equal part in the conversation? I do not only mean the spoken voice, but refugees who work in other grammatical forms of intervention. We have to break apart the dominant influence of language: not everything can be put into words. So what forms of grammatical intervention do I mean? Aesthetics, music or theatre, for example. These expressions are important in their own right and in their own forms of political interventions. How do we allow such voices to come through into the conversation? This is a profound question of both ethics and aesthetics. I also think that this is a good starting point for rethinking the political, because there is always a beyond, a way to reinvent language and aesthetics. Then we can develop a more poetic understanding of politics where we are not just repeating the familiar tropes, but actually having a more open and honest conversation with one another. In such a conversation we should recognise that we are all fundamentally different. That is a positive thing. That is where the idea of humanity comes from – that we are all different. And that is good. It should be celebrated and affirmed.

Hasko's story is the centre piece of the refugee triptych as he addresses the viewer most directly and espouses through his own telling what refugees require, namely, to shed the label of 'refugee' as it obscures their individuality and shared humanity. Flamboyant Hasko takes his agency for granted. 'Would it surprise you to know that I'm an artist? Why, I'm one of Syria's best', he tells us, only, unlike his painting, he himself was not allowed to cross borders. Hasko sets a fine example for Europe to follow when he welcomes the viewer into his newly rented apartment in Denmark from where he awaits family reunion. He provides hospitality and reaches out 'I'm Hasko by the way, join me for a walk?', he suggests and spins a yarn about former happy days in Damascus, his participation in a protest rally that broadcast him 'fist high in the air' on the national news, his terrifying ten-day boat journey across the Mediterranean and his trek through Europe, indulging in the pretence of being 'like any other backpacker'. Hasko is sketched as confident and does not ask for recognition, he has won it already in his life and looks us in the eye without hesitation. Perhaps this is why he can refuse to take hostility personally when he sees us fleeing close encounters with refugees, like the woman in the street he wants to help; 'What do you suppose that woman saw when she looked at me? Crazy Arab I suppose, just like in the news.' He knows that such responses come from irrational fear of the sea-invading hordes, 'We see pictures in the news, just like you.' Knowing well his human worth and that his identity cannot be reduced to that of refugee, he tails his comment that 'I could have flown [me and my family] here – Business class! Like civilized people, with a glass of wine and the children watching *Jurassic Park*' with a rhetorical rebuttal of what we think we see when we come across people like him, 'But of course, we refugees are "nothing but a burden".' Thus, as our close encounters with Khalid, Hasko and Mohammad subtly draw us into their lives, the aesthetic visualities of the refugee triptych make us empathise with fellow human beings whose ordinary lives have been catapulted into extraordinary circumstances. We have every reason 'to expand the concept of us' and 'enlarging the circle of the we'; to offer welcome is a basic act of solidarity. In that sense, there is a 'gentle radicalness' embedded in the stories told, as Burrell and Hörschelmann point out, concluding that in the 'era of "fake news" and simplified narratives, it is radical to be nuanced, radical to be sensitive, and radical to push so hard for a politics of care' (2019: 61–2).

**In conversation, Daniel Trilling says**: Refugees are people so obviously they have agency, yet they are often represented in ways that strip them of it, even in humanitarian discourses. So how can we find a way of representing people that restores it? To me, whether you use the word dignity, agency or humanity is not so important – it is actually about the relation between people. I feel that a situation in which people are treated with dignity is a situation where there is a relation that is reciprocal.

It is easy to celebrate humanitarianism while avoiding politics if the focus is very narrow and on the immediate acts of humanitarian aid. It is easy, for instance, to focus on the moment of saving drowning people in the Mediterranean – although in Europe, even that has become contentious now. But the person who is saved does not stop existing after the dramatic moment of rescue. They go on existing. And the politics around that does not stop either. The rescued person has to live somewhere and has to live with other people. So, decisions about where people seeking asylum should live, and in what circumstances, are often made for them. People who offer help can have different motivations: some rescue NGOs might say that their work is just about saving lives, while other NGOs will say that we are here to highlight the fact that the wider political situation is intolerable. Religious groups might intervene because of particular views on the nature of human life or morality. But there are wider political contexts attached to all these perspectives. I think that shows that humanitarianism cannot be completely divorced from politics. It is not only about saving lives.

The notion of solidarity, a term more strongly associated with the political left, is often mentioned in this context, too. In the current British government, for instance, ministers might talk about humanitarian actions, but they would never use the word solidarity. But I think it is a useful word because it opens up that idea of a reciprocal relationship, and raises the question of what we would have to change about the world to achieve it.

## THE DISTANT OTHER IN CLOSE PROXIMITY

'The relation between what we see and what we know is never settled', says John Berger in *Ways of Seeing* (1983: 7). Differentiating between seeing and looking, he identifies the former as a result of the latter: 'To look is an act of choice. As a result of this act, what we see is brought within our reach, though not necessarily within arm's reach' (8). This is a useful point of departure for the last section in this chapter where we turn to Richard Mosse's audio-visual art installation *Incoming* (2017) and the BBC series *Exodus: Our Journey to Europe* (2016) with specific reference to Hassan Akkad's contribution. We do not offer detailed analysis of these productions but rather reflections on their emotional impact as we zoom in on a few especially affective moments. Our brief discussion is alert to the radical politics of care that can emanate from the viewer's witnessing, or what may be termed the moral spectatorship of the refugee plight (Dahlgren, 2016). These documentaries represent two different means of recording the refugee journey to Europe; one is filmed from a distance using a high-tech thermal surveillance camera, the other is filmed close-up with a low-tech camera phone. Highlighting the potential of the visual to challenge, indeed profoundly disturb, our cognitive responses, we are interested in exploring what we see when we look at these representations of the refugee journey. Coupling this with the issue of solidarity, we contend that Mosse's conceptual documentary inherently enacts solidarity with refugees whereas Akkad's on-the-spot documentary urgently calls for it.

In *Incoming*, the 'storytelling photographer' Richard Mosse tells 'a series of stories' (Mosse, 2020) of epic mobility using a heat-capturing, high-tech camera that is designed for detection, border enforcement and search and rescue, a camera 'not designed for storytelling purposes' (Mosse, 2018b). With his own 'transgressive' storytelling approach, Mosse, however, engages in the ongoing refugee crisis in an intimate manner that forces the audience to look and to see – 'to confront our act of viewing' (Mosse, 2018a). John Berger writes that '[w]e never look at just one thing; we are always looking at the *relation* between things and ourselves' (1983: 9, our italics). When we experienced *Incoming* in August 2019 at Gl. Strand Gallery in Copenhagen we were reminded of this insight. We were (awe)struck by how Mosse's panoramic and telescopic representation of the human figure was disturbingly exalted. Mosse says that he wanted to 'unsettle the audience' by creating an uneasy 'sense of complicity' (2018b). His use of a thermographic surveillance camera that can film bodies from over 30km away allows the viewer to look from a (safe) distance while at the same time coming (uncomfortably) close to the spectral objects viewed. The effect of zooming in on body heat is one of an intimacy so profound that we can 'peer directly into somebody's soul' (Martin, 2019: 19), into the haunting and ghostlike figures of the incoming refugees. Mosse represents the figure of the refugee in line with Giorgio Agamben's notion of *zoë*, or bare life, highlighting the simple fact of a common biological nature that unites all human beings. Furthermore, the viewer is made to consider Judith Butler's reflections on what constitutes a grievable life. Immersing ourselves in the monochrome appearance of the figures on the screen also reminded us of Robert Young's suggestion that current refugees are the new subalterns who are bound up in a contrary logic of visibility-invisibility (2012). Agnes Woolley's comments on how representations can 'cloud as much as they clarify' in that 'the tension between occlusion and revelation is most ethically and politically pressing in relation to disenfranchised groups who have only limited access to the means of self-representation' (2014: 3) also resonate with viewers. Indeed, the high-tech camera used in this art documentary is 'an apt metaphor for the vast and ungraspable refugee crisis – the lives that "register" but are not "seen"' (Lange, 2017). Thus, we agree with Anthony Downey's observation that 'the thermal images before us compel us to reflect upon what we are seeing and what we are missing' (2017: 24).

In Chapter 1 we reflected on how the refugee is perceived as a disturbing figure that creates tensions in nation-states. Such tensions seem to spill over into Mosse's film. Our response to the combination of the monochrome 'colour scheme', the slow-paced movement of the interrelated triptychonic screens and Ben Frost's 'abstract' and mesmerising score is heightened when we watch the recognisably human yet uncannily ghostly figures. We peek into the soul, close up yet from a distance, of a man performing the ritual of prayer. This is a quotidian event, but it is turned into an extraordinary moment that forces us to see this man again, to recognise him, in a way that we would not expect since all facial details are missing. What we *can* see are his movements in shimmering black-and-white and the milky-looking water that cleanses his face. In spite of this defamiliarising effect, or perhaps because of it, we arrest our responses as we linger somewhat uneasily on the private expression of faith right in front of our eyes. In this way we cannot help but reflect on the relation between us and the evocative representation of a man praying; we register him, and we see him, but in a complicit manner. Viewers cannot *not* look as we are drawn into the unhomely universe that surrounds us when we watch the art documentary. The ambivalences and ambiguities involved in 'turning suffering into spectacle' (Martin, 2019: 3) are effective as we respond to the unsettling combination of the visual and the audible, the figurative and the abstract, wrapped up in a monochrome aesthetic style. We are witnesses to the chaos of the arrival of rubber dinghies in almost total darkness with refugees huddled onboard. We cannot look away from the heart-breaking attempts to rescue drowning children, again in darkness, but with the hammering, hypnotic score invading our ears. Looking, we are reminded of Khaled Hosseini's *Sea Prayer*: 'Because you, /you are are precious cargo, Marwan, /the most precious there ever was. I pray the sea knows this./Inshallah' (2018). We eavesdrop and spy unseen on the refugees caught up in the 'permanently temporary', 'frozen transience' (Bauman's terms) of a refugee camp in Berlin's Tempelhof, and are startled when we witness ordinary scenes of children playing because they seem unreal in such a hellish place.

At the heart of this 'cold' black-white-grey documentary is heat. Heat circulates in the stories told, connecting the panels in the cinematic triptych, and connecting people through human touch. Heat can be interpreted in many ways: heat is home, humanity and life. Niall Martin reads Mosse's thermal imagery from a combined political and aesthetic perspective, suggesting that it 'puts into circulation an enhanced understanding of heat as a form of contact [… and it] reminds us of the productive nature of touching and being touched [… that] involves rethinking political space' in adequate ways that respond to the current refugee crisis (2019: 16). When Mosse zooms in on the powerful image of a heat print from the warm human hand on a cold, close-to-death body he reveals that it is as ephemeral as life itself in such dramatic circumstances. But the heat of that hand print is also, we argue, a metaphor for solidarity. The warm residue of touch acts as a conduit, as it were, of common humanity, of kinship and of a realisation of what being in solidarity with somebody actually means. Heat thus speaks directly to the tensions at play and to the viewer's uneasy emotive response.

Another friction that commentators have reacted to is the tension between ethics and aesthetics. It *is* possible to critique Mosse for aestheticising suffering. We can ask, as Iain Chambers does in the catalogue to the exhibition *Sink Without Trace* (London, 2019), when he responds to art that faces 'what history refuses to register and has rendered ghostly', how do we not reduce artistic objects so that they are 'only susceptible to aesthetic evaluation' (2019: 40)? Chambers suggests that the art on display in *Sink Without Trace*, and we would argue, *Incoming*, too, exceeds 'the academic frame' as it 'renders aesthetics in ethical terms' (42). Hence our affective and almost cathartic response to Mosse's film: it gives us a 'perceptual shock' (Mazzara, 2019: 45) that holds us in its grasp. Mosse employs what we might call a heightened aesthetics because of what he describes as his need for 'new images' and 'an adequate strategy' (2020) that would enable him to 'to communicate complicated narratives' (2018c). Combining photojournalism, documentary photography and art, Mosse uses aesthetics as a communicative tool, because to him, 'aesthetics is the opposite of anaesthetics' in that it can 'awaken the senses' in a productive way, as a call to action (2018a). Ethics, aesthetics and politics are thus combined in this art documentary as an example of how to participate in the refugee debate. And for Mosse, using a surveillance camera against itself, as it were, not for long-distance detection, but for intimate emotional engagement, is *his* cultural response to the refugee crisis. To Agnes Woolley, '*Incoming* lays bare both the dehumanising and the humanising aspects of [digital] technologies' (Woolley in Cox et al., 2020: 425). Diego Ramirez, however, is critical of the 'ethical dimensions' of Mosse's work, pointing to what he calls a 'conceptual gulf' (2018) in *Incoming*. Even though Mosse advocates for empathy and social justice for refugees, Ramirez argues, his work 'demonises the figure of the refugee by situating it within a digital hell' (2018). To Ramirez, Mosse's 'hyperbolic aesthetic' ends up dehumanising the subjects he wants to humanise: 'the artist tells us to care about these people and their reality, while the video shows them as non-people' (2018). This, however, was not our response to *Incoming*. Mosse explains that there is a '*feeling* of ethical violation' in it and that the intention is to 'push the viewer in certain directions emotively and viscerally, which can be by turns disorienting or surprising' (Photoworks, 2020). It is this disorientation that we feel can help reorient responses to the human figures that are the subjects of the refugee crisis and, hopefully, push viewers towards an understanding of human solidarity as beginning with the simple recognition of kinship – touching the bare life that unites us all on this planet.

The BBC series *Exodus* is a 'participatory project' co-produced by KEO Films and refugees from Syria, Afghanistan and Gambia who make use of camera phones to document their hazardous journey to Europe. In combination with en route interviews and post-journey studio recordings where traumatic memories finally pour into the open, *Exodus* is yet another example of 'a terrifying, intimate, epic portrait of the immigration crisis' (2017). This is documentary realism at its starkest as the refugees take us where only they go and where no reporters or camera crews can follow, across sandstorms in the 'Sea of Sahara' in a smuggler's pickup jeep, inside a dark container on a truck headed for the UK or on unseaworthy inflatable dinghies from Turkey to Greece. In contrast to *Incoming*, the use of relatively simple mobile-phone technology allows for immediate close-up witnessing of the most harrowing part of the refugee journey. For refugees of the current crisis, a smart phone is indispensable. It is relatively inexpensive, lightweight and portable, as Bruce Bennett observes, and it has 'numerous mobilizing functions' (2018: 24) in that its applications facilitate communication via the social media of WhatsApp or Facebook, orientation via GPS when a rescue operation is urgent or when invisible national borders in foreign landscapes are crossed (25–6), just as it enables Skype conversations with smugglers and fellow refugees, or family and friends left behind. A mobile phone is part and parcel of the refugee survival kit. In *Exodus*, however, the camera phone serves a significant additional function as a filming device for storytelling and self-representation which makes sure that the individual voices of the self-filming refugees are recorded in an unfiltered manner. As Bennett argues, 'greater intimacy and affective charge' is secured when refugees speak directly to the recording camera with the effect that 'the restlessly bobbing, low-resolution, wide-angle lens of the phone, situates us in [their] location in a way that a high-definition film or video camera can't replicate' (22). Most importantly, then, 'the embodied quality of camera-phone video insists upon the presence of the user and, by extension, the viewer' (22).

One of the most affectively charged episodes of the series is Hassan Akkad's real-time filming of his first abortive crossing of the Aegean Sea with 63 people onboard a dinghy intended for 30. The journey is ill-omened from the start. An eerily subdued atmosphere of stillness, only interrupted by engine sound, unison prayer and softly spoken calls for fellow passengers to sit still and be patient, grows into panic when water begins to fill the dinghy; children scream, adults plead to please call the emergency services and young men, including Hassan Akkad, jump into the sea holding on to the side of the dinghy while others use plastic bottles to scoop out water to delay sinking – and then the screen blackens. The video shot lasts less than four minutes but feels like prolonged hours of terrifying doom, as Akkad's exclamation 'Oh my God' keeps droning in the viewer's ears. As Siobhan Brownlie comments: 'The handheld footage is unstable with Hassan's body close up, low-angle shots, constant moving due to the boat's movements, crowded heads and limbs of men and women some of whom are wearing hijab, shots of hands clasped, rubber tyres, and [wide-eyed] children in coloured life-jackets' (2020: 47). What do we see when we look at this recording? We emphatically do not see 'distant others' (Chouliaraki's term) as we look at the horrified ordinary people who are no different from us, yet words to describe their fear and stifled despair escape viewers who are dumbstruck in suspense until Hassan Akkad appears in a flash-forward studio recording to tell us that all passengers were rescued by a Turkish patrol ship. But no one knows this when Hassan Akkad records; death seems imminent. Akkad's successful attempt to cross the next day is, surprisingly, not included in *Exodus*, but he tells us in his 2016 talk at 'Being The Story' that the 45 people onboard were intercepted by the Greek marine forces who 'broke the engine, stole the fuel tank' and sailed away. Akkad and other able-bodied men 'swam for seven hours, pushing the boat until Lesbos' (Akkad, 2016). As he recalls, upon setting foot on European ground and as we see in *Exodus* when he films his onward journey for England, 'expectations did not align with reality'. There was no organised reception, there was only chaos.

To recall Berger's words, then, looking at Akkad's handheld footage of his 87 days of illegalised journeying brings what we see 'within our reach' and this is indeed an uncomfortable sight range that makes for deep thinking about the moral collapse of Europe that we are, or should feel, required to act on. In the viewers' mind, the anti-migration metaphors of floods and flows are made to seem utterly disrespectful and cruel, we think only about the power of water to kill and let sink without trace. Akkad and his fellow passengers made it, unlike more than 20,000 other migrants who since 2014 were also forced to travel by the deadly sea route only because they did not possess a passport. We come to see the Mediterranean Sea as the contemporary Middle Passage, a fluid graveyard or the 'liquid archives' of 'histories that are suspended and sedimented in the aquatic realm' (Iain Chambers, 2019: 41). Yet such metaphors are in themselves potentially violating when what refugees need is not the language of metaphor but solidarity and concrete interventions on our part to offer safe alternatives to this inhumane and fatal means of passage. Yet the act of seeing, as Frederica Mazzara contends, 'has the potential to make the invisible and unsayable, visible and sayable' (2019: 45) while calling on the viewer to 'enact that visibility' (Bal and Hernández-Navarro in Mazzara, 2019: 45). In *Exodus*, when Akkad, at an emotional breaking point in hostile Europe, speaks directly to his camera and says '[e]very night I think of those who died on the way. ... I feel that those are the people who keep me going – for you to die while trying to escape death is something that is really hard to accept ... . I feel like this is all meant to be heavy', his upfront words cannot remain unaddressed. 'Governments failed us', as he said in a follow-up address to a British audience, 'but you people didn't, [it is] the power of people helping people, the solidarity of people helping people' that makes a difference (Akkad, 2016).

**In conversation, Brad Evans says**: I want to think about humanitarianism in the context of what Mark Duffield calls the humanitarian industry, and to reflect on the changing nature of humanitarianism. If humanitarianism grows out of the wealth the West accrued from once colonised countries, then there is an asymmetrical relationship by definition. Part of the problem with humanitarianism has been an unwillingness to recognise that this asymmetrical relationship exists. We know now that humanitarianism is a power relationship. It should be stripped away from all kinds of conditionality. If you want to help, help, in spite of any risks involved. It is better to have those risks than to impose conditionality, which is not humanitarianism at all. It is a financial and a political contract. You can do aid in a way that is more humanitarian, more reciprocal. But then we have to change the fabric of what humanitarianism means, and we have to recognise unequal relations of power as well as the histories of colonisation and of exploitation – and the continued lived effects of those histories. Another problem with humanitarianism is that the ethics involved has been destroyed by wars on terror and the idea of humanitarian warfare. The idea that we can change the world for the better has also been a casualty of the war on terror.

According to Bennett, the political aesthetics of *Exodus* relies heavily on the integration of phone footage into the 'epistolary, self-reflexive and critically juxtaposed narrative structure' (Naficy in Bennett, 2018: 18) of the series. Bennett calls attention to the self-filming refugees as 'guerilla film-makers' (21) whose 'self-reflexive concern with narration' may be said to reveal 'a fundamental concern with representation and advocacy, as the individualized story offers up a stubbornly irreducible particularity as a strategic response to the dehumanizing stereotypes of bogus asylum-seekers and pathetic refugees' (27). As their stories are the only 'portable' property refugees have left on the journey, they employ phone footage as an effective audio-visual means of storytelling to convey the reality of what it means and feels like to be in flight. In Bennett's words, '[t]he continual cross-cutting between different stories emphasizes the temporality of migrant experience, which is structured around interruption, delay and immobility, as much as it is by the movement that seems deceptively straightforward on animated maps' (28) that cannot fully represent often 'long, frustrating periods of stasis' (28). While this pinpoints the ontological uncertainty of being a refugee, the visuality of witnessing it at close-hand through the illicit live 'reportage' of refugees forces the viewer into a cognitive processing of the faulty conception that refugees are distant others when, quite plainly, they are just fellow human beings. We see that when we look at their footage and when we listen to the detailed stories of their past lives at home in the countries they have fled. As Brownlie observes, this points to 'the power of restorying' to provide a bond between those who film and tell and those who see and listen 'through the viewer being called to draw on memory of shared human experiences: family, friendship, emotions of fear, anger and love' (2020: 52). *Exodus*, she argues, 'enacts the creation of a new story giving rise to a particular vision ... which is able to argue implicitly but powerfully for a more humane attitude towards refugees and migrants' (52). For refugees, the stories filmed and told come to stand in the place of a historical archive of the refugee experience. Brownlie alludes to this as a refugee 'collective memory product' (47) but also contends that *Exodus* provides a 'public memory artefact' (51); one that can hopefully invite a wider audience into 'explorative thinking' (51), to recall Berger's words, about the always unsettled relation between what we see and what we know.

This chapter has explored how solidarity with refugees is a matter of collaborative efforts to work for justice in recognition of human rights as universal rights. As Hassan Akkad reminds us in *Exodus*: 'Anyone can become a refugee. Anyone. It's not something that you choose; it's something that happens to you. And just like it happened to me, it could happen to you' (2016). We think of the collaborative efforts inherent in all the works discussed in this chapter to showcase the power of what Gilbert calls 'potent collectivities' to promote change through 'the production of relations, experiences and affects of solidarity' (2020). Again, solidarity is enacted by people, with people and for people and, to be meaningful, it must involve action. As we stated at the outset, however, solidarity has no single definition and for the EU that continues to criminalise human movement, the gesture of solidarity with refugees is not deemed to be affordable. As William Maley observes, '[i]f the sufferings of refugees are to be ameliorated, it is not very likely that politics will show the way. Rather, it is through the recovery of moral sentiment that a path might be found' (2016: 182). From *Refugee Tales* to *Exodus*, refugees and artist-activists walk this very path and exhibit storytelling as a means by which the political and the aesthetic combine in ways that are soundly ethical. Storytelling is part and parcel of this walk, a matter of both testimony and witnessing, thus implicating both teller and listener. As highlighted throughout this chapter, such interaction debunks the idea of refugees as distant others and invariably deflates common stereotypes. As we explore in the next chapter, this interaction leads instead to recognition of the most basic bond between us: our shared humanity.

# 4

# Recognition – Refugee Literature and Defamiliarisation

In the previous chapter we explored the effects of hearing and seeing in connection with artistic and activist responses to the ongoing refugee crisis. We have also already gestured to the word 'recognition'. Our intention here is to home in on that term, keeping in mind Sara Ahmed's pointer that to recognise means 'to know again, to acknowledge and to admit' (2000: 22). We are now concerned with the effects of saying – with what refugee literature says and how it says it. The overarching question we ask in this chapter is: How does refugee literature facilitate recognition? According to J.J. Bola, recognition is 'the job of art. To hold up a mirror and validate our experiences. That's what makes us feel more human. We're here. We're breathing' (Bola in O'Shea-Meddour, 2019: 15). The proposal we pursue in an attempt to answer this query is that we can (begin to) understand how refugee literature opens up for recognition by unpacking the defamiliarising ways in which it makes us, as it were, stop and think as a result of the way literature says what is says. We are interested in how refugee literature demands a cognitive and imaginative readjustment of the vocabularies that characterise refugee talk. To us, this perspective is part of the 'ethical turn in literary studies' that has placed, as Lyndsey Stonebridge holds, 'a lot of emphasis on "responsibility" and "obligation" in recent years' (2018: 14). To this we adjoin 'recognition' – keeping in mind, as Stonebridge adds, that 'ethics traffics with politics' (14). Indeed, Anna Bernard insists in her exploration of genres of refugee writing that 'we must consider not just what these [refugee] texts say, but how they say it, and understand advocacy as a driver of aesthetic innovation as well as a political project' (Bernard in Cox et al., 2020: 67).

The literary technique that Victor Shklovsky termed 'defamilia-risation' draws attention to how and what texts say. David Lodge explains its effect thus: 'What startles us into a new way of seeing is a new way of saying, and we can only appreciate the novelty of *that* against what is habitual and expected in any given context' (1991: 15). Refugee literature, we argue, throws readers out of their habitual and often thoughtless responses to migration and to the figure of the refugee by treating these phenomena in unex-pected ways so that readers can begin to know them again, only this time in a more nuanced way. Through this 'new way of saying', literature facilitates a renewed way of thinking that is aesthetically thought-provoking and ethically challenging. Defamiliarisation, or 'making strange', is an illuminating perspective on the efficacy of refugee literature. Shklovsky argues that since our 'perception becomes habitual' and 'automatic' in our everyday life (Shklovsky in Lodge, 1991: 19), art has a special function; its purpose is 'to recover the sensation of life; it exists to make one feel things' (20). Consequently, the 'technique of art is to make objects "unfamil-iar"' so that our perception is arrested (20). With recourse to Leo Tolstoy's work, Shklovsky details how that writer 'describes an object as if he were seeing it for the first time, an event as if it were happening for the first time' (21). This technique, then, encourages readers to rethink that which has been rendered so ordinary and familiar that we do not even notice it anymore. The power of litera-ture is its capacity 'to disturb, defamiliarize or shake our beliefs and assumptions' (Bennett and Royle, 2004: 35). Defamiliarisation, we thus contend, opens up a space for recognition by making strange and different that which has become familiar through force of habit and repetition. We have already explored the tired tropes of victim and villain, of deserving and undeserving refugees – effectively a vocabulary of *mis*recognition – that lull us into mundane and default responses. By disarranging such habitual reader responses, the defamiliarising aspects of refugee literature open up for the habit-disturbing and upsetting process of knowing something and someone again. We are thus forced to engage with the vocabularies of refugee talk in potentially unsettling ways.

Before we begin, however, we need to reflect on what refugee lit-erature is, and we do so via Claire Gallien's inspirational ideas. As we go forward, we concomitantly explore refugee writers' self-imposed duty to remember, the troping of time, and non-refugee writers' potentially problematic relationship with what can be termed refugee thematics. We comment briefly on striking and defamiliarising narrative patterns before we zoom in on six contemporary refugee novels in three separate sections. This detailed exploration of how literature *actually* defamiliarises allows us to demonstrate what we mean when we argue that refugee literature opens up for recognition through its defamiliarising techniques. In short, we explore how these literary texts disturb 'our world', by focusing on their capacity 'to refigure, reform, revolutionize' (Bennet and Royle, 2004: 80) and their effect on readers to acknowledge that there are fresh ways of knowing that which we think we know already.

## OBSERVATIONS ON REFUGEE LITERATURE

While there is no easy way to define 'refugee literature', Claire Gallien's thoughts are useful. She encourages postcolonial scholars to engage in 'a refugee poetics and aesthetics … by confronting consensual yet politically, ethically, and ideologically problematic modes of representation of forcibly displaced people, and by showcasing and analysing what literature and the arts propose in terms of alternative discourses, voices, and imaginaries' (2018a: 722). It is such alternative discourses that this chapter focuses on. Gallien insists that this engagement is not only important, but also beneficial, because refugee literature has 'long-term impact' since its 'uprootedness and extraterritoriality interrogate default literary geographies defined along national borders and the default monolingual imaginary of national languages' (722). Refugee literature also 'lends itself to extraterritorial readings' since it 'defines places of departure as much as places of transit and arrival' and is likely to be engaged in 'subverting national linguistic and literary borders' (2018b: 740). Such extraterritoriality is a reminder of Arendt's point that refugees expose the crisis of nation-states since they upset the established trinity of people-state-territory. In this context, we should also keep in mind Agnes Woolley's reminder that refugees are 'not metaphors of rootlessness, but socially situated subjects' (2014: 4). Even so, refugee literature cannot easily be subsumed under the rubric of any national literature. Small wonder, then, that it is concerned with borders as experiences of 'danger and death' and not, as postcolonial studies has tended to argue, as interstitial spaces where creativity occurs (Gallien, 2018b: 741). In fact, the current refugee crisis provides a new purview for postcolonial writers, Homi Bhabha holds in connection with such writers' capacity to speak 'truth to global power', because 'they speak neither for the nation nor the globe; their purview is the colony, the city, the neighbourhood, the region – and more recently, the refugee camp' (Appiah and Bhabha, 2018: 189).

But what is refugee literature? Gallien draws on Corina Stan's suggestion that refugee literature refers to 'texts by and about refugees, which represent migration as part of a shared world' (2018a: 723). Gallien elaborates that refugee literature 'is not (only) a literature of despair that dwells on the moral hypocrisy of the west', nor is it 'only a form of testimonial literature depicting traumatic events' (725). More importantly, it is 'a literature where seminal experimentations with forms, genres, languages, and national literary constructions occur' (725). To exemplify Gallien's points, we briefly include Hoda Barakat's *Voices of the Lost*. The novel asks a number of questions that go to the heart of cultural responses to refugee crises:

> How well can we ever know people who have lived through civil wars? How much can we ever really know about the violence and destruction, the losses, the devastation? The overpowering fear they must feel every day? Can we ever really understand how they are transformed, which things change inside them, and which things harden? (2021: 175–6)

Barakat's experimental response to such questions is to fashion her text around a series of unfinished letters circulating between unnamed refugee and migrant characters in the first part, turn to the unnamed recipients of the letters they never receive in the second part and to end with a postman who wonders what you do when homes and houses have been destroyed: '[W]ho do you write to? What address do you use?' (195). In this playful novel, then, Barakat illustrates that refugee literature is not only a testimony of despair and trauma but also a demonstration of literary experimentation that defamiliarises the reader's response to what is becoming familiar tragic territory.

Arthur Rose argues that a genealogy of refugee writing 'emerges when it is understood as an intervention into refugee discourses as a problem of style' (Rose in Cox et al., 2020: 55), also drawing attention to the aesthetic aspects of refugee literature. Gallien takes such insights further and proposes that refugee literature 'can be taken to mean not only writing by refugees, but also the publications of former refugees turned residents or nationals, as well as those who have not experienced forced displacement' (2018b: 742). This is indeed a 'broad definition', and surely provocative to some readers. Yet for Gallien it is a way of bringing 'creative heterogeneity and dissonance into the category', thus making 'readers more aware of and attentive to the politics of representation' (742). That is why it is a definition that we align ourselves with since we are interested in the ethical and aesthetic implications of the politics of representation. At the same time, however, we are mindful of Sam Durrant's point in connection with 'the imaginative interiorisation' in much of the literature written in response to the current crisis (Durrant in Cox et al., 2020: 614). According to Durrant, 'we seem to get more or less direct access to refugee experience and the refugee seems to be included in the realm of grievable life by virtue of her common humanity' (614). While this move is 'laudable' (614) such interiorisation also disregards the exceptionality of the refugee that Arendt wrote about in the 1940s. Consequently, we must remain vigilant when it comes to the ethics as well as the politics of representation. We bear this in mind as we reflect on literary experimentations in this chapter, highlighting the chosen texts' formal and stylistic aspects and how they critically intervene in refugee talk.

**In correspondence, Simon Gikandi writes:** How can we speak of literary figures or signs when the crisis of humanity swirls around us? This is a difficult question and has become increasingly so in the midst of our current crisis when there is a compulsion for us to do something visible and active. My view on this question may not be comforting.

The distinction between literary scholars and anthro-pologists is important and needs to be maintained. Many anthropologists might say they, too, work with figures, so I think the distinction to be made is between those who work with representations and those who do empirical work. The role of literary scholars is not to represent things as they are but as they could be, or as they are imagined and come to us through figures and images (this is a debate that goes to the beginning of literary criticism in Plato and Aristotle). We should be less defensive of our work and insist on its essential value, which is connected to the imaginative and figurative language. Empiricists will provide demographi-cal studies of refugees; social science will provide the facts and diagnosis; historians will provide the background; legal scholars will locate the narratives of refugees in inter-national law; but writers of fiction will provide imaginary narratives of refugees and literary scholars will try to add to our understanding of the situation through the explication of these texts. In short, we need to remind ourselves what kind of knowledge and understanding the study of these literary representation, films, and photographs bring to the discourse on the figure of the refugee and to insist on the role of the imagination in staging the ethical questions the crisis has brought about.

I think it is important for us to be mindful that what we study are figures not real people. My main complaint about literary criticism at the moment is that the figural is conflated with the real. Although this makes us seem socially relevant, it distorts what we can do most effectively: When we look at the picture of a dead Syrian child being pulled from the sea, we are not talking about the child (although we have his name) but how his figuration by a photographer has the capacity to generate a melancholic dialectic with immense power to move us and to bring about change.

Sara Ahmed has a point in her discussion on the 'figure' of the stranger: When we read the story of an African refugee in Northern Britain in Caryl Phillips' A Distant Shore or follow the lives of Zimbabwean refugees in Brian Chikwava's Harare North, we recognise them as strangers with 'linguis-tic and bodily integrity.' But that, to me, is not a problem but an opportunity; it is, indeed, the work of literature – to make us imagine refugees as people with histories, relationships, and desires. When we see them in a list of names at the local refugee center, they are just numbers; when we see them walking awkwardly down our streets, we see only their strangeness. In the fiction they are recognised as human, people with linguistic and bodily integrity.

Ahmed might argue that by giving the refugees integrity, we distort their conditions of existence, that we imagine them as we would like them to be and find comfort in a distortion. My counter to this is that the language of representing strangers used by those who do not want them in their midst is premised on their animality. Rescuing their linguistic and bodily integrity is an important first step in understanding the crisis of humanity. The figure does not replace the real thing, but it is an essential supplement (addition).

We now want to draw attention to three general observations we have made in our study of refugee literature. We notice that there is a tendency in refugee writers or writers with a refugee background or legacy – writers with 'refugenes' – to feel a duty to remember. For example, in *The Sympathizer*, Viet Thanh Nguyen notes the link between being a refugee and memory and how the refugee is duty-bound to remember. As the narrator wryly insists, 'the most important thing we could never forget was that we could never forget' (2015: 239). In *The Displaced*, Nguyen holds that since displaced people are unwanted where they come from and where they come to, they risk becoming unremembered strangers. This is where 'the work of writers becomes important, especially writers who are refugees or have been refugees – if such a distinction can be drawn' (2018: 17). As a child refugee, he takes this duty seriously: 'I remember all these things because if I did not remember them and write them down then perhaps they would all disappear' (14):

I cultivate that feeling of what it was to be a refugee, because a writer is supposed to go where it hurts, and because a writer needs to know what it feels like to be an other. A writer's work is impossible if he or she cannot conjure up the lives of others, and only through such acts of memory, imagination, and empathy can we grow in our capacity to feel for others. ... This is a writer's dream, that if only we can hear these people that no one else wants to hear, then perhaps we can make you hear them, too. (2018: 17, 22)

That this duty is often a burden is made abundantly clear in Hassan Blasim's story 'Ali's Bag', when his refugee narrator explains in dark tones how forging a career as an author of refugee literature becomes an incurable cancer: 'More than once it had occurred to me that I will spend my life writing about the events and surreal happenings I have experienced along the routes taken by undocumented migrants. It's my cancer and I do not know how it can be cured' (2016: 60). Blasim's strange description of the duty to remember as cancer is a good example of the defamiliarising aspect of refugee literature that we consider in this chapter.

Second, we have detected a foregrounding of the complexities of time in refugee literature, so much so that it is becoming a recognisable trope, possibly even a defining characteristic of such writing. In Nguyen's *The Sympathizer*, for example, the striking layering of 'refugee time' and 'refugee space' that characterises the temporal-spatial logic of refugee living is perfectly illustrated in a clock that hangs in a local restaurant:

carved from hardwood into the shape of our homeland [Vietnam]. For this clock was a country, and this country was a clock. ... Some craftsman in exile had understood that this was exactly the timepiece his refugee countrymen desired. We were displaced persons, but it was time more than space that defined us. While the distance to return to our lost country was far but finite, the number of years it would take to close that distance was potentially infinite. Thus, for displaced people the first question was always about time: When can I return? ... Refugee, exile, immigrant – whatever species of displaced human we were, we did not simply live in two cultures, as celebrants of the great American melting pot imagined. Displaced people also lived in two time zones, the here and the there, the present and the past, being as we were reluctant time travelers. But while science fiction imagined time travelers as moving forward or backward in time, this timepiece demonstrated a different chronology. The open secret of the clock, naked for all to see, was that we were only going in circles. (2015: 199)

In another example, this time from Roma Tearne's 'The Colour of Pomegranates' (Tearne in Popescu, 2016), we note how the story operates with a double-and-simultaneous temporality: there is official clock time that frames the story, beginning with '25 March 2003' (2016: 191) in Baghdad and ending in the Jungle in Calais, '30 September 2015' (201), when time is also paused: in Calais, '[t]ime on this occasion stood still' (201). Disturbing this general clock time is personal time:

> He walked slowly into time, sleeping when it was dark, rising to start up again at first light. He carried very little into this new life, only those few things that had survived the water. A wristwatch belonging to his wife. Time was still ticking under its broken glass. No bomb could stop that. (Popescu, 2016: 199)

We shall see more of such temporal-spatial disjunction in the literary discussion in this chapter.

The third observation we have made is that many writers *without* refugee background feel drawn to a sweeping 'refugee thematics'. Contemporary novels are full of refugee talk as a quotidian topic for conversation, whether the setting is Britain, Ireland or the US. A few examples will suffice. In Ali Smith's *Winter* we come across this conversation:

> Choice, she said. Yes, he said. Is this like when we were talking about the people who drowned trying to cross the sea running away from war, and you said we didn't need to feel responsible because it has been *their choice* to run away from their houses being burned down and bombed and then *their choice again* to get into a boat that capsized? she said. (2017: 55)

In Sally Rooney's *Conversations with Friends* the characters chat about refugees:

The others were talking about refugees. Evelyn kept saying: some of these people have degrees, these are doctors and professors we're talking about. I had noticed before this tendency of people to emphasise the qualifications of refugees. Derek said: whatever about the others, imagine turning doctors away. It's insane. What does that mean? said Bobbi. Don't let them in unless they've got a medical degree? (2018: 111–12)

And as a last example, we include this passage of widespread refugee talk from Valeria Luiselli's *Lost Children Archive*:

The broadcasters are calling it an immigration crisis. A mass influx of children, they call it, a sudden surge. They are undocumented, they are illegals, they are aliens, some say. They are refugees, legally entitled to protection, others argue. This law says that they should be protected; this other amendment say that they should not. Congress is divided, public opinion is divided, the press is thriving on a surplus of controversy, nonprofits are working overtime. Everyone has an opinion on the issue; no one agrees on anything. (2019: 39–40)

In fact, the refugee crisis has become *the* contemporary story for many writers. Authors respond with sympathy to what is seen as 'the central moral question of our time' (Wood, 2017) as we notice in, for example, Karen Campbell's *This Is Where I Am* (2013), Jason Donald's *Dalila* (2017) or Donal Ryan's *From a Low and Quiet Sea* (2018). Venturing into this thematics, however, comes with risk, as we can glean from the less-than-sympathetic review of *From a Low and Quiet Sea* by Parul Sehgal. Ryan's Syrian refugee protagonist is, according to Sehgal, 'the product, it seems, of the author's immense pity for – but scant actual curiosity about – the figure of "the migrant"'; to her, Ryan comes perilously close to being what James Wood calls a 'moral flâneur' (2017). We could say the same about Gavin Extence's *The End of Time* (2019). According to a BBC interview, the author 'has previously tackled topical issues', and 'his Syrian refugee novel' is 'fuelled entirely by online research, with Extence spending hundreds of hours in his attic office reading articles, scouring photographs and watching videos' (Leatherdale, 2019). The interview explains that the danger when you write 'topical books' is that 'the topics can become outdated': "'Sadly the plight of refugees is still topical and I think it will be for a long time yet," Extence says' (2019). There is something utilitarian, possibly even ethically problematic, in this literary approach to the 'topical', especially when Extence explains that his next book is on the topical issue of autism.

**In conversation, Mohsin Hamid says**: The idea of refugee literature and of being a refugee is very interesting to me. The term refugee, of course, is a legal term. It implies that someone has the right to be protected by the laws that protect refugees and that there are certain people who are legitimate refugees and others who are not. So, my preferred term is migrant – and migrant literature. I think migrant is a broader term that encompasses those who might not qualify legally for refugee status. I prefer the term migrant because it widens up the domain. When we begin to examine who is a migrant and what migrant literature is, what we see is that there are certain people who move from one place to another and they can be called migrant and, of course, some of them can legally be called refugees. But in fact, all of us migrate through time. And the notion that every human being is a migrant is central to my under-standing of the nature of humanity, to what it is to be human and to my own writing – particularly to *Exit West*. Rather than saying we need to begin by expanding our compassion for the legal category of person that is a refugee, I would take a slightly different and broader approach, and say: let us begin by expressing compassion for ourselves and to recognise that we are all migrants, that we all suffer the pain of migration. If we stop denying this within ourselves, we can begin to extend to others the recognition that they, too, are us, and that they are like us – that they, too, are experiencing the reality of being a migrant. If we can think in those terms, we have a much broader category which includes everyone. So rather than telling non-refugees to accept refugees, I am more interested in allowing those who do not think of themselves as migrants to realise that in fact they, too, are migrants and that their animosity or resistance towards migrants and refugees is, in fact, an animosity or resistance towards themselves and towards their own lived experience.

## DEFAMILIARISING NARRATIVE PATTERNS

Before we turn to the selected novels as case studies, we want to reflect on what may be termed a search for an appropriate narrative pattern, template or model for refugee literature. Sarajevo-born, US-based Aleksandar Hemon explains how migration 'generates narratives; each displacement is a tale; each tale is unlike any other ... the world of refugees is a vast narrative landscape. ... What literature does, or at least can do, is allow for individual narrative enfranchisement' (Hemon in Nguyen, 2018: 92). This narrative-generating migratory story of refugees is, not surprisingly, described in sweeping, epic terms. To Peter Tinti and Tuesday Reitano, such tales can be seen as 'a modern parable of our times' (2018: 1). Homer's *Odyssey* has become a central source text, fashioned, as it is, around familiar refugee experiences of wandering, time, loss, violence and hope. Parvati Nair suggests that the notion of an 'odyssey' has become part of a 'global imaginary not as a process, but as the framing condition of the refugee' and that it 'triggers in readers an expectation of prolonged drama, as in the classic stories of quest' (Nair in Cox et al., 2020: 415). Perhaps this is so, or perhaps it is not so much the drama and the quest, as it is the dangerous, ongoing stop-and-start journey that resonates. As Claire Gallien writes: 'Their [refugees'] journeys recall the *Odyssey*, but without the promise of return, and the Mediterranean Sea, as used to be the case with the Black Atlantic, has become a cemetery' (2018b: 736). Let us ponder the return to the *Odyssey* (and to Virgil's *Aeneid*), before we touch briefly on the *Titanic* trope and the mythic narrative as examples of narrative patterns that exploit familiar sources in defamiliarising ways.

In 1944, Arendt used the classic tale of hazardous movement to explain her own experiences. She writes of 'Ulysses-wanderers' (1994: 118) drawing attention to the ancient history of seeking refuge even if the experience might be different from that 'great prototype' (118). Behrouz Boochani, too, employs the term 'odyssey' in the early chapters of his autobiography *No Friend but the Mountains* (2018) before the terms 'prison' and 'cages' take over when he finds himself incarcerated on Manus Island. Charlotte McDonald-Gibson's *Castaway*, too, mobilises the idea of 'an odyssey to Europe' (2017: 4) – where migrants and refugees are embroiled in the 'new business of hope and dreams' (15). And most powerfully, Patrick Kingsley calls his investigation into the current refugee crisis *The New Odyssey* (2017). In an interview he comments on the title as a template:

> I was trying to remind the reader that these great journeys are not just something from our age but also from centuries and millennia past. And one way of reminding people of that is to evoke the title of a famous migration like the *Odyssey*. However, if it had been better known I might have called it 'The New Aeneid'. ... Ironically, Aeneas is fleeing from the same war as Odysseus was leaving from, but he is actually trying to find a new home, rather than going back to his old one. So for me the *Aeneid* was a slightly better template because Aeneas is in essence a refugee. (Kingsley in Simon, 2016)

Kingsley elaborates on that 'classic' pattern in *The New Odyssey*, explaining that for him, the current refugee journey:

> deserves to be considered a contemporary *Odyssey*. ... [T]heir voyages through the Sahara, the Balkans, or across the Mediterranean ... are almost as epic as that of classical heroes such as Aeneas and Odysseus. ... Today's sirens are the smugglers ... the violent border guard a contemporary Cyclops. Three millennia after their classical forbears created the founding myths of the European continent, today's voyagers are writing a new narrative that will influence Europe, for better or worse, for years to come. (2017: 11)

There is one moment in *The New Odyssey* that explicitly encourages readers mentally and imaginatively to cross and conflate time and space. Such a gesture opens up for empathetic recognition in an unexpected manner, playing on readers' emotional investment in the story told and their affective responses to it:

> Not for the last time, I'm reminded of the classical heroes I used to read about at school. This sight in particular [of newly arrived refugees on a Lesvos beach] summons up images of Aeneas, the Trojan who fled a burning Troy, voyaged around the Mediterranean for years, before eventually settling in Italy and starting the dynasty that would eventually build the Roman empire. As Aeneas leaves Troy, he has a lion's pelt on his back, his dad Anchises on his shoulders, and his little son Iulus tugging on his hand. Tall, upright and stoic, [Syrian refugee] Maher looks like Aeneas today. Except that instead of a lion's fur, Maher wears a plastic life jacket. And instead of just one child, Maher has four. (2017: 178–9)

As discussed in Chapter 2, we follow the 'protagonist', Syrian refugee Hashem's journey to safety in Sweden. Kingsley's choice of template, however, has an interesting effect on the representation of this real-life character. While the author emphasises that he does not want to turn him into a symbol, for the reader Hashem occupies several positions simultaneously, in an unsteady and defamiliarising way: he is the character Hashem in the book and the real Hashem in Sweden right now, that is to say, a named individual and an ordinary Syrian. But he is also, symbolically, an everyman and an epic hero. He fulfils all of the roles Kingsley has created for him. For the reader, Hashem slides between being a literary figure set up in the context of the *Odyssey*, a latter-day, heroic Ulysses wanderer, but also Hashem, the ordinary Syrian searching for safety. This instability slows down the reader's perception and precipitates a more profound engagement with this familiar-unfamiliar refugee 'figure'.

Rereading the classics helps to disturb, perhaps even revolutionise, the way we think about the mobilities involved in the current refugee crisis. Simon Armitage's poem 'On the Existing State of Things' resources Virgil's the *Aeneid* and makes strange that intertextual return for the reader. Charon, the ferryman who ships the souls of the recently dead across the river Styx to Hades has now become a ruthless people smuggler in Armitage's imagination: 'But Charon trafficked as he pleased, first these, then those,/ordering others to stand back from the boat' (Armitage in Popescu, 2018, 217, ll. 20–1). There is certainly no denying that a return to those European foundation myths is illuminating. These are stories about time and loss, violence and hope that have become the central thematics of refugee literature. They engage in what Helon Habila calls 'the politics of travel': 'When the Greeks in *The Iliad* set out to conquer Troy – they're heroes, we celebrate them. When the [colonialists] came to Africa, they came to explore and to conquer – they're heroes. But when we go [to the West] – we're migrants, we're refugees. The politics of travel' (Habila in Wood, 2019).

Another narrative pattern that exploits a familiar phenomenon is the return to the *Titanic*. Claire Chambers (2019b) draws attention to the literary use of the *Titanic* – both the ship that could not sink and James Cameron's film *Titanic* (1997) – with recourse to Hassan Blasim's story 'The Truck to Berlin' (from *The Madman of Freedom Square*, 2016) and Abu Bakr Khaal's *African Titanics* (2014), which we will return to. For now we touch briefly on the defamiliarising employment of that term. To Chambers, the *Titanic* is reconfigured as rickety boats and inflated dinghies which she terms 'necroboats' (2019b) that cross the Mediterranean – a contemporary Black Atlantic or Middle Passage– and more recently The English Channel. Blasim has the narrator in 'The Truck to Berlin' tell us: 'Obviously you already know many similarly tragic stories of migration and its horrors from the media, which have focused first and foremost on migrants drowning. My view is that as far as the public is concerned such mass drownings are an enjoyable film scene, like a new *Titanic*' (2016: 68). Blasim alerts us to how the representation of the refugee crisis can turn into a ubiquitous spectacle of violence that desensitises us so we barely register it. Again the evocation of a known story, the *Titanic*, in an unfamiliar context destabilises our habitual response in ways that open up for cognitive readjustment.

Rounding off this consideration of refugee literature, we want to mention what may be called 'the mythic narrative pattern', with reference to Marina Warner's *The Leto Bundle*. This novel also takes us on an 'odyssey' (2002: 310), an epic journey from 400 BC to the 1990s in the footsteps of a time-travelling Ulysses wanderer called Leto who is looking for refuge for herself and her twins: 'Until someone takes me – not for a stranger, not for an intruder; until someone takes me in, takes me home … I'll never rest. That's the curse I bear' (29). Like all refugees, Leto dreams of *a new life* where she and her children can *become anything we want, where we can put on a new life like a suit of clothes, if only we could find some* (174, italics in original). The novel speaks to the universal human concern with home and belonging that has become a central theme in refugee literature. As David Farrier puts it: 'There is perhaps no refugee imaginary more essential, more poignant, or with greater capacity to shape lived experience than *home*. Home is the wound made in the act of leaving, and the hope that keeps the journey going' (Farrier in Cox et al., 2020: 501). It is to ideas of home that we now turn in our reading of Dina Nayeri's *Refuge* (2017) and J.J. Bola's *No Place to Call Home* (2018).

## HOME AND BELONGING

As child refugees, with only scattered memories of flight, Dina Nayeri and J.J. Bola know what Nguyen means by the duty to remember the loss of home and a secure sense of belonging. They would also agree with child refugee Gulwali Passarlay who says in his memoir: 'I had a deep sense of duty. People needed to understand what refugees go through, and if I was given a chance to inform them, then I had to take it' (2019: 358). As literary writers, Nayeri and Bola seem compelled to 'go where it hurts' to prevent their refugee (hi)stories from becoming 'unremembered'. If their parent generation, like refugees in the painful moment of the current crisis, may shy away from recollecting the past in narrative form, their children feel the need to puzzle together fragmented stories. Although Nayeri and Bola refer to their novels as fiction, they also confirm that biographical experiences went into the making of their protagonists (Murphy, 2017 and O'Shea-Meddour, 2019). What they share with their protagonists is the quest to know themselves again by working out, indeed getting to know and understand, their refugee pasts and how these impact on a sense of home and belonging. This becomes an important venture for Niloo in Nayeri's *Refuge* and Jean in Bola's *No Place to Call Home*. Unlike Niloo who struggles to come to terms with her refugee legacy throughout Nayeri's novel, Jean was only a toddler when his family fled and is therefore, in the first part of Bola's novel, unaware of the existential pain inherent in such a legacy. Both novels, however, point to the memory work of autofiction as a central aspect of refugee literature.

Dina Nayeri calls herself an 'Iranian Exile' in her debut novel *A Teaspoon of Earth and Sea* (2013: 421). *The Ungrateful Refugee*, however, opens with the sentence: 'We became refugees' (2019: 3). Reading Nayeri we quickly become alert to the shaky foundations of identificatory labels that are linked to the author's personal history. In *Teaspoon*, Nayeri outlines a 'set of Immigrant Worries' (2013: 97) linked to the 'exile panic that comes from standing at too many borders with dangerously thin piles of paperwork' (101) and how this is coupled with the 'unwanted stepparent' called the 'immigrant curse' (102). In the autofiction *Refuge* the same worries take centre stage in the 'fantastic refugee saga' at the heart of the novel (2017: 35). The characterisation of Iranian-born protagonist Niloo, who became a refugee at the age of eight and is, in the novel's present of 2009, a successful academic living in Amsterdam, is bound up in the contrary logic of the freedom to move and longing to settle. Indeed, the narrative demonstrates how for neurotic Niloo being exposed to the experiential contradictions of being an exile and, at the same time, a refugee, 'the self splits' (Senior, 2017). In order to alleviate this unsteadiness, Niloo constantly has to protect what she calls her 'Perimeter', her safe space, and she goes nowhere without her backpack, even as she wonders 'what is this urge to set off alone toward some imagined home?' (2017: 120). In the course of the novel, she self-consciously reflects on what 'home' means for her: 'For decades she's tried to make homes for herself, but she is always a foreigner, always a guest – that forever refugee feeling, that constant need for a meter of space, the Perimeter she carries on her back' (222). Her internally warring refugee/exile identity, to quote Arendt on refugees, changes with such a frequency 'that nobody can find out who we actually are' (1994: 116). As an adult reconnecting with fellow Iranian refugees in Amsterdam, Niloo thinks of herself 'as an Iranian immigrant again, a child refugee, not an American expat – the difference having to do with options, purpose and personal control' (2017: 207). It is this feeling of 'purpose and personal control', laced with the reluctant sense of duty to remember the past, that drives the novel forward. As we get to know Niloo, we are reminded that while the label 'refugee' is temporary and intertwined with agency in a complex manner, it is also central to a (stable) sense of self. The novel demonstrates that being a refugee is aligned with time, too:

> When you learn to release that first great windfall after the long migration, when you trust that you'll still be you in a year or a decade, even without the treasures you've picked up along the way, always capable of more – when you stop carrying it all on your back – maybe that's when the refugee years end. (2017: 252)

*Refuge* details how Niloo learns to carry less weight on her back.

**In conversation, Dina Nayeri says**: The experiences of being a refugee stay a part of you forever. But at some point, you move toward what is singularly and ultimately you, and you begin to take more power over those defini- tions. It stops becoming about being a refugee or not and you stop paying attention to those words. Are you or are you not a former refugee? I feel empowered. I have a voice. I have an education that I can trust and so as a result, I do not feel a lot of sharp pains from that time anymore. But at the same time, I have habits that come from that time. This is a duality that I deal with all the time. As a person who has passed the trauma of her refugee years, I often wonder whether home is a place, a state of being, a state of mind, or simply safety? For me home is constantly changing, perhaps because of the number of times that I have been uprooted. Personally, I have found that place of safety in myself, in my habits, and in my family. In many ways you are haunted by who you were. But I think that is true of everyone. As healing happens, we move toward our singular selves and so these labels fall away.

The heavy weight of the trauma of Niloo's refugee years properly begins with the night in the homeless shelter of Jesus House, on 'her first night in America' in 'a single sleep, a hiccup, that came and went between two good lives', in her Iranian childhood and her American youth (37). This 'black interlude night' 'returns' (37) even in the narrative present in Amsterdam, and remains an uncanny reminder of a troubling and not-yet-reckoned-with past. The memory of Jesus House and the refugee story that it stands for haunt Niloo to such a degree that her present exile, or expat, identity is constantly shadowed by her childhood refugee identity, which she cannot lay to rest or allow herself to forget. André Aciman offers a serviceable vocabulary of exile that helps to illuminate the predicament of Nayeri's protagonist: 'This is what we mean by the word *alibi*. It means elsewhere. Some people have an identity. I have an alibi, a shadow self' (2011: 192). Niloo also has an alibi; her shadow self is Niloo the child refugee, the figure that spooks the novel and complicates dearly-achieved experiences of refuge – always understood as both a state and a place of safety in the novel.

In fact, Niloo seems to have found safety in Amsterdam with her cosmopolitan, American-French husband Gui whom she met as a student in the US. Here she lives a successful life as an American expat academic in a middle-class life accompanied by an appropriately tasteful style of living. Yet, she still nurtures her Perimeter and goes nowhere without her backpack, which of course signals that there is still memory work to be processed. However, when she stumbles on Zakhmeh, a Persian storytelling squat frequented by Iranian exiles and refugees, 'without homes, always under threat of deportation' (2017: 77), memories of her own refugee background begin to impact even more forcefully on her carefully constructed equilibrium. The more time she spends in Zakhmeh, the more she begins to understand her own semi-repressed history. She slowly realises that she has a duty to remember this past, for her own sake and for that of her fellow refugees, since she realises that such memories help to forge sustaining communities for her:

> She is part of an important movement; she has friends linked to her by blood, culture, and native words; she feels something

like purpose. It seems that for years she has lived under a mild, teetering sedation, waiting for a spell to break, for something to puncture her skin, releasing the weariness and bringing her back to the waking world. (2017: 211–12)

Here is a purpose in life for her, and a strangely homely community that shakes her out of her hard-fought-for exilic existence. By breaking the spell cast over her life since the night at Jesus House, the Zakhmeh community has opened up an important space of recognition, even of reckoning, for her where she can begin painful memory work and try to process her split self. In order to do so, however, she needs to recalibrate how she thinks about home and belonging.

Nayeri's defamiliarising way of exploring the thematics of home and belonging is especially striking at the end of the novel. As a result of Niloo's increasingly time-consuming engagement with the Zakhmeh community and the effect it has had on her sense of self in the novel, she has lost the tiny community of two she had established with her husband. Their marriage is falling apart. The marriage has, of course, always struggled with how to accommodate Niloo's experiences of complex ontological, temporal and geographical instability. We can make sense of this radical instability again via Aciman's useful vocabulary, this time by how he twists the term 'parallax' – it is more than:

a disturbance in vision. It's a derealizing and paralyzing disturbance in the soul – cognitive, metaphysical, intellectual, and ultimately aesthetic. It is not just about displacement, or of feeling adrift *both* in time and space, it is a fundamental misalignment between who we are, might have been, could still be, can't accept we've become, or may never be. … The past interferes and contaminates the present, while the present looks back and distorts the past. (2011: 189–90)

Parallax, in other words, describes what we understand by a radical defamiliarisation, a situation where both our point of observation *and* that which we observe are unstable. In *Refuge*, the repeated Rilkean verse-line 'Beware o wanderer, the road is walking too' (2017: 188, 203, 285–6, 307) attests to this temporal and geographical instability that profoundly affects Niloo's search for refuge and for a solution to the misalignment that names her 'parallaxical' existence. It is tempting to suggest that the ending of the novel indicates one way in which home and belonging can be calibrated and attuned to Niloo's experiences of being *both* a refugee and an exile.

Anna Gotlib sees 'memory and nostalgia' as 'central drivers in coming to know and define oneself' and that 'turning to them by those who were torn from their pasts in often violent ways may be the beginning of finding new voices' (Gotlib in Oliver et al., 2019: 249). To her, nostalgia is a longing not 'only for a place but also for a time or for a certain state of being' (249). However, it is not a longing to recreate the past in the present but rather the kind of longing enacted when the refugee 'embraces her own ambiguities, the ongoing confusion and convergence of her own backward-looking desires and present realities, and weaves them into a new kind of story, a new kind of self that is reflective of its own fragility, strangeness, and contingency' (250). This forward-looking state of being is descriptive of how Niloo recognises the possibilities for developing a new kind of story and new kind of self. While Zakhmeh has provided her with a sustaining affiliative community, the last chapter, 'Village Building', ends with a filiative reunion between Niloo and her parents in a converging gesture that gathers together the temporality (past and present) and the geography (Iran, the US and Amsterdam) of the novel. Focalised through the father, we are told that while '[i]t is not easy, to build a village' (2017: 285) this is exactly what the family attempts in an unplanned and haphazard way, joined together on the *sofreh*, that homely and familiar Iranian image of sharing, hospitality and conviviality in the novel. Here they are, in Niloo's flat in Amsterdam 'far from all they had known, around a familiar *sofreh* as if drawn together by magnets in their shoes. … They were three and three was enough. They were a village' (320). Such a defamiliarising way of describing home and belonging alerts us to the necessity of recognising that refugee experiences entail a radical rethinking of what familiar phenomena mean. In this private, peaceful moment we observe a benign and humble version of Simon Gikandi's 'dislocated locality'.

Gikandi's suggestion that 'locality itself has been globalized' (2010: 32) has bearings on how we think about home and belonging. In its closing scene, we witness a (possibly temporary) feeling of contentment and safety, where the global and the local are braided together in a moment of refuge for three Iranians a long way from 'home'. We may say that for Niloo, in this moment at least, the split self converges.

*No Place to Call Home* works to facilitate recognition through defamiliarisation differently from *Refuge*, and it does so in two interrelated ways. At the level of genre, it reads as a young adult (YA) novel concerned with the coming-of-age of protagonist Jean who lives with his Congolese family in North London faced with the well-known challenges of migrants to fit in and laboriously nurture a sense of belonging in a new place. Our genre expectations are defamiliarised, however, when it turns out that Jean and his family are not regular 'postcolonial' migrants but refugees with a traumatic back-story that the parents have worked hard to repress and keep a secret from their children. As the plot is spatially and temporally divided into London and Kinshasa parts, the reader knows this before Jean finds out and is therefore guided by the narrator to contemplate the novel as a family refugee story and trace Jean's emotional sense of disorientation when he discovers the family secret and later on is moved to enact, on his parents' and community's behalf, the painful duty to remember what would otherwise remain unchronicled. Jean is a migrant who becomes haunted by the defamiliarising figure of the refugee, in particular as it transpires that his father may be facing deportation. When he takes refuge in diary writing as an affective means of memory processing, we recognise him, or know him again, as the son who must turn the deep anxieties of his father and his generation, into narrative: '*We [refugees] are on the outside looking in, looking into ourselves. Looking in not knowing what we see, not even recognising who we are … And in the end, we are all looking for the same place: somewhere to call home*' (2018: 326–7, italics in original).

In the London Congolese community, to be a refugee is a self-imposed taboo, as is hinted at when an additional textual layer of defamiliarisation works through language. In church, Congolese pastor Kaddi prays for many things, but

most resonating was the prayer for citizenship; an incanta-
tion for those without papers. ... It was the climb to the top of
the mountain, it was Daniel escaping the lion's den, or Jonah
being freed from the stomach of the whale, it was reaching the
Promised Land after years of wandering the desert, a miracle on
equal par. (2018: 118)

As the pastor's wisdom goes, while waiting for citizenship can feel
like a 'perpetual purgatory' (119), to be deported 'was a curse,
an eternal damnation ... quite simply a sign that the person had
sinned and was now bearing the consequences of their actions'
(118). The pastor's biblical oratory disturbingly translates the
refugee experience into a parable of believers and sinners that
can all too readily be aligned with the distinction between worthy
and unworthy asylum seekers that migration authorities ascribe
to. Small wonder that most characters in the novel are 'suppress-
ing something; hiding their backgrounds' (O'Shea-Meddour, 2019:
13). But this is of no real concern to Jean until the day of revelation when his father tells him that he cannot go on a school trip
to France because he does not have a passport, 'We are refugees,
son' (2018: 201). '[V]oice breaking, falling apart like an abandoned
building with no foundation to hold it up', Jean asks "What is a
refugee?"' (202). From then on, his father's short and simple answer
that '[a] refugee is simply someone who is trying to make a home'
(202) becomes haunting because as a place of safety, Jean realises,
home exists neither here (London) nor there (Kinshasa). In this
confessional moment, it is not just Jean's voice that falls apart; for
him, home, too, collapses like 'an abandoned building' and he is
left to pick up the ruins and 'go where it hurts' to ponder the implications of having no place to call home.

Other revelations lead to other ruins as people disappear from or
turn up in the Congolese church community, no questions asked.
But it is when the family takes what remains of refugee Madeleine
and her family into their household that Jean is propelled into
the urgent duty to remember. Sent off to photocopy Madeleine's
testimony to the authorities, he cannot resist the temptation to read
it and is held captive by the detailed horrors and deadly 'smells' of
her story, 'he breathed it in, the taste rested on his tongue and his

stomach turned almost causing him to throw up' (223). Thus 'over-whelmed from this out of body experience where, for the first time, for a moment, it was as though he went into the body of another life and became them. Someone he knew' (224). Madeleine's 'papered' memories prey upon Jean's mind, making him feel 'he was no longer in his room, but in Kinshasa, in the prison, the imagined sound; the screams and the stomping boots echoed in his head and through the room' (224). His coming-of-age conflates his recognition of his own 'refugenes'. As he writes in his diary: *It's scary ... There is so much I don't know ... I have so many questions. I want to ask my dad or mum about this but I don't think I can. I am scared* (224, italics in original). Jean's by-proxy memory of Madeleine's refugee story latches on to his need to know and help remember that of his parents. Yet when the family house turns into a temporary refuge for forsaken countrymen, a floodgate of repressed trauma stories of house guests is opened up, and we understand '[h]ow difficult it is to remember' (181). This is affectively portrayed in the moment when a mature man like Tonton, who had kept the murder of his wife and daughter by Congolese soldiers a secret, 'broke down and wept like an orphaned child' and Jean's father 'wrapped his arms around him, and they held each other, these two men like giant rocks worn down by tears that flowed beneath them' (181). The painful duty to remember is always impeded by the tempta-tion of willed forgetfulness. It is, however, the combined efforts of narrator and protagonist that complete the required memory work of Bola's novel; the narrator pieces together the parents' past lives and traumatic event in Congo that Jean has no access to, while Jean is left with the job of reckoning the affectivity of having 'no place to call home', at least in the commonly understood sense of home as an undisturbed place of safety. That is why Jean's mother feels constantly reminded 'how she did not belong here, that this place was not hers' (172) and why his father tells him that the past is a secret only so that 'you will not have to feel fear at every moment, like how we feel' (324).

Jean employs writing as a private space of escape when there is a 'weight fill[ing] inside him he was desperate to unload' (324), but not quite knowing how to. Yet it becomes a place where he can turn emotional turmoil into emotive prose and reach out again, towards his family, his community and fellow refugees in general. As O'Shea-Meddour points out, 'the story begins in a place where [Jean] is struggling to speak but ends with a very powerful diary entry in which he writes fluently and intimately about his emotions' (2019: 15). The epilogue, to be thought of as a stand-alone extension of Jean's diary or the author's personal afterthought, or both, considers the luck of those who never had 'to remember home through your mother's tears or the rage of your father's voice when it shakes'. A refugee who tries 'to remember whether you left home, or if it left you' has no such luck; rather 'home haunts you as though a ghost'. How, then, is the reader to understand the following lament that speaks to this haunting: 'Home should never break you in two so wherever you go you are never whole; half of you remains where you left it, and the other half is rejected where you arrive. You are a split flat-sided pendulum suspended in the air on both sides.' Clearly, the loss of home splits the self. Although the pendulum is an image of movement and not perspective, we might borrow again from Aciman's parallaxic imagery and suggest that the split flat-sidedness of the pendulum speaks to 'a fundamental misalignment between who we are, might have been, could still be, can't accept we've become, or may never be' (2011: 189). If home is a haunting ghost, the split self can never aspire to heal unless the tight bonds between the conceptual pair of home and belonging are loosened in recognition of the ways in which home is more a state of mind than a place, and that belonging grows from deep attachments to family and community. We need alternative imaginings of home and belonging. As Bola insists: 'I want us to … remove the fixation of home being just one place. It's a feeling … "Home" shouldn't have to be just one place or one thing' (Bola in O'Shea-Meddour, 2019: 15). A careful reading of *No Place to Call Home* should be alert to how remembering 'trauma is the moment when [Bola's] characters come together' (O'Shea-Meddour, 2019: 13) and a new communal sense of belonging may be envisioned. This is not tied to a sense of home as a fixed location. Rather, the hospitality of Jean's family that, despite its cramped household space, takes in people in need suggests that home can be a 'feeling of togetherness' emerging from emergency. Even if this is temporary, it is a sense of home that takes the idea of refuge seriously.

## BUGS AND GAMES

Wendy O'Shea-Meddour argues that '[t]here is a clear and often voyeuristic appetite for refugee experiences that centre on brutality, trauma and a dramatic, high-tension "escape story," but the period that follows is often overlooked' (2019: 12). The novels we will now consider turn the reader's voyeuristic appetite against itself. Eritrean-born, Denmark-based Abu Bakr Khaal and Iraqi-born, Finland-based Hassan Blasim write about their own refugee experiences in unexpected ways that provocatively play with European reader responses. A reading together of *African Titanics* (Arabic 2008/English 2014) and *God 99* (Arabic 2018/English 2020) undercuts the habitual manner in which migration is understood. Both writers rely on dark humour and shocking irony that shake readers out of their customary reader responses as we are forced to think again about the intricate connections that link Europe with Africa and the Middle East and acknowledge that the vocabularies we use to describe these geopolitical and human webs – migration, migrants, refugees, traffickers – need to be denotatively and connotatively unpacked and repacked again in order to maintain explanatory traction. In contrast to the intimate relationship we develop with Nayeri's Niloo and Bola's Jean, we are afforded relatively little access to the interiority of Bakr Khaal's and Blasim's narrating protagonists. Instead, we follow them on picaresque-like routes where we observe them as conversational partners engaged in exploring aspects of the complex mobilities at the heart of refugee experiences. The novels offer 'alternative discourses' as they insist in their specific and somewhat idiosyncratic ways that we all begin to recognise the fact that migration is part of an inevitably webbed world.

In the opening of *African Titanics*, a 'half-testimony, half-fiction novel' (Gallien, 2018b: 737), the first-person narrator Abdar reflects on what he sees as the quasi-mysterious phenomenon of migration. He has managed to stay put in Eritrea, in what he calls, analeptically, his 'sheltered years' (2014: 4), but as the novel begins, he is on the brink of migration. He needs to rethink mobility in order to understand how 'the dangerous lure of migration' (4) entraps even reluctant individuals, himself included. Migration, the narrator acknowledges, is 'a pandemic. A plague. And not a single young soul was left untouched' (3). This infection is not only highly contagious, it is also 'the work of a dark sorcerer emerging from the mists of the unknown' whose 'magnificent bell' calls 'one and all to its promised paradise' (3). It is this hypnotic, ongoing sound of the bell that is 'infecting our minds with the migration bug' (3), the narrator explains. He is unable to protect himself against the contagious tolling of the sorcerer's bell as he is 'plucked from Eritrea, swept across the Sudanese border and on into Libya in the dark of the night' (3). He feels doomed to a 'ceaseless roaming' on migration's 'endless road' (4). Migration is here reconfigured as a highly contagious pandemic and this naturally plays havoc with any sense of agency and choice, and, coupled with the magic of a sorcerer's spell, there is a sense of predetermination and fate at play in the text. The characters are doomed to embark on the perilous journey to Europe.

Accompanying the physical border-crossing journey, the narrator also embarks on a process of imaginative and cognitive recognition of where this pandemic originates and how to make sense of the 'seductive bell' (5) that pulls migrants towards their destiny. Together with his fellow migrants, Abdar needs to rethink migration, and he realises that the bell that is 'luring us away from our quiet lives (which still counted as lives after all)' bears a 'startling similarity' to the bell 'owned by the wicked wizard who'd lived in Europe long ago' (5). Abdar knows that while in Europe, African lives are largely regarded as disposable and barely register as 'grievable lives', to use Judith Butler's term; his sheltered pre-migration life is a treasured memory, part of his story and his sense of dignity. However, he also realises that this European wizard enchants everyone to follow in his footsteps. He is, in so many ways, the personification of the intricate connective tissues between (former) coloniser and (former) colonised. He is also the incarnation of the bug that drives the recalcitrant pandemic. Migration is the result of this intertwined history, and it affects not only our Eritrean narrator but all of postcolonial Africa. Bakr Khaal encourages us to take one provocative step further, by reconfiguring migration, not as unidirectional, but as uncontrollable, multidirectional and future-oriented, as we would expect of a pandemic, affecting all of humanity. Fellow migrant, Liberian storyteller Malouk tells the narrator: 'But there will always be migration so long as there are human beings on earth. Show me a land that hasn't been trodden by a migrant's foot. And I personally wouldn't be surprised if Africa became the next destination for lost souls, even as they leave it today' (70). There is a logic to this making-strange of the phenomenon of migration, as the narrator intuitively recognises in his response: 'True,' I added, 'This land will be man's final refuge just as it was his first cradle' (70). Africa as refuge – a place and a state of safety – is not currently how the continent is envisioned. Africa is in the novel, then, imagined as humanity's natural home; it is where we begin as a *Homo sapiens*, and where we will find shelter (again) and rest after we have thrown off the migration bug. Integral to the defamiliarising effect of this novel's alternative discourse of migration is to encourage the reader to recognise that in an unpredictable and interconnected 'liquid world', to use Zygmunt Bauman's metaphor, anything is possible and everyone is liable to be affected by the migration pandemic, this 'epidemic of collective madness' (Chambers, 2019b).

Janet Wilson sees the novel as a 'turbulent story of thwarted expectations, loss, and death [that] foregrounds the delusional impulses that gave rise to such wholescale departure in ways that may seem alien to modern globalised readers' (2017: 3). One way of counteracting that alien impression is to draw on that which is familiar to a modern audience. Bakr Khaal cleverly opts for the *Titanic*. He might also, as Derek Duncan suggests, invoke the less well-known but equally tragic ship, the *Zong*, in his description of Malouk's sinking ship (2019: 102). In the novel, the migrants cross the desert and the sea – 'they're about equal' (2014: 28) – even as they know about 'unlucky ships' (6) and 'doomed vessels' (61), the 'rubber dinghies' that the narrator names 'Titanics' (in the plural) (15). Crossing the Mediterranean, set up as a modern-day version of the Black Atlantic and the Middle Passage, these 'necroboats' (Claire Chambers' term) are doomed in an eerie echo of the way that the passengers are doomed to embark on perilous journeys, unable as they are to withstand the migration pandemic. The narrator shares willingly from the 'impressive amount of information' (15) he has gleaned about the journeys across land and sea.

Fellow migrants, however, critique the use of the term 'Titanics'. They do not like how this ship has been pluralised and demoted. Nor do they like the fact that the dinghies are named for the most famous *sinking* ship. They would like a more 'optimistic' appellation such as 'Noah's Ark perhaps. Or any other ship that never sank' (60–1). But the pluralised Titanics term sticks: '[e]ven those who had not heard the term Titanics applied to the boats routinely referred to them as The Doomed' (61). Just like the well-informed narrator, the migrants know the risks taken and the dangers ahead: 'Many of my fellow travellers could not bear to hear of shipwrecks and drowning and would grow restless whenever we began discussing our dubious chances of survival' (61). They know that on the 'unlucky boats', it is 'pure blind luck' (106) that gets them safely to the other side. Commenting on how far removed the West is for the characters in the story, 'epistemologically, ontologically', Wilson suggests that '[s]ymptomatic of this disconnection is the characters-in-flight's ignorance of their status as refugees' (2017: 5). However, there is also a sense in which the characters *do* know what is going on and that they feel an intrinsic connection to Europe as a result of the long history of colonisation. From a defamiliarisation perspective, the employment of the *Titanic* is a deliberate literary gesture that twists our conception of that which we consider familiar and known. By constantly vacillating between the words 'migrants' (2014: 46, 70, 82, 96) and 'travellers' (43, 47, 61) the narrator wants to signal that while you can be both, or neither, you can also be 'simply a man' (82), as Abdar calls himself when he is in Tripoli on a break in the great game of migration. These terms are, of course, (temporary) labels, not (fixed) identities. And they can be applied to us all.

A 'bleak panorama of violence, grief and madness' (Barekat, 2020), Hassan Blasim's *God 99* also treats migration in ways that make readers slow down the reading pace in our exposure to the author's 'unapologetically brutal prose' with which he 'wants to jolt the reader into thinking about language' (Popescu, 2020). The narrator, an Iraqi-born refugee writer residing in Finland named Hassan Owl, admits at the start of this strange, autofictional and experimental novel that he has been planning to develop a blog project about refugees but has not been able to get funding. That is, 'until disaster struck and vast numbers of refugees flooded into Europe, bringing about a small miracle for me. The doors of finance opened up here in Finland, because the migrants or refugees might have voices, faces and stories to tell' (2020: 10). We are familiar with this provocative, in-your-face, acerbic wit from his poem 'A Refugee in the Paradise That Is Europe' that we referenced in Chapter 1. In *God 99*, the refugee crisis offers a windfall of refugee stories. These stories become interlaced with Owl's own, and because of his unflinching honesty we get to know some extroverted aspects of the character well. Sometimes he plays the role of 'nice, quiet refugee writer' (162), but mostly he hangs out in bars and talks to people.

When 'stubbornly unsentimental' (Barekat, 2020) Owl travels to Baghdad to interview ordinary individuals whose lives have been affected by the American intervention in Iraq, when 'everything came to into the country except peace, which stood waiting at the door, reluctant to enter' (Blasim, 2020: 31–2), he is mistaken for a foreigner. A local man berates him: 'You expats come back to the country and you're like foreign orientalists always carrying around with you a bottle of mineral water and a rucksack, looking at everything in surprise, as if you've never been here' (51). Owl is simultaneously an expat (in Baghdad) and refugee (in Finland), and in Finland, he is as exposed to spectacles of violence as the next (European) man. When Owl lies 'naked in bed' with one of his girlfriends, he describes how he 'scrolls through Facebook on my iPhone. Pictures of drowned refugees in Greece. My brother in Baghdad has written an angry comment about government corruption. A friend in northern Finland has posted a picture of a cat looking at itself in a mirror in surprise' (57). The juxtaposition of these images is startling on the page, yet also unsurprising, as they mirror how social media lumps together and flatten unrelated events, as if they are the same and have the same impact. They cease to mean anything of importance, noticed in passing, but not registered. The nonchalant scrolling indexes a familiar, even cynical, media-induced habituation. But it is the next comment that upsets the reader's affective response to this commonplace bed-scene: 'The picture of the cat looking at itself in the mirror is stuck in my mind' (57). This is Blasim's sly way of defamiliarising our lazy, unthinking and unfeeling responses to the refugee crisis: for us, spectacles of violence and exposure of political corruption cannot compete with images of cute cats.

As part of his research for his blog, Owl spends a lot of time in conversation with fellow refugees – old and new – in Finland, and they talk about what it means to be a refugee in ways that supplement, but also problematise, the refugee ontology we outlined in Chapter 1. From an old Syrian refugee he is told that '[n]ew refugees are shattered' and '[t]alking about integration often strikes them as some kind of joke, or sometimes as something that threatens a new nightmarish experience. It's not easy for people to shed their skin. ... New refugees are still in shock when they arrive and it's often too soon to talk about integration' (82). There is an eerie echo from Dina Nayeri's observations on skin-shedding, self-destructive assimilation here (see Chapters 1 and 2). There is also the uneasy effect on the reader of Blasim's realism: recently arrived refugees are shattered and shocked, yet are expected to cope with their trauma immediately upon arrival. It is too much to ask, too soon, the novel insists, yet this is an established European approach to newly arrived refugees. In a passage that continues the reflection on refugee situations, Owl is told that:

> [w]hen you lose your home and your sense of security you become sensitive, lazy and suspicious of everything, your willpower breaks down and your ability to think properly is distorted. You latch onto other people's faults while you try to deal with your own life, which has messed you around and maybe crushed you. Aren't humans in general really migrants who carry around shattered fragments of their peace of mind deep inside them? Do the fragments cut you and poison your blood? (2020: 212)

The repetition of the word 'shattered' encourages us to consider how this moment mirrors Owl's conversation with the Syrian refugees. The list of incongruous adjectives is a conspicuous gloss on what it feels like to become a refugee: if you become sensitive, lazy and suspicious, then this is unlike how we have discussed the refugee ontology. The sliding from 'you', that is, refugees,

REFUGEE LITERATURE AND DEFAMILIARISATION

to 'humans in general' is also striking, pointing to an inclusive nomenclature that we shall see developed to its full potential in Mohsin Hamid's *Exit West*. The quotation suggests that migrants are merely humans pained by life. However, such observations remain outliers in this novel; it is preoccupied with other ways of thinking about migration, for example, as a high stake game of violent border crossing where the lot of refugees is not at all like the lot of general humanity.

> **In conversation, Gulwali Passarlay says:** Depending on where you come from, your life is in many ways like a game. For an Afghan, every day is a game and a chance for us. Then the refugee journey itself is also like a game. For example, when we attempted to get into lorries and escape from the Jungle in Calais, we called it a game. To human smugglers the whole journey is a game. This was the coded language that the smugglers used. On my journey I realised that those smugglers are pretty heartless people. They were liars. They kept us in suspense. We came to a point that even when they were telling us the truth, we did not believe them. For them the whole thing is just a game. But for refugees it is a different kind of game. They just hope they will reach safety eventually – and then they will overcome the game.

Labelling the dangerous journey to Europe a 'game' is becoming a recognisable trope, as we see, for example, in Gulwali Passarlay's *The Lightless Sky*: 'It was a perverse game, and I was trapped playing it for as long as it took – as long as I could keep going. It was the game without end. They [the French police in Calais] thought it was funny' (2019: 309). In *God 99*, Blasim describes how he 'won a free trip with the traffickers' in a game of chess (2020: 113). This marks the beginning of a harrowing description of attempts to cross borders and enter into Europe that are all-too-familiar aspects of the migration game. The violent encounters with Fortress Europe embody Europe's attempt to clamp down on migration. Many of the characters in this novel, however, see this encounter as the result of an intertwined world:

The West has to pay the price for the destruction it has wrought on several continents. The mass migrations and the refugees that are flooding in that direction today, travelling to Europe on foot, are, I believe, leading the largest demonstration against injustice and capitalism so far this century. It's a demonstration by land and sea. ... Let refugees sleep in the skull of the octopus of capitalism. (2020: 146–7)

Migration is here reconfigured as a mass demonstration against brutal neoliberal policies and the tentacular and exploitative 'mushroom cloud of capitalism' (148) that is as destructive of peaceful lives as Bakr Khaal's migration bug. It is a human demonstration that willingly crosses African deserts and risks lives at sea fully aware of the high stakes involved; the migrants and refugees have nothing left to lose. Blasim's ruthless prose opens up for a painful reckoning for Western readers: Europe is responsible for this demonstration of extreme pecuniary inequality and social injustice, and Europe needs to recognise this. The novel, then, demands that Europeans admit their part in the migration game.

The chapter titled 'The Son's Game and the Father's Game' focuses on a refugee father and his Finnish-born son, and it picks up and develops the violent border experiences in the dangerous migration game just described. The son is a games designer who is turning the refuge journey into a computer game where the player faces many obstacles: 'You will meet fable and reality in a maze of time in a place called Earth' and 'you win points when you cross a border' (183). However, the son tells Owl, '[r]eaching your destination is not the end of the story. At this point you reach the last and most important stage – being able to convince' (184). We have already explored this stage in the previous chapter; it is where luck affects the outcome of the story you tell about yourself and if it will be believed or not. This has bearings on how you will be storied, too, as we explored in Chapter 3. Blasim does not dwell on this stage. Instead, he juxtaposes the son's story of the refugee journey computer game with the refugee father's different game, written as it is in a declaration with the intention of inspiring international activists to set up a group called 'Traffickers without Borders'. The son explains:

The gist of the declaration was that everyone should have the automatic right to live in any village in the world, in a world without borders, passports or regulations, without being challenged on grounds of security, culture or ethnicity. People would have the right to live in and move around in any miniscule village they chose on this vast planet called Earth. (2020: 186–7)

We might read this as an announcement of what Kelly Oliver calls an 'Earth Ethics' that we referred to in Chapter 1. We might even argue that Blasim's 'alternative discourse' should become an inherent part of the rethinking exercises of Jeremy Harding and Sonia Shah about rights, resources and migration, mentioned in the same chapter. Blasim's engagement in the politics of representation embroiled in the refugee crisis is especially evident in his striking, almost oxymoronic, moniker 'traffickers without borders'. Such a way of saying certainly affects our way of seeing. The label indexes Peter Tinti and Tuesday Reitano's insistence, in their study of the role smugglers play in the global migration game, that if we want to move beyond the default narratives of good and bad, of victim and villain that are so characteristic of refugee talk, 'we must start by examining smugglers dispassionately for what they are: service providers in an era of unprecedented demand' (2018: 6). Human traffickers and smugglers 'profit from the desperation of others' but they also 'save lives, create possibilities and redress global inequalities' (5). In the refugee father's serious yet playful declaration, traffickers without borders are indeed service providers in the great migration game. They not only help migrating individuals, they also help to construct a borderless world of equal rights to move and to settle – equal rights to refuge. Perhaps these traffickers point to a world to come, described by Agamben as a Europe guided by 'the *refugium* of the individual' rather than the '*ius* of the citizen' (1995: 118)?

In his review of *God 99*, Barekat holds that '[i]f there is any hope at all in these pages, it lies in literature, which forms "a bastion against winds and waves"' (2020). Certainly, for the narrators of *African Titanics* and *God 99*, literature and storytelling – trafficking in words – are the arenas of hope, bringing people together through acts of saying and hearing that nudge participants towards the recognition of a shared world, even if it is cruelly inequitable in its present incarnation.

## BORDERS AND CATEGORIES

Helon Habila's *Travellers* (2019) and Mohsin Hamid's *Exit West* (2017) are a compelling pair of novels to consider in the last section of this chapter. Both arrest our habitual thinking about the current refugee crisis through the defamiliarisation of its associated vocabulary and trajectories of migrant movement. Indeed, to rehearse Shklovsky's point, a new way of 'saying' promotes a new way of 'seeing' that comes to reconfigure the worn-out ideas that the refugee vocabulary has entrenched, most significantly the idea of Europe under siege and the refugee as an antagonistic and disturbing presence. The titles of the novels anticipate a process of reconfiguration: *Travellers* as a democratising nomenclature that includes refugees rather than seeing them as illegitimate trespassers into otherwise 'wholesome' European nations, and *Exit West* as a double entendre stipulating that as refugees are indeed exiting their unsafe homes to seek refuge in the West, their unwelcome reception could lead to the disappearance, the exit, of the idea and ideals of the democratic West.

Habila comments that his choice of title for the book was deliberate: 'I didn't call it ... Refugees or Migrants because I know there is so much politics, and these words have become overpoliticised and sometimes are used in a pejorative sense to reduce people to one category ... I wanted to represent the totality of the travel experience' (Habila in Wood, 2019). He researched the material for the novel through interviews with refugees during a fellowship in Berlin at the time when the current refugee crisis began to gather momentum with the 2013 *Lampedusa* migrant shipwreck, drowning more than 360 migrants. Habila appears, in fact, to have much in common with the unnamed narrator of *Travellers*, a Nigerian migrant academic from the US whose close-hand encounter with refugees gradually draws him into deep thinking about the violating effects of what Outlwile Tsipane terms 'the commonly drawn caricatures that people who cross borders for a better life suffer under' (Tsipane, 2019). The narrator arrives in

Berlin with his African-American artist wife Gina whose one-year fellowship project (called Travellers) is to result in a series of portraits of 'real migrants' (Habila, 2019a: 4), a term that the novel contests as inherently fraudulent. On the grounds that 'his face was too smooth' (4) and inexperienced to qualify as a 'real migrant', Gina rejects the first prospective sitter Mark, a film student from Malawi on a German scholarship whose visa has expired and rendered him illegal, but is instantly attracted to Libyan asylum seeker Manu whose 'face was lined, prematurely old … each one of [the lines] an eloquent testimony to what he had left behind, to the borders and rivers and deserts he had crossed to get to Berlin' (5). It is the physical traces of emotional scars that testify to human suffering and a fatalistic crossing of entrenched borders that appeal to Gina's artistic sense of 'gravitas' (40). When her curious, cosmopolitan husband, however, takes an interest in rejected Mark, wondering 'what his story was' (8), the novel 'takes a nomadic turn' (Tsipane, 2019); caught up with, or in, travel, the narrator becomes the conduit for a kaleidoscope of migrant voices and stories in and beyond Berlin that has him not only witness but become embroiled in 'gravitas' in more profound ways than his wife's artistic project can muster.

Transgender Mark was Mary before exiling herself to Europe and doomed if returned to Malawi, nightclub bouncer Manu was a doctor in Libya before he and his daughter were separated from his wife Basma and son in a shipwreck but stubbornly hopeful that they will, as vowed, reunite on a future Sunday at Checkpoint Charlie, Portia was a former African student in London and daughter of a late renowned exile poet before she revisits Europe from Zambia in search of answers to the death of her brother David who had mysteriously renamed himself Moussa from Mali upon arrival in Switzerland, Karim from Somalia is on an endless quest via prolonged transits in Yemen, Syria, Turkey and Bulgaria to bring his scattered family to Germany, and Nigerian Juma is on hunger strike in a British removal centre in protest of imminent deportation when, before dying, he delivers his story in writing to the narrator. These are intertwined stories that connect through the itinerant narrator to bring out what Habila calls the totality of the(ir) travel experience along circuitous routes: 'the beginning, how it transpired, the current moment, and the as-yet-unknown end' with the characters all 'somehow com[ing] across another by chance, enjoying an intrinsic solidarity' (Tsipane, 2019). Their stories echo Hemon's point that 'the world of refugees is a vast [bordered] narrative landscape' that awaits 'individual narrative enfranchisement' (Hemon in Nguyen, 2018: 92). At the stylistic level, Habila honours this by having his narrator intermittently relinquish his first-person narrative privilege and hand it over to those who have stories to tell. As the telling proceeds, however, and as foreshadowed on the novel's dustjacket, 'the divide between the self-chosen exiles and those who are forced to leave home becomes ever more fragile, until it is crossed, with frightening consequences'. Thus, in the novel's crucial defamiliarising narrative move, the confident narrator's cosmopolitan persona breaks down when he himself becomes a mistaken identity. Changing trains after having listened to Karim's story on a ride from Switzerland to Germany, the narrator loses his bag with passport and green card and ends up paperless on the wrong train in a carriage transporting rejected asylum seekers back to a camp in Italy.

When the 'man of the world' narrator becomes, by default, an 'undocumented' detainee, the defamiliarisation of his subject position pushes his own story within the story into an existential limbo, yet one that eventually culminates in insights that allow him to know himself again and to recognise fellow 'travellers' in a new way. Helga Ramsey-Kurtz observes that '[w]ith his story thus annulled, the protagonist seems without an identity. In surrender to the near-cancellation of his existence, he has retreated into complete inaction' (2020: 174). Standing by the fence staring at the sea 'change colour with the dying sun' (Habila, 2019a: 206), he appears to be, the camp director believes, slowly dying from meaningless waiting. His former privilege of observing suffering from a distance has been annulled: 'Who is to say if I'm not dead already, the people around me could be shadows, wraiths, like me. If I am alive, then I am barely alive' (208). Yet, the narrator does survive his 'refugee' experience to endure 'whatever comes' (208) and is reborn from his dream nightmare of being at sea and witnessing in horrifyingly close proximity hundreds of people drowning. The nightmare resonates with the horrors of the Lampedusa shipwreck, envisioned as a contemporary Middle Passage:

> Bodies floating face-up, limbs thrashing, tiny hands reaching up to me … they float amidst a debris of personal belongings, toys, shoes, shirts, and family pictures all slowly sinking into a bottomless Mediterranean. I drift past, and they drift past, and God drifts past, paring his nails … *I had not thought death had undone so many.* I repeat the line over and over, rolling it over my tongue like a prayer, till my whisper turns into a scream. (2019a: 234)

The tormented line from T.S. Eliot's *The Waste Land* adds to the list of literary texts that most main characters take refuge in to lend expression to, and possibly soothe, their emotions of loss and pain. It makes sense, therefore, to suggest that the formerly confident narrator is reborn from his trials, and in the process also facilitates the rebirth of the main characters, as Arendtian 'Ulysses wanderers' who, echoing Tennyson's 'Ulysses' and the novel's epigraph, 'cannot rest from travel'. Indeed, to borrow two additional lines from Tennyson, 'To rust unburnish'd, not to shine in use' (2006, l. 23) contradicts the travelling instinct in human nature 'To strive, to seek, to find, and not to yield' (l. 70). In more prosaic terms, Habila contends that '[t]ravel is a perfect metaphor for the human condition' (Habila in Wood, 2019) and that 'travel is about trying to be understood … and trying to understand others' (Habila, 2019b). The insight the narrator gains from his camp experience has to do with this aspect of travel, veiled almost prophetically in the anticipation of the moment when 'someone would step up to me, a familiar face, or a total stranger … And they would tell me a story, a fable, a secret, something so pithy, so profound, that it is worth the wait. Listen, they would say, listen carefully' (2019a: 208). We agree with Ramsey-Kurz who posits that 'for Habila's protagonist, learning to listen to other people's stories properly and compassionately means to distance himself from the abstract projections of refugee subjecthood he himself endorses as the cosmopolitan intellectual he represents at the outset' (2020: 168). As the restless reverberations of the main characters' painful travel come together anew in the narrator's mind, they do so, as it were, with a sense of empowering 'gravitas'. Perhaps this is what Tsipane is getting at when suggesting that through the novel's 'didactic elegies ... we are able to learn and relearn; they become the crucial ground of historical contestation, before history has even had the chance to freeze the happenings of the current moment inside a settled narrative' (2019).

It is, we argue, when we (re)view all characters, including the narrator, as contemporary 'Ulysses wanderers' that the conflation of the figures of refugee, migrant or exile into the unspecified figure of the traveller becomes a powerful repellent of prejudiced refugee talk and anti-migration rhetoric. The democratising category of traveller is empty of socio-political content and performs in the novel a conceptual and cognitive shake-up of fixed assumptions about others. And this, as we see in the narrator's changed perception and renewed attention, promotes recognition. Different as their reasons for travelling are, all travellers are driven by their quest for a safe or liberating space to find themselves at home in, 'something just beyond the horizon, something outside their grasp' that they 'keep searching for' (Habila, 2019a: 141) whatever the obstacles encountered. Admittedly, '[t]here is nothing of wander-lust in the crossing of borders when you have been uprooted from an environment you have always called home' (Tsipane, 2019) and, certainly, real material borders of the 'barbed-wire' kind discussed in Chapter 1 are part of the characters' stories. Yet Habila reconfigures the idea of border through the unfamiliar, if not defa-miliarising, framework of casting refugees, migrants or exiles as travellers, thus defining them by what they *do* rather than who (we think) they are. This again collapses the conceptual borders that keep migrant people apart from each other and from us, each in their own insulated category of people to be surveilled, managed or held accountable for their presence in Europe. Such borders are both arbitrary and permeable in the novel. Shared stories of travel experiences, however different and unique, becomes part of a continuum of human migration through time and space. This is the radical impulse of *Travellers*. People defined in terms of cate-gories, Habila says, 'are just statistics' and 'I thought maybe if I talk to these people, from the stories they're telling me, maybe I'll be able to show them in their totality as human beings .... And that's really how the book started' (Habila in Wood, 2019).

*Exit West* shares with *Travellers* the desire to disturb our conventional thinking about refugees and their trajectories through the technique of defamiliarisation. As a contribution to the emerging genre of refugee writing, Hamid's novel pursues this in a different manner. We first get to know the novel's protagonist couple Nadia and Saeed in the presumably Middle-Eastern besieged 'city of their birth' (unnamed because it stands in for any home location that citizens are forced to leave when their lives are endangered) and we follow them after their flight, first to Mykonos, next to London and then to Marin. While their travel destinations replicate well-known refugee routes, such 'transitory locations' are not, as Arthur Rose observes, represented in familiar ways: 'the camp in Mykonos is likened to "a trading post in an old-time gold rush" ..., the squat in London to a "university dormitory" ... and the shanty town in Marin produces "sounds like a festival"' (Rose in Cox et al., 2020: 58–9). This defamiliarising manoeuvre arrests the reader's 'automatic' perception along the lines of our previous reference to Shklovsky who contends that the purpose of art is to throw us out of habit and 'to recover the sensation of life; it exists to make one feel things', in this case in tune with the protagonists' first impressions upon encountering unfamiliar milieus. In his combined realistic and near-futuristic narrative, Hamid employs, however, a far more radical exercise of defamiliarisation when he has his protagonists, and others in flight, avoid borders of the conventional kind and escape instead through magical 'black doors' that pop up irregularly in unforeseen public and private places around the world. An obvious point to make from this is that migration cannot be policed or prevented, even when it feels as if 'the whole planet [is] on the move' (Hamid, 2017a: 167) and migrants participate in a 'remodelling of the Earth itself' (177). But most importantly, the magical doors are Hamid's way of avoiding that his characters will suffer the refugee fate that their lives are reduced to their perilous, traumatic crossing into the West as victims of pity or scorn, with no concern for their lives before and after the crossing.

Although, as the omniscient narrator informs us, '[i]t was said in those days that a passage [through doors] was both like dying and like being born' (98), and without downplaying the many terrifying experiences of loss and pain that led up to it, the doors allow instantaneous transfer between places that compacts otherwise long, soul-drenching periods of waiting in uncertainty into intense brief moments of unarrested passage into the possibility of pursuing a new life. Michael Perfect suggests that as conventional borders dissolve in the novel, the doors 'serve as a means of imagining a post-nation future' (2019: 195) where state sovereignty has finally lost its grip on human movement because of 'the black holes in the fabric of the nation' (Hamid, 2017a: 126). While this is a valid reading of the novel's global orientation, we suggest that in concrete terms it is part of the novel's general push towards a renewal of categories through defamiliarisation, most specifically that of 'refugee'. Observing Saeed and Nadia from a distance, Saeed's beard and his devotion to prayer and the long black robe that Nadia wears from the first to the last page would automatically lead to the assumption, or misrecognition, that they pose a danger to Western societies. As we develop a close relationship with them in the course of their travels, however, we recognise that this could not be further from the truth. Nadia is not religious. She transgresses the most conservative ideas of female chastity and simply wears the robe to protect her personal space and freedom to explore the world. Saeed is not a fundamentalist. For him, prayer is a spiritual ritual that affirms his connectedness with family and loved ones that inspires him 'to believe in humanity's potential for building a better world, and so he prayed as a lament, as a consolation, and as a hope' (202). Saeed and Nadia are in that sense, like the rest of us, human beings who need to be recognised for who they are and aspire to become. Recognition is the cue word for them as they adjust to new trying environments – seeking 'acceptance ... or at least tolerance' (145) – and for us as readers as we sympathise with their endeavours, after they split up, to begin new lives with new people in Marin. '[B]eing seen' by the new love in her life, Nadia is 'struck ... with a shock of recognition, as though a door was opening up' (215) just as Saeed's new lover is attracted to his faith and 'the expansiveness of his gaze upon the universe [and ...] people of the world' (218–19), a recognition of his personal qualities that 'prompted him to want to listen and speak' (219).

Significantly, the novel deliberately does not identify Saeed and Nadia as refugees; we know they are, but they are not represented as such. They are to be aligned with Habila's more comprehensive category of travellers. Contrary to *Travellers*, however, Hamid's novel works effectively to defamiliarise the entire idea of migration. In a daring proposition, when commenting on an old woman's confusion about seeing Palo Alto, where she has lived all her life, changed beyond recognition, the narrator ponders that 'she too had migrated, that everyone migrates, even if we stay in the same house our whole lives ... We are all migrants through time' (209). In the grander scale of the novel's temporal-spatial conception of the world, natives can become migrants just as migrants can, over time, become natives. Nativeness is therefore 'a relative matter' (196) that can make the conceptual and cognitive borders between the categories of native and migrant implode, thus also questioning the purpose and sanctioning of material ones.

The universalising idea that 'we are all migrants through time' has troubled some critics who worry that Hamid disregards 'the specificity of [refugee] trauma in his well-intentioned phrase' (Chambers, 2019a: 238) and that this evokes 'a reductive view of refugees, emptying out refugees' distinctive experiences of violence, dispossession, and devastating loss' (Lagji, 2019: 218). On the other hand, as Lagji admits, Hamid's bold assertion is an open invitation to 'attend [thoughtfully] to our shared *time*, even if our shared *space* is divided by political and national boundaries' (225). Hamid is obviously aware that the world of today is one of divided spaces – thus his reasons for writing the novel. When '[p]urity seems to be all the rage', he argues, 'the most fundamental requirement' of a literary writer is to 'to explore the worst' but also 'to find hope' (Hamid, 2017b), notably through the radical hopefulness that comes from viewing migration as an integral part of humanity: 'Perhaps thinking of us all as migrants offers us a way out of this looming dystopia. If we are all migrants, then possibly there is a kinship' to be recovered, '[a]ccepting our reality as a migratory species will not be easy. ... But the potential is great. A better world is possible' (Hamid, 2019). In *Exit West* violence and hope are like the forcefully inscribed two sides of a coin that, depending on events and circumstance, flips towards one or the other side in refugee imaginaries. To recalibrate refugee talk, however, it is important to decriminalise and normalise migration. Utopian as Hamid's universalising take on migration may sound, it is pertinent to pursue an imaginative readjustment of our habitual thinking concerning human movement. As has been detailed throughout this chapter, it is precisely the capacity of literature to think against the grain of accepted ideas and realities and imagine other, as-of-yet unrealised possibilities of coexistence. To return to Anna Bernard's point, refugee literature is committed to advocacy by being 'a driver of aesthetic innovation as well as a political project'. As it is the artistic licence of writers to reimagine 'what is' along the lines of 'what if', the idea that 'we are all migrants through time' should be understood in that context as a proposition that carries transformative power to make us think again in more reconciliatory terms about our shared humanity.

Critical interventions into refugee talk tend to highlight the urgent need to humanise refugees. This appears to us a condescending misnomer. Moving now towards the end of this book, we hope our readers will agree, as has been latent in all preceding chapters, that it is not refugees that have to be humanised. They are, of course, human. Rather, it is the categories we insert them into, the barriers we set up to exclude them, and the language we use in talking about them that needs to be humanised. And urgently so. We might take heed from the hostile nativists in *Exit West* who eventually give up on driving refugees out of London and come around to the necessity of decency, because with 'the denial of coexistence' they would not be able 'to speak with head held high of what their generation had done' (2017a: 164) to exterminate the idea and democratic ideals of the 'West'. We need to develop a new humanism for the twenty-first century that is attentive to the current challenge of human migration; one that is hopeful, morally and ethically sustainable, and in tune with human rights and justice. In promoting this need, however, we must think carefully about what that would entail. To this we devote the last pages of *Refugee Talk*.

# Framing Hope

Claire Chambers calls Ghassan Kanafani 's 1962 story, 'Men in the Sun', the 'Ur-text of refugee hardship' (2019b) and it is not difficult to see why. Invoking what Gil Loescher identifies as 'the world's oldest and largest protracted refugee situation' (2021: 6), the story describes Palestinian refugees in flight:

> The huge lorry was carrying them along the road, together with their dreams, their families, their hopes and ambitions, their misery and despair, their strength and weakness, their past and future, as if it were pushing against the immense door to a new, unknown destiny, and all eyes were fixed on the door's surface as though bound to it by invisible threads. (Kanafani, 1999: 63)

This is a narrative about familiar aspects of refugee literature, also that coming out of the present moment: of people smuggled across deadly deserts or waters, of 'nothing but wait[ing]' (26), of 'feelings of loneliness and hope' (43) – the kind of hope that holds together everything inside the refugee (36). We want to end this book by turning to hope as perhaps the most important aspect of the refugee experience and certainly as a central word in a recalibrated refugee lexicon. Indeed, we pursue the idea that hope is integral to the new humanism of the twenty-first century that we gestured towards in Chapter 1, especially with reference to ideas inherent in Kelly Oliver's 'earth ethics', Zygmunt Bauman's 'one planet, one humanity' credo, Étienne Balibar's 'decolonisation at home' and Sonia Shah's anti-sedentarist reconfiguration of migration as a solution to the current refugee crisis. In correspondence with us, Dina Nayeri writes: 'Hope is the driving force for humanity, and it becomes increasingly central to life, the lower you fall, the more ways you're displaced. That is really all there is to say about it' (12 November 2020).

**In conversation, Gulwali Passarlay says**: We live in this world with hope. If you lose hope, you lose your humanity. On my journey, the thing that kept me going was hope – hope and faith. If we lose hope, then we are in serious trouble. Every situation that you are in is not going to last forever. You just have to keep the faith and keep that hope alive. Hope is important for our own survival, for our own well-being, and for our own mental health. But hope is also important when it comes to helping others. So being hopeful myself and trying to get people to not lose their hope has become my mission in life.

We lose our humanity when we stop caring. Kindness, hope, faith and solidarity matter in an interconnected world. Solidarity is really important. We all need allies, people who stand with us and who will use their power to challenge people's negative attitudes. As human beings we have it within our hearts to do the right thing and to touch people's lives. It is just that we need a little triggering point. Ultimately, I have faith that people are good.

I hope the ongoing Covid-19 pandemic teaches us what matters the most. What is really important is having your family near you, being safe and secure. We see clearly now that human interaction makes a difference. We need to find a way to expand the idea that as a human species, whether we like it or not, we are all interconnected. Refugees have been living in a pandemic for years. I have not seen my family for the last fourteen years. So, I hope that in the future there will be more sympathy, empathy, understanding, compassion, kindness and solidarity among people. We all need to remain hopeful that things will be better tomorrow. But we have to work on our todays and touch people's lives in positive and encouraging ways by helping and supporting those in need. Let us not take anything for granted, not our peace, security or freedom. Millions of people across the world are hoping to see a brighter tomorrow, away from the misery of war. They are also hoping for an end to this global pandemic. Let us all continue to be hopeful and kind to ourselves and to those around us. We all need encouragement so we do not give up but keep going forward in these uncertain times and in this strange world.

However, we want to say more about hope. In Chapter 1, we also referenced Paul Mason's call for 'a narrative of hope' (2019: 262). This is a narrative that is contingent on humanity: '[A]ll humans have the capacity to think "beyond" their surroundings. The capacity to imagine what's not there is constant' (139). To help us reflect on hope, we want to draw Ernst Bloch's ideas into the discussion. Written in exile in the US during the 1930s and 1940s, *The Principle of Hope* (1959) bundles together the emotion of hope with a rethinking of utopia and visions for a better world, individually and collectively understood – it is an 'encyclopaedia of hopes' (Vol. 1, 1995: 17). Bloch explores what he calls 'expectant emotions' and he zooms in on hope, promoting it as active and superior to the 'passive' emotion of fear: 'The emotion of hope goes out of itself, makes people broad instead of confining them' (3). Hope is an integral part of the 'world-improving' (91) pursuit of the idea that a better life might be possible. In this sense, hope is 'provocative', since it 'does not accept renunciation' (3). For Bloch, hope is 'the most authentic emotion of longing' (75). Furthermore, since hope is the central 'counter-emotion against anxiety and fear' it is *'the most human of all mental feelings'* and *'refers to the furthest and brightest horizon'* (75, italics in original). Indeed, the 'anticipatory ... operates in the field of hope' (12), disposed as it is to moving forward, while dreaming of a better life (11). Central to an understanding of Bloch's ideas, however, is the disappointability of hope because of its proclivity for risk-taking and chance (Richter, 2006). According to Bloch, 'hope must be unconditionally disappointable' not only because it is future-oriented, and thus 'committed to change rather than repetition', but also because it always incorporates 'the element of chance, without which there can be nothing new' (Bloch in Richter, 2006: 51). To Bloch hope does not 'make peace with the existing world' (50). Consequently, as Richter writes, it 'cannot be thought undialectically, without an eye to that which, within it, already threatens to undo it, even in the moment of its articulation. Hope is processual, dependent for its existence on the danger of its own undoing even while striving to overcome that danger' (51). Transposed into refugee situations these ideas help to explain how agency, risk-taking and hope are intimately connected and stubbornly refuse defeat.

Yet Bloch insists that hope is not only an emotion. It is also '*a directing act of a cognitive kind*' (1995: 12, italics in original) and thus he connects hope to thinking, a mental activity he defines as 'venturing beyond' (4, 5). '[R]eal venturing on' is bound up in 'the future dimension' that contains both passive fear and active hope (4). Finally, in Bloch's vision there is a utopian aspect to hope, understood as *both* emotion and mental activity: 'The imagination and the thoughts of future intention ... are utopian, ... in the newly tenable sense of the forward dream, of anticipation in general' (12). This 'anticipated better life', the 'wished-for', is imagined both 'in psychological and material terms' (13). In fact, '[a]s long as man is in a bad way, both private and public existence are pervaded by dreams of a better life than that which has so far been given him' (5). Bloch calls that which man hopes for, and dreams of, 'the Not-Yet-Conscious' (11, 13). For him, this is not an empty daydream, nor is it 'conformist or escapist' (Bloch in Richter, 2006: 50): 'The road is and remains that of socialism, it is the practice of concrete utopia' (1995: 17).

> **In conversation, Mohsin Hamid says**: I think hope or optimism is something that is politically essential. Without hope and a sense of optimism we leave the stage open to those who wish to suggest that the future is pessimistic and negative and who try to take us back to nostalgic visions of purity, when there were only one kind of people and we all looked the same, had the same religion, and the same belief. I think the reactionary political forces that resist migration and that are anti-refugee tend to be strengthened by a feeling of hopelessness and a lack of optimism. So, I think that hope and optimism are very important. As for hope sustaining refugees on their journeys – a journey is many things; among other things, it is a narrative and a story that has within it the idea of hope. It is a story that has much more potential for sustenance. That is why hope is vital both at the level of the individual migrant or refugee and the level of society and politics.

Hope is central to Parvati Nair's discussion of Stephen Burgess' painting 'Refugee Rescue':

By highlighting the idea of hope, Burgess successfully aligns the aesthetic with the affective. In turn, this alignment leads to a revised ethics of vision, whereby the figure of the refugee is framed in terms of hope, that is, a positive narrative that connects her or him to the viewer. The limitations of media representations, prone to repeated sensationalism in refugee contexts, often mean that hope, indeed humanity, is too often stripped away. Instead, artwork ... brings to light the fact of hope as a connecting vector between opposites: refugee and citizen, subject and viewer. (Nair in Cox et al., 2020: 416)

In her engagement with 'the persistence of hope as the bedrock from which courage, tenacity and determination arise', Nair elaborates on hope as sustenance and survival for refugees (412). Hope 'orients refugees', assists and empowers them, and remains a central source of agency (412). Moreover, recognising the persistence of hope as a 'key aspect of the refugee experience' is 'a vital step in dignifying' it (413). The perilous journeys refugees undertake are bound up in risk and resilience (413), but it is hope that is 'a life-sustaining force' in the search for a better life (416). Nair insists that 'the recognition of hope as a shared human dynamic' (417) binds us together as fellow humanity.

Inspired by Nair's insistence that hope be firmly anchored in the experiences of being a refugee *and* as something we share as human beings, and if hope is an expectant emotion bound up in dreams of a better life, perhaps we may venture the idea that it should form the backbone of a new humanism? If hope is 'a connecting vector' between refugees and non-refugees, it should be foregrounded as something we *all* need to cultivate in the present moment of refugee, climate – and pandemic crises. Should hope, then, be reinscribed as constitutive of the language of human rights and as a resource that sustains global solidarity? Daniel Trilling notes that 'the universal language of human rights is a promise, even if it is a partly unfulfilled one – and the more rigidly we enforce distinctions between the deserving and undeserving, the more likely we are to accept the violence done in our name' (2018a: 260–1). Accordingly, in preceding chapters, we have referred to Brad Evans and Zygmunt Bauman's suggestion that we need a new humanism for the twenty-first century. We have also indicated that this new humanism remains unqualified and short of actual content and direction. If we aspire to think more deeply about a new humanism for the twenty-first century, we suggest, as a start, that the terms humanity, responsibility, solidarity, recognition and hope become integral to the lexicon of a new humanism. These terms are deeply intertwined and contingent. Under the banner of a *shared humanity conditioned by hope*, responsibility, solidarity and recognition go hand in hand in actively promoting change and ethically sustainable solutions to global problems, refugee crises included. And if this particular coupling is activated as an intermediary first step, the 'new' in new humanism would signal, first of all and at long last, consensus to stop paying mere lip service to the already solid humanist ideas that we embrace, but in reality, do not practice. This in itself would hold promise for the steps to follow. And it would be an honest and, we hold, un-naive, forward-looking beginning point.

**In conversation, Brad Evans says**: What does a new inclusive humanism look like? It is certainly not rooted in identity politics, which can only accelerate fundamental divisions between people. In the context of the refugee crisis, we see the pitting of the precarious against the vulnerable. Now you have the truly vulnerable refugee pitted against the precarious workers in certain so-called broken, white communities. Unless we can bridge those gaps, then politics is lost. And that is where a new humanism needs to start. It is not going to be resolved by the contemporary fetishisation with identity politics by the 'religious' left. Instead a global conversation about new humanism needs to start with two terms. The first is art. I truly believe that politics is an art and not a science. For me, Frantz Fanon, for example, is a poet. The second term is conflict. Conflict is different from violence. Without conflict, we do not have creativity. We have to have space where ideas can conflict, and come into tension with one another in a non-violent way. The political has to be about the clash of ideas in a non-violent, respectful way. We do not move forward as a society without that.

**In conversation, Mohsin Hamid says**: I am not sure what exactly a new humanism for the twenty-first century means. The term would need to be defined for me. I would say, though, that we do need to engage in a global conversation about the themes that are central to human existence in a way that is open to everyone, and that is not circumscribed by a particular religious, linguistic or cultural tradition. Very often themes about human existence and human nature and what we might call spirituality or existential questions are conducted inside of very narrow frameworks. I think one of the important needs that we have at the moment is the birth of a global conversation and global ways of articulating these fundamental aspects of humanity that are currently so often articulated only in fragmented tribal languages – the language of Christianity or of Islam, the language of Denmark or of Pakistan, of Urdu or English. Now we need to have these conversations in a way that anyone can participate regardless of their background and that they can understand what is being said. When they can engage with what is being said, then we can truly have a conversation. If this is what is meant by a new humanism for the twenty-first century, then I certainly would be in support of it. But for me, it is very important to use simple language and not get stuck on terminology that is difficult to understand. I would say that having narratives about the essential nature of human existence and questions that were formerly, or perhaps even currently, considered spiritual topics is essential to the continued existence of our species, our ability to comprehend each other and to move forward together as one humanity.

We would like to promote the idea that a new humanism needs to be considered as a pedagogical, political, ethical and imaginative project that, while moored in the present, is future-oriented, or at least, focused on the future as imagined in the present moment. Furthermore, a new humanism has to be attuned to both individual and social emancipation. It should work as a revitalised and broadened *social contract* that reinstates hope and freedom as intrinsic to humanity, indeed, as central as dignity and agency. A new humanism relies on the power of the imagination to envision and formulate the content of such an all-embracing and all-inclusive project. As Evans and Giroux write in *Disposable Futures*, 'a pedagogical confidence to imagine another world is both possible and desirable' (2015: 140). They want to 'rethink the concept of the political itself' (xiv) as part of their analysis of the spectacle of violence. Perhaps surprisingly, there is an optimistic undercurrent in this analysis that suggests a serviceable vocabulary that is helpful in the formulation of a new humanism: 'love, cooperation, community, solidarity, creative wonderment, and the drive to imagine and explore more just and egalitarian worlds than the one we have created for ourselves' (xiv).

**In conversation, Kate Evans says**: In general, I think love is an underrated revolutionary force. You could probably use love to cut through things in a politically incisive way. Love is a very good way of separating the good from the bad in politics. Politics has been reduced to flag waving, to symbols that make people feel safe and to threats that make them feel unsafe. Right wing thinking is based on fear and control, not love and solidarity. Solidarity is difficult during a pandemic, when we are all individually isolated from each other. In spite of this, you can reshape the national conversation to be about generosity. If you attempt to make society more equal, then you can be directly involved in alleviating the suffering of the people who do not have enough within society.

**In conversation, Brad Evans says**: Hope is a term I struggle with because I find it too pessimistic. When we are talking about hope, we are talking about time. Hope is for a time to come, for a politics to come, for a better world to come. Part of my issue with hope is that it can lead to inertia. Hope can stigmatise action. As a political concept, I think a better term is love. To me, the idea that politics begins with security is a misnomer. Without love, you would not want to secure anybody. In order to move forward with hope in the politics of our current time, we need to recover more such ancestral ideas, through a connection to a deep past. There is something really important in that long history of love, and in the ways in which love itself can be mobilised as a political term – of course also for the furtherance of power and the disposability of life. We might feel embarrassed talking about concepts such as optimism, hope and love. But I think we need this different vocabulary in a rethinking and re-narrating of what politics means. Love is central here. Let us say you walk down the street and ask ten random people what sovereignty (to take an established political term) means they could not give you a definition. But most of them could tell you what love means.

This vocabulary is familiar to readers of Paulo Freire's *Pedagogy of the Oppressed*, where Freire talks of 'human liberation' and 'critical consciousness' in the same breath as 'love, dialogue, hope, humility, and sympathy' (2017: 10–11). For Freire, dialogue is central to human liberation, but its efficacy requires 'love for the world and for people' (62), 'humility [...and] faith in humankind' (63) and, crucially, 'hope' (64) and 'trust' (142). Dialogue both creates and relies on a democratic platform, a 'horizontal relationship' (64), where the participants are teachers and students, talkers and listeners at the same time. For Freire, then, dialogue remains central to his own pedagogical project of awakening a critical consciousness in people that will help realise human liberation. We should not shy away from Freire's lofty ideas – and ideals. Instead we should be inspired to translate them into a serviceable new humanism that can be put to practical use. The story of Little Amal is an excellent example of a cultural response to the ongoing refugee crisis, and indeed a spectacular happening that turned such ideas into celebratory practice. The giant puppet girl Amal (the name means 'hope' in Arabic) left the Syrian border in July 2021 and walked 8000km across Europe arriving in the UK in October 2021, marking 'a journey of hope for refugees'. Organised by the Good Chance Theatre Ensemble as an 'Atlas of the Future' event, Little Amal was welcomed on her route by thousands of people and hundreds of cultural and educational workshops pivoting on the 'potential, success, respect, hospitality and kindness' that dialogical encounters between refugees and citizens of host societies can foster when both parties are given the chance to be, simultaneously, teachers and learners, talkers and listeners. Amal's walk, and our walk with her, turned the spectacle of violence into one of welcome and possibility: 'where politics often fails, art succeeds in connecting us with our shared humanity' (Atlas of the Future).

**In conversation, Daniel Trilling says:** What can we learn from the 2015 refugee crisis? That a crisis of this sort is not only produced by wars and persecution in the countries people leave, but by the border policies of the countries they encounter. This dynamic has to change and we need to open up legal routes by which people can come and claim asylum. It is important to understand that for as long as there are things pushing people to move, people will continue to move. Why not create a world in which we collectively work together to stop people being forced to leave their homes? Why not create a world in which people can move if they choose to? Those two things are not mutually exclusive.

In contemplating a new humanism for the twenty-first century we can also draw inspiration from Edward Said's thoughts from *Humanism and Democratic Criticism*, in which he explores 'the relevance and future of humanism in contemporary life' (2004: 5), with humanism understood as an 'activity' (7) and a 'worldly practice' (75). What Said writes can be read as a proposal for how to formulate one aspect of new humanism: 'What concerns me is humanism as a useable praxis for intellectuals and academics who want to know what they are doing, what they are committed to as scholars, and who want also to connect these principles to the world in which they live as citizens' (6). Of course, Said's emphasis on intellectuals and academics is less radical than Freire's democratic platform, but we recognise the familiar worldliness of Said's endeavour. We also need to reference Said's brief aside that seemingly homogeneous countries such as Sweden (and we include Denmark, where we are writing from) 'are now permanently altered by the huge waves of migrants, expatriates, and refugees that have become the single most important human reality of our time the world over' (47). If we practice humanism it has to be critically alert to this 'permanently altered' globalised, multicultural and messy world. Said goes on to argue that humanism is 'critique that is directed at the state of affairs in, as well as out of, the university ... and that gathers its force and relevance by its democratic, secular, and open character. For there is, in fact, no contradiction at all between the practice of humanism and the practice of participatory citizenship' (22). Yet, the latter is, obviously, the crux of the matter for refugees whose participatory entitlement is denied them as long as it hinges on citizenship status. A humanism that is attuned to twenty-first century challenges must act to reject that exclusivist prerequisite. According to Said, humanism achieves its critical relevance through 'a means of questioning, upsetting, and reformulating so much of what is presented to us as commodified, packaged, uncontroversial, and uncritically codified certainties' (28), especially how this comes across in 'the products of language' (28). Humanism remains, Said insists, 'a resistance to *idées reçues*, and it offers opposition to every kind of cliché and unthinking language' (43). On this view, perhaps our manner of exploring the crises in meanings of words that constitute the refugee lexicon can be seen as an act of critical humanism?

**In conversation, Homi K. Bhabha says**: For Fanon, the question of a new humanism is a rallying cry. However, I wonder if the project of a new humanism is really what one requires, unless it is a critique of certain aspirations of humanism, which have been compromised. Humanism has a long history, not only to do with humanity, but also with cultural values. The histories of empire, racism, poverty, inequality, the ecological devastation of the planet, the travails of democracy and the current refugee crisis are phenomena that humanism was supposed to address, including, of course, the idea of the dignity and equality of human beings. We have seen that this aspiration has fallen short. Humanism is always tied to universalism. But if we are designating people as refugees, migrants, minorities, the displaced, and the marginalised, then we are already in some ways talking about the violation of universalism. Does one want to go from the problematic status of a universalist humanism to yet another mode of thinking about humanism? In fact, what would one get out of a new humanism? I am not sure, partly because if you call it a new humanism, then it is already tied to the notion of humanism. Most discussions around what humanism could be today show that humanism is in a self-contradictory and aporetic relation to itself. You cannot really speak about humanism without putting it on trial or under erasure, because this concept is so contested in itself. To live up to its much-vaunted Enlightenment principles, Levinas once said, Europe has to critique Europe, and thus reconstruct itself by engaging with its alterity.

To return to Evans and Giroux, we can also think about a new humanism along the lines of what they call 'counter-narratives of participation, liberation, historical memory, community, and autonomy' that constitute a 'humanity of struggle' (2015: 133). Such counter-narratives have to harness 'a new radical imagination that is able to mobilize alternative forms of social agency' (xv) and they have to critique 'a politics of contempt and a culture of cruelty' (94). Contempt and cruelty have, of course, been amply demonstrated in Europe's responses to the refugee crisis – in 'the violence done in our name', to echo Trilling's words. A new humanism for the twenty-first century would therefore necessarily aspire to be a 'critique of violence adequate to our deeply unjust, inequitable, and violent times' (3). In point of fact, it might be an example of the 'more radically poetic and politically liberating alternatives' (xv) that Evans and Giroux call for.

Liberating alternatives to violent times are illustrated in Mohsin Hamid's lucid indictment of Europe in his radical and poetic ideas on a hopeful future. Europeans, he writes, have to 'dispense with the delusion that theirs can remain pleasant countries and unattractive countries at the same time' (2015). One way for Europeans to rid ourselves of this delusion is to 'articulate a vision of an optimistic future as a migrant friendly society' (2015). When we realise that we all have ancestors who 'left the precise spot where our species first evolved' we are in Hamid's globally inclusive vision all 'a great and powerful hope' (2015). This observation links up with his compelling thought experiment:

What if … we're willing to build some sort of global architecture that allows us to jointly solve problems, and we don't have to replicate the 20th century's battle between nations or the 19th century's battle between empires? I think that this less-frightening future will be based upon a much more radical equality than we have today, and a much more radical optimism than we seem to be articulating. (Hamid in Chandler, 2017)

While radical equality and optimism may be considered 'disappointable' hopes in the context of current world affairs, the solidarity and generosity of spirit required to begin to envision such goals can nevertheless grow unexpectedly and unfold unconditionally in unforeseeable places and contexts of the present – as small moments in the grander scale of things, but big in terms of affective human interaction across experiential borders. This is what artist Kate Evans experienced in the Jungle in Calais and why, as an activist, she insists on the power of equitable 'people' moments to effect a radical change of perception in cross-cultural encounters. Her ingenious linking of solidarity with a conceptual renewal of what is understood by 'common class interest' reveals this:

Solidarity is key to social change, and I think the current focus on 'identity' within radical politics, while it is really useful for unpicking the particularities of intersecting oppressions, can also atomise and divide us with its intensely individualistic focus. The best counter to that, that I can see, is the concept of 'common class interests,' and in terms of welcoming the immigrant, the foreigner, the 'other,' the common class to which we all belong is that of humanity. So everything that breaks down difference and which fosters understanding helps. I really enjoyed being able to make portrayals of the incredible generosity that I encountered at Calais, from people who had very little. Making a depiction of Kurdish hospitality both humanised the subjects of my comic and also completely subverted that 'they just want our benefits' trope, because here were people who didn't want to take, who actively wanted to give. (Personal correspondence, 20 April 2021)

Inherent in this personal encounter is also a strong hint that we Europeans need to reciprocate the welcome Evans experienced from refugee quarters. In thinking about 'common interests' we cannot afford to leave Europe out of the equation. If hope sustains risk-taking refugees in flight, then reimagining migration may be a risk worth taking for Europe as an alternative to the destructive 'border-fetish' that is currently promoted as an efficient problem-solving strategy. Without 'gloss[ing] over the problems', Europe needs what Regina Polak calls 'resource-oriented narratives' in its approaches to migration issues: 'Europe [too] needs hope. Without resource-oriented narratives, without mental and spiritual empowerment, Europeans run the risk of failing. Europe will not solve the crisis without learning to see flight and migration as an opportunity' (2018: 245) for the current century.

Our contemplations so far have privileged a vocabulary of hope and optimism. Alexander Betts and Paul Collier would most likely suggest that such an approach is based on the 'principles of the heart', and call for a reality check in the shape of what they label the 'principles of the head' (2018: 102). As they argue: 'Just as the heartless head is cruel, the headless heart is self-indulgent. The lives of refugees are plunged into nightmare: in responding, we owe them both our compassion and our intelligence' (124). Betts and Collier offer a substantiated proposal to rethink refuge and a broken refugee system from a combination of ethical (philosophical) and rational (concrete) perspectives that will be beneficial to both refugees and host societies. In their view, Europe has failed to 'engage adequately' (35) with the refugee crisis by not looking beyond the emergency of the situation: 'refuge must be understood as not only a humanitarian issue but also one of development. Put simply, it is not just about indefinitely providing food, clothing, and shelter. It has to be about restoring people's autonomy' (10) through carefully planned and internationally coordinated resettlement plans, education and job programmes whereby refugees are integrated into, and contribute to, the continued development of their host societies. Betts and Collier's proposal draws on what they designate as 'compassion' (100), 'solidarity' (105) and 'need' (118) as the 'principles of the heart' that they want to align with the 'principles of the head' that require properly organised international coordination of refugee protection, global partnership, fair burden-sharing and multiple aid agencies qualified in promoting post-conflict reconstruction and resettlement. What their proposal amounts to, then, is a new global architecture of aid work. This makes overlooked political sense, yet to pursue it further lies outside the remit of this book's inquiry into cultural responses to the current refugee crisis. Still, Betts and Collier's contribution towards what Bauman terms global solutions to local problems is also, we find, resonant with hope for a better and more equitable future for refugees. We may in fact press the point again that it is not only refugees who need this, so do we Europeans whose moral integrity and reputation have become an open sore of inhumane neglect in recent years. As Betts and Collier contend, acting with compassion and solidarity 'in response to the need for refuge is not some new demand upon mankind, or an implausible emotion that modernity has to invent from scratch. It is something hardwired into our humanity' (97). It is inexcusable that in today's world where 'due to 24/7 media, the internet, and broadcast news, we know more about suffering elsewhere than any previous generation' – yet we are persistently 'turning our backs to it' (97–8). The call is on us: 'The alternative to the politics of the ostrich is to embrace change. Our politicians now need to pay sufficient attention to rethinking refugee policy for it to actually get changed. That change cannot be cosmetic' (236).

Principles of hearts and heads notwithstanding, refugee stories continue to demonstrate that hope is a stubborn feeling indeed – as we see in, for example, Hamed Amiri's *The Boy with Two Hearts: A Story of Hope* (2020) and Hassan Akkad's *Hope Not Fear* (2021). We want to end by returning one last time to Gulwali Passarlay's memoir of his journey to safety as a child refugee. *The Lightless Sky* is undergirded by hope. In the epilogue, reflecting on how 'faith and fate' (2019: 375) brought him to the UK, casting his eyes back to his origins and forward to his future, the word 'hope' is foregrounded: 'More than anything, this book is about faith, hope and optimism. I hope too that it is about dedication and commitment towards fellow human beings. A story of kindness, love, humanity and brotherhood' (374). This message resonates with Passarlay's personally inflected hopeful philosophy. For Passarlay, this philosophy is per definition connected to that enlarged circle of we that is humanity: 'The enemy of love is not hate, it is indifference. The enemy of love is turning away from those in need. The enemy of love is doing nothing when you can help your fellow man' (376). His philosophy is also integral to the ongoing conversation that emanates from his activism and from his writing. We see this in his personal address to the reader towards the end of his story: 'I want to thank you for reading my book and for being part of my journey' (377). If we work together to make life better for our fellow human beings, Passarlay believes, we can 'change the world', and achieve his 'single dream' – 'that a child in the future will read this book and ask, "What was a refugee?"' (378).

# Bibliography

Websites last accessed 2 June 2021.

'A Perilous Journey.' 2015. PositiveNegatives production. *Guardian*, 11–13 November.

Aciman, André. 2011. 'Afterword: Parallax.' In *Alibis: Essays on Elsewhere*. New York: Picador (185–200).

Ackroyd, Peter. 2005. *Chaucer. Brief Lives*. London: Vintage.

Agamben, Giorgio. 1995. 'We Refugees.' Trans. Michael Roche. *Symposium*, Summer, 49:2 (114–19).

Agamben, Giorgio. 1998. *Homo Sacer: Sovereign Power and Bare Life*. Trans. Daniel Heller-Roazen. Stanford, CA: Stanford University Press.

Agamben, Giorgio. 1999. *Remnants of Auschwitz. The Witness and the Archive*. Trans. Daniel Heller-Roazen. New York: Zone Books.

Ahmed, Sara. 2000. *Strange Encounters: Embodied Others in Post-Coloniality*. London: Routledge.

Akkad, Hassan. 2016. '"My Journey to Europe" – Being The Story Event.' 4 November.

Akkad, Hassan. 2021. *Hope Not Fear*. London: Bluebird.

AlAmmar, Layla. 2021. *Silence Is a Sense*. London: Borough.

Amiri, Hamed. 2020. *The Boy with Two Hearts: A Story of Hope*. London: Icon.

Appiah, Kwame Anthony and Homi K. Bhabha. 2018. 'Cosmopolitanism and Convergence.' *New Literary History*, 49:2 (171–98).

Arendt, Hannah. 1970 [1968]. 'On Humanity in Dark Times: Thoughts about Lessing' [1959]. In *Men in Dark Times*. London: Jonathan Cape (3–31).

Arendt, Hannah. 1978. *The Life of the Mind*. San Diego, CA: Harvest/Harcourt.

Arendt, Hannah. 1994 [1943]. 'We Refugees.' In *Altogether Elsewhere: Writers on Exile*. Ed. Marc Robinson. Boston, MA and London: Faber and Faber (110–19).

Arendt, Hannah. 1998 [1958]. *The Human Condition*, 2nd edn. Chicago, IL: University of Chicago Press.

Arendt, Hannah. 2006 [1963]. *Eichmann in Jerusalem: A Report on the Banality of Evil*. London: Penguin.

Arendt, Hannah. 2007 [1944]. 'The Disenfranchised and Disgraced.' In *The Jewish Writings*. Ed. Jerome Kohn and Ron H. Feldman. New York: Shocken Books (232–5).

Arendt, Hannah. 2017 [1951]. *The Origins of Totalitarianism*. London: Penguin.

Atlas of the future: A Journey of Hope for Refugees: https://atlasofthefuture.org/project/little-amal-the-walk/

Baerwaldt, Neske. 2018. 'The European Refugee Crisis: Crisis for Whom?' 20 March: www.law.ox.ac.uk/research-subject-groups/centre-criminology/centreborder-criminologies/blog/2018/03/european-refugee

Bakr Khaal, Abu. 2014. *African Titanics* [Arabic 2008]. Trans. Charis Bredin. London: Darf Publishers.

Balibar, Étienne. 1998. 'The Borders of Europe.' Trans. J. Swenson. In *Cosmopolitics: Thinking and Feeling beyond the Nation*. Ed. Pheng Cheah and Bruce Robbins. Minneapolis, MN: Minnesota University Press (216–29).

Balibar, Étienne and Frank Collins. 2003. 'Europe, an "Unimagined" Frontier of Democracy.' *Diacritics*, 33:3–4 (36–44).

Barakat, Hoda. 2021 [2017]. *Voices of the Lost*. Trans. Marilyn Booth. London: Oneworld.

Barekat, Houman. 2020. '*God 99* by Hassan Blasim, Review.' *Guardian*, 8 December.

Barr, Helen. 2019. 'Stories of the New Geography: The Refugee Tales.' *Journal of Medieval Worlds*. 1:1 (79–106).

Bauder, Harald and Lorelle Juffs. 2020. '"Solidarity" in the Migration and Refugee Literature: Analysis of a Concept.' *Journal of Ethnic and Migration Studies*, 46:1 (46–65).

Bauman, Zygmunt. 2004. *Liquid Love*. Cambridge: Polity.

Bauman, Zygmunt. 2012 [2007]. *Liquid Times: Living in an Age of Uncertainty*. Cambridge: Polity.

Bauman, Zygmunt. 2017. *Strangers at Our Door*. Cambridge: Polity.

Bennett, Bruce. 2018. 'Becoming Refugees: Exodus and Contemporary Mediations of the Refugee Crisis.' *Transnational Cinemas*, 9:1 (13–30).

Bennett, Andrew and Nicholas Royle. 2004. *An Introduction to Literature, Criticism and Theory*, 3rd edn. Harlow: Pearson.

Berger, John. 1983 [1972]. *Ways of Seeing*. London: BBC.

Berry, Mike, Inaki Garcia-Blanco, Kerry Moore et al. 2015. *Press Coverage of the Refugee and Migrant Crisis in the EU: Content Analysis of Five European Countries, Report prepared for the United Nations High Commission for Refugees*, December.

Betts, Alexander. 2013. *Survival Migration: Failed Governance and the Crisis of Displacement.* Ithaca, NY and London: Cornell University Press.

Betts, Alexander and Paul Collier. 2018. *Refuge: Transforming a Broken Refugee System.* London: Allen Lane.

Bhabha, Homi K. 2018. 'Dignity in Distress: Thoughts on Migration and Morality.' Trinity College, Dublin, 25 September.

Bhabha, Homi K. 2019. 'The Barbed Wire Labyrinth: Thoughts of the Culture of Migration.' *Philosophy and Social Criticism*, 45:4 (403–12).

Bhabha, Homi K. 2000. 'The Vernacular Cosmopolitan.' In *Voices of the Crossing.* Ed. Ferdinand Dennis and Naseem Khan. London: Serpent's Tail (133–42).

Blackburn, Simon. 2003. *Ethics: A Very Short Introduction.* Oxford: Oxford University Press.

Blasim, Hassan. 2016. *The Madman of Freedom Square* [Arabic 2009]. Trans. Jonathan Wright. Manchester: Comma Press.

Blasim, Hassan. 2018. 'A Refugee in the Paradise That Is Europe.' *Wasafiri*, 33:1 (43).

Blasim, Hassan. 2020. *God 99* [Arabic 2018]. Trans. Jonathan Wright. Manchester: Comma Press.

Bloch, Ernst. 1995 [1959]. *The Principle of Hope.* Vol. One. Trans. Neville Plaice, Stephen Plaice and Paul Knight. Cambridge, MA: MIT Press.

Bola, J.J. 2018. *No Place to Call Home.* London: OWN IT!

Boochani, Behrouz. 2019. *No Friend but the Mountains.* Trans. Omid Tofighian. London: Picador.

Brooks, Maya. 2020. 'Advocacy: The Aesthetic of Solidarity.' CIRCA, the NCMA blog, 23 July.

Brownlie, Siobhan. 2020. *Discourses of Memory and Refugees: Exploring Facets.* London: Palgrave Macmillan.

Buchanan, Sara et al. 2003. 'What's the story? Results from Research into Media Coverage of Refugees and Asylum Seekers in the UK.' Article 19 (The Global Campaign for Free Expression).

Burrell, Kathy and Kathrin Hörschelmann. 2019. 'Perilous Journeys: Visualising the Racialised "Refugee Crisis,"' *Antipode*, 51:1 (45–65).

Butler, Judith. 2006. *Precarious Life: The Powers of Mourning and Violence.* London: Verso.

Butler, Judith. 2020. *The Force of Nonviolence. An Ethico-Political Bind.* London: Verso.

Butler, Judith and Stephanie Berbec. 2017. 'We Are Worldless without One Another: An Interview with Judith Butler.' *The Other Journal*, 26 June.

Campbell, Karen. 2014 [2013]. *This Is Where I Am*. London: Bloomsbury.

Chambers, Claire. 2019a. 'The Doors of Posthuman Sensory Perception in Mohsin Hamid's *Exit West*.' In *Making Sense of Contemporary British Muslim Novels*. London: Palgrave Macmillan (213–52).

Chambers, Claire. 2019b. 'Titanic Refugee Fictions.' *Discover Society*, 6 November.

Chambers, Iain. 2019. 'War on the Waters.' *Sink Without Trace – Exhibition on Migrant Deaths at Sea*. Exhibition Catalogue, P21 Gallery, London, 13 June–13 July (40–3).

Chandler, Caitlin. 2017. '"We Are All refugees": A Conversation with Mohsin Hamid.' *The Nation*, 30 October.

Chouliaraki, Lilie. 2017. 'Suffering and the Ethics of Solidarity.' In *Alleviating World Suffering – the Challenge of Negative Quality of Life*. Ed. Ronald E. Anderson. Social Indicators Research Series, Vol. 67. Cham: Springer (49–60).

Chouliaraki, Lilie and Tijana Stolic. 2017. 'Rethinking Media Responsibility in the Refugee "crisis": A Visual Typology of European News.' *Media, Culture & Society*, 39:8 (1162–77).

Collier, Paul. 2013. *Exodus. Immigration and Multiculturalism in the 21st Century*. London: Penguin.

Cox, Emma, Sam Durrant, David Farrier, Lyndsey Stonebridge and Agnes Woolley, eds. 2020. *Refugee Imaginaries. Research across the Humanities*. Edinburgh: Edinburgh University Press.

Dahlgren, Peter. 2016. 'Moral Spectatorship and Its Discourses: The "Mediapolis" in the Swedish Refugee Crisis.' *Javnost – The Public – Journal of the European Institute for Communication and Culture*, 23:4.

Davies, Dominic. 2017. 'Comics Activism: An Interview with Comics Artist and Activist Kate Evans.' *The Comic Grid – Journal of Comics Scholarship*, 7:1 (1–12).

Deutsche Welle. 2019. Online news, 18 September: www.dw.com/en/italy-france-agree-on-automatic-distribution-of-migrants/a-50489114

Donald, Jason. 2018 [2017]. *Dalila*. London: Vintage.

Dorfman, Ariel. 2020. 'Songs of Loss and Reinvention.' *The New York Review of Books*, 3 December.

Downey, Anthony. 2017. 'Scopic Reflections: Incoming and the Technology of Exceptionalism.' *The Curve: Richard Mosse*. London: Barbican.

Dreher, Tanja. 2009. 'Listening across Difference: Media and Multiculturalism beyond Politics of Voice.' *Continuum*, 23:4 (445–58).

Duarte, Melina. 2019. 'The Ethical Consequences of Criminalizing Solidarity in the EU.' *Theoria*, 86:1 (28–53).

Duley, Giles. 2018. 'I Can Only Tell You What My Eyes See.' *Wasafiri*, 33:1 (3–8).

Dummett, Michael. 2001. *On Immigration and Refugees*. London and New York: Routledge.

Duncan, Derek. 2019. 'In the Wake: Postcolonial Migrations from the Horn of Africa.' *Forum for Modern Language Studies*, 56:1 (96–109).

Engelbert, Jiska, Isabel Awad and Jacco van Sterkenburg et al. 2019. 'Everyday Practices and the (Un)making of "Fortress Europe": Introduction to the Special Issue.' *European Journal of Cultural Studies*, 22:2 (133–43).

Erll, Astrid. 2020. 'Literary Memory Activism in an Age of Migration: The Refugee Tales': https://lecturenet.uu.nl/Site1/Play/eb6650eafdd34657a539881931e1fc7f1d

Erpenbeck, Jenny. 2018a. *Go, Went, Gone* [2015]. Trans. Susan Bernofsky. London: Portobello.

Erpenbeck, Jenny. 2018b. 'Blind Spots: The 2018 Puterbaug Keynote.' *World Literature Today*, July.

Evans, Brad. 2017. 'Dead in the Waters.' In *Life Adrift: Climate Change, Migration, Critique*. Ed. Andrew Baldwin and Giovanni Bettini. London: Rowman & Littlefield (59–78).

Evans, Brad and Zygmunt Bauman. 2016. 'The Refugee Crisis Is Humanity's Crisis.' *New York Times*, 2 May.

Evans, Brad and Henry A. Giroux. 2015. *Disposable Futures: The Seduction of Violence in the Age of Spectacle*. Open Media Series/City Lights.

Evans, Brad and Julian Reid. 2014. *Resilient Life: The Art of Living Dangerously*. Cambridge: Polity.

Evans, Kate. 2017. *Threads from the Refugee Crisis*. London: Verso.

*Exodus: Our Journey*. 2016. BBC Series.

Extence, Gavin. 2020 [2019]. *The End of Time*. London: Hodder.

Fanon, Frantz. 1986 [1967]. *Black Skin, White Masks* [1952]. Trans. Charles Lam Markmann. London: Pluto Press.

Fanon, Frantz. 1990 [1965]. *The Wretched of the Earth* [1961]. Trans. Constance Farrington. London: Penguin.

Farrier, David. 2011. *Postcolonial Asylum: Seeking Sanctuary before the Law*. Liverpool: Liverpool University Press.

Fassin, Didier. 2016. 'From Right to Favor.' *The Nation*, 5 April.

Fiddian-Qasmiyeh, Elena, Gil Loescher, Katy Long and Nando Sigona, eds. 2014. *The Oxford Handbook of Refugee and Forced Migration Studies*. Oxford: Oxford University Press.

Freire, Paolo. 2017 [1970]. *Pedagogy of the Oppressed*. Trans. M.B. Ramos. London: Penguin.

Gallien, Claire. 2018a. '"Refugee Literature": What Postcolonial Theory Has to Say.' *Journal of Postcolonial Writing*, 54:6 (721–6).

Gallien, Claire. 2018b. 'Forcing Displacement: The Postcolonial Interventions of Refugee Literature and Arts.' *Journal of Postcolonial Writing*, 54:6 (735–50).

Georgiou, Myria and Rafal Zaborowski. 2017. 'Media Coverage of the "Refugee Crisis": A Cross-European perspective.' *Council of Europe Report, DG1(2017)03*.

Gikandi, Simon. 2010. 'Between Roots and Routes: Cosmopolitanism and the Claims of Locality.' In *Rerouting the Postcolonial: New Directions for the new Millennium*. Ed. Janet Wilson, Cristina Sandru and Sarah Lawson Welsh. London: Routledge (22–35).

Gilbert, Jeremy. 2020. 'Potent Collectivities: Aesthetics of Solidarity.' 8 April: https://crisisandcommunitas.com/?crisis=potent-collectivities-aesthetics-of-solidarity

Godin, Marie, Katrine Møller Hansen, Aura Lounasmaa, Corine Squire and Tahir Zaman, eds. 2017. *Voices from the 'Jungle': Stories from the Calais Refugee Camp*. London: Pluto Press.

Gotlib, Anna. 2017. 'Refugees, Narratives, or How to Do Bad Things with Words.' *Kennedy Institute of Ethics Journal*, 27:2 (E-65–E-86).

Greussing, Esther and Hajo G. Boomgaarden. 2017. 'Shifting the Refugee Narrative? An Automated Frame Analysis of Europe's 2015 Refugee Crisis.' *Journal of Ethnic and Migration Studies*, 43:11. (1749–54).

Gross, Bernhard, Kerry Moore and Terry Threadgold. 2007. *Broadcast news coverage of asylum April to October 2006: Caught between human rights and public safety*. Project report, Cardiff School of Journalism, Media, and Cultural Studies.

Gumbel, Peter. 2020. *Citizens of Everywhere. Searching for Identity in the Age of Brexit*. London: Haus.

Habila, Helon. 2019a. *Travellers*. London: Hamish Hamilton.

Habila, Helon. 2019b. 'Helon Habila Discusses *Travellers* at Politics and Prose.' 25 August: www.youtube.com/watch?v=qVLwYzaLofE

Hamid, Mohsin. 2015. 'The Turmoil of Today's World: Leading Writers Respond to the Refugee Crisis.' *Guardian*, 12 September.

Hamid, Mohsin. 2017a. *Exit West*. London: Penguin Random House.

Hamid, Mohsin. 2017b. 'What Makes a Man Booker Novel? Mohsin Hamid on *Exit West*.' *Guardian*, 14 October.

Hamid, Mohsin. 2019. 'In the 21st Century, We Are All Migrants.' *National Geographic*, August.

Harding, Jeremy. 2012. *Border Vigils: Keeping Migrants Out of the Rich World*. London: Verso.

Harpham, Geoffrey Galt. 1995. 'Ethics'. In *Critical Terms for Literary Study*, 2nd edn. Ed. Frank Lentricchia and Thomas McLaughlin. Chicago, IL: University of Chicago Press (387–405).

Heidenreich, Tobias, Fabienne Lind, Jakob-Morritz Eberl and Hajo G. Boomgaarden. 2019. 'Media Framing Dynamics of the "European Refugee Crisis": A Comparative Topic Modelling Approach.' *Journal of Refugee Studies*, Special Issue, 32:1 (i172–i182).

Herd, David and Anna Pincus, eds. 2016. *Refugee Tales*. Manchester: Comma Press.

Herd, David and Anna Pincus, eds. 2017. *Refugee Tales*, Vol. II. Manchester: Comma Press.

Herd, David and Anna Pincus, eds. 2019. *Refugee Tales*, Vol. III. Manchester: Comma Press.

Herd, David and Anna Pincus, eds. 2021. *Refugee Tales*, Vol. IV. Manchester: Comma Press.

Herxheimer, Sophie and Bidisha. 2018. 'Interview with Sophie Herxheimer.' *Wasafiri*, 33:1 (52–60).

Hill, Samantha Rose. 2020. 'Hannah Arendt and the Politics of Truth.' *OpenDemocracy*, 25 October.

Hollenbach, David. 2019. 'Refugees and the Scope of Solidarity.' Georgetown University Berkley Center for Religion, Peace and World Affairs, 11 November.

Hopkins, Katie. 2015. 'Rescue Boats? I'd Use Gunships to Stop Migrants.' *The Sun*, 17 April.

Horsti, Karina. 2019. 'Refugee Testimonies Enacted: Voice and Solidarity in Media Art Installations.' *Popular Communication*, 17:2 (125–39).

Hosseini, Khaled. 2018. *Sea Prayer*. London: Bloomsbury.

*Humanity on Trial*. 2019. Dir. Jonas Bruun.

Hussein, Asad. 2020. 'Chasing the Mirage.' *The New York Review of Books*, 9 April.

Islam, Shada. 2020. 'Europe's Migration "Crisis" Isn't about Numbers. It's about Prejudice.' *Guardian*, 8 October.

Jones, Reece. 2017. *Violent Borders. Refugees and the Right to Move*. London: Verso.

Kanafani, Ghassan. 1999 [1962]. 'Men in the Sun.' In *Men in the Sun and Other Palestinian Stories*. Trans. Hilary Kilpatrick. London: Lynne Rienner (21–74).

Karolewski, Ireneusz Pavel and Ronald Benedikter. 2018. 'Europe's Refugee and Migrant Crisis: Political Responses to Asymmetrical Pressures.' *Politique Européenne*, 60.

Kaye, Ronald. 2001. '"Blaming the Victim": An Analysis of Press Representations of Refugees and Asylum-seekers in the United Kingdom in the 1990s.' In *Media and Migration: Constructions of Mobility and Difference*. Ed. Russell King and Nancy Wood. London: Routledge (E-book, chapter 4).

Kingsley, Patrick. 2017 [2016]. *The New Odyssey: The Story of Europe's Refugee Crisis*. London: Faber and Faber/Guardian Books.

Kingsley, Patrick. 2019. 'Witness or Participant? The Ethical, Practical and Linguistic Challenges of Reporting on the Refugee Crisis.' Harvard University, 16 May.

Kirby, Emma Jane. 2016. *The Optician of Lampedusa*. London: Allan Lane.

Kluth, Andreas. 2018. 'A New Refugee Crisis Could Break the EU.' *Bloomberg Opinion*, 3 March.

Koser, Khalid. 2016. *International Migration: A Very Short Introduction*, 2nd edn. Oxford: Oxford University Press.

Lagji, Amanda. 2019. 'Waiting in Motion: Mapping Postcolonial Fiction, New Mobilities, and Migration through Mohsin Hamid's *Exit West*.' *Mobilities*, 14:2 (218–32).

Lange, Christy. 2017. 'One Take: Incoming.' *Frieze*, 185, 4 March.

Leatherdale, Duncan. 2019. 'Gavin Extence: Sheffield Author on His Syrian Refugee Novel.' *BBC News*, 22 September.

Lee, Christopher J. 2011. 'Locating Hannah Arendt within Postcolonial Thought: A Prospectus.' *College Literature*, 38:1 (95–114).

Levi, Primo. 2013 [1963]. *If This Is a Man/The Truce* [1958]. Trans. Stuart Woolf. London: Abacus.

Levinas, Emmanuel. 1969 [1961]. *Totality and Infinity: An Essay on Exteriority*. Trans. Alphonso Lingis. Pittsburgh, PA: Duquesne University Press.

Lim, Audrea. 2021. 'We're Trying to Recreate the Lives We Had.' *Guardian*, 25 February.

Loescher, Gil. 2021. *Refugees: A Very Short Introduction*. Oxford: Oxford University Press.

Ludji, Irene. 2018. 'The Ethics of Solidarity and Human Rights: Insights from the World Council of Churches on United Nation Reform.' *The Ecumenical Review*, 70:2.

Luiselli, Valeria. 2019. *Lost Children Archive*. New York: Vintage.

Maley, William. 2016. *What Is a Refugee?* London: Hurst.

Marquez, Xavier. 2012. 'Spaces of Appearance and Spaces of Surveillance.' *Polity*, 44:1 (6–31).

Martin, Niall. 2019. 'As "Index and Metaphor": Migration and the Thermal Imagery in Richard Mosse's *Incoming*.' *Culture Machine*, 17 (1–19).

Mason, Paul. 2019. *Clear Bright Future: A Radical Defence of the Human Being*. London: Allen Lane.

May, Simon. 2021. *How to Be a Refugee. One Family's Story of Exile and Belonging*. London: Picador.

Mazzara, Frederica. 2019. 'Can Art Subvert the "Ungrievability" of Migrant Lives?' *Sink Without Trace – Exhibition on Migrant Deaths at Sea*. Exhibition Catalogue, P21 Gallery, London, 13 June–13 July (44–6).

McDonald-Gibson, Charlotte. 2017. *Castaway: Stories of Survival from Europe's Refugee Crisis*. London: Portobello.

Morton, Stephen. 2018. 'Postcolonial Refugees, Displacement, Dispossession and Economies of Abandonment in the Capitalist World System.' In *The Bloomsbury Introduction to Postcolonial Writing: New Contexts, New Narratives, New Debates*. Ed. Jenni Ramone. London: Bloomsbury (215–36).

Mosse, Richard. 2017. *Incoming*.

Mosse, Richard. 2018a. 'Richard Mosse on "Brilliant Ideas".' 19 March: www.bloomberg.com/news/videos/2018-03-19/richard-mosse-on-brilliant-ideas-video

Mosse, Richard. 2018b. 'NGV Triennial. Richard Mosse.' 18 April: www.youtube.com/watch?v=6QOyFAqs_rM&t=25s

Mosse, Richard. 2018c. 'Nowness: Photographers in Focus.' 19 August: www.youtube.com/watch?v=Ng4koDgq2No

Mosse, Richard. 2020. 'MACK Live: Ricard Mosse.' 15 May: hwww.youtube.com/watch?v=Kt9_-xyG5K8

Moulin, Carolina. 2012. 'Ungrateful Subjects? Refugee Protests and the Logic of Gratitude.' In *Citizenship, Migrant Activism and the Politics of Movement*. Ed. Peter Nyers and Kim Rygiel. London: Routledge (54–72).

Mukherjee, Reshmi. 2019. 'Threads: From the Refugee Crisis: Creative Nonfiction and Critical Pedagogy.' *Assay: A Journal of Nonfiction Studies*, 5:2.

Murphy, Sinead. 2017. 'Dina Nayeri's *Refuge*.' *Refugee History*, 17 August.

Nayeri, Dina. 2013. *A Teaspoon of Earth and Sea*. London: Allen & Unwin.

Nayeri, Dina. 2017. *Refuge*. New York: Riverhead Books.

Nayeri, Dina. 2019. *The Ungrateful Refugee*. Edinburgh: Canongate.

Newman, Frances. 2017. 'Threads from the Refugee Crisis – Review.' *Socialist Review*, 427, September.

Nguyen, Marguerite and Catherine Fung. 2016. 'Editor's Introduction: Refugee Cultures: Forty Years after the Vietnam War.' *MELUS: Multi-Ethnic Literature of the U.S.*, 41:3 (1–7).

Nguyen, Viet Thanh. 2015. *The Sympathizer*. New York: Grove Press.

Nguyen, Viet Thanh. 2018. *The Displaced. Refugee Writers on Refugee Lives*. New York: Abrams Press.

O'Brien, Paraic. 2020. 'Humility and Humanity Are Key to Ethical Reporting on the Global Refugee and Migrant Crisis.' *Ethical Journalism Network*, 22 August.

O'Connor, Flannery. 1971 [1955]. 'The Displaced Person.' In *The Complete Stories*. New York: Farrar, Straus and Giroux (194–235).

O'Shea-Meddour, Wendy. 2019. 'In Conversation with JJ Bola.' *Wasafiri*, 34:1 (12–15).

Passarlay, Gulwali. 2019 [2015]. *The Lightless Sky. My Journey to Safety as a Child Refugee*, revised edn. With Nadene Ghouri. London: Atlantic Books.

Oliver, Kelly. 2017. *Carceral Humanitarianism: Logics of Refugee Detention*. Minneapolis, MN: University of Minnesota Press.

Oliver, Kelly, Lisa M. Madura and Sabeen Ahmed, eds. 2019. *Refugees Now: Rethinking Borders, Hospitality, and Citizenship*. London and New York: Rowman & Littlefield.

Passerin d'Entreves, Maurizio. 2001 [1994]. *The Political Philosophy of Hannah Arendt*. London: Routledge.

Perfect, Michael. 2019. '"Black Holes in the Fabric of the Nation": Rfugees in Mohsin Hamid's *Exit West.*' *Journal for Cultural Research*, 23:2 (187–201).

*Photoworks*. 2020. 'Interview: Incoming by Richard Mosse': https://photoworks.org.uk/incoming-richard-mosse

Polak, Regina. 2018. 'Turning a Curse into a Blessing? Theological Contributions to a Resource-Oriented Narrative on Migration in Europe.' In *Religion in the European Refugee Crisis*. Ed. Ulrich Schmiedel and Graeme Smith. London: Palgrave Macmillan (243–63).

Popescu, Lucy, ed. 2016. *A Country of Refuge*. London: Unbound.

Popescu, Lucy, ed. 2018. *A Country to Call Home*. London: Unbound.

Popescu, Lucy. 2020. '*God 99* by Hassan Blasim Review.' *Guardian*, 22 November.

Popoola, Olumide and Annie Holmes. 2016. *Breach*. London: Peirene Press.

PositiveNegatives: positivengatives.org

Ramirez, Diego. 2018. 'Racial Phantasmagoria: The Demonization of the Other in Richard Mosse's "Incoming".' 23 November: https://necsus-ejms.org/racial-phantasmagoria-the-demonisation-of-the-other-in-richard-mosses-incoming/

Ramsey-Kurz, Helga. 2020. 'Precarity in Transit: Travellers by Helon Habila.' *Current Writing: Text and Reception in Southern Africa*, 32:2 (168–77).

Refugenes: www.helprefugees.org

Refugee Tales: www.refugeetales.org

Richter, Gerhard. 2006. 'Can Hope Be Disappointed? Contextualizing a Blochian Question.' *symploke*, 14:1–2 (42–54).

Rooney, Sally. 2018. *Conversations with Friends*. London: Faber and Faber.

Ryan, Donal. 2018. *From a Low and Quiet Sea*. London: Doubleday.

Said, Edward. 1994. *Representations of the Intellectual*. The 1993 Reith Lectures. London: Vintage.

Said, Edward. 2000. 'Reflections on Exile.' In *Reflections on Exile and Other Essays*. London: Granta (180–92).

Said, Edward. 2004. *Humanism and Democratic Criticism*. New York: Columbia University Press.

Said, Edward. 2014. *Freud and the Non-Europeans*. London: Verso.

Scheufele, Dietram A. and David Tewksbury. 2007. 'Framing, Agenda Setting, and Priming: The Evolution of Three Media Effects Models.' *Journal of Communication*, 57:1 (9–20).

Schmid, Johannes C.P. 2019. 'Documentary Webcomics: Mediality and Contexts.' In *Perspectives on Digital Comics: Theoretical, Critical and Pedagogical Essays*. Ed. Jeffrey S.J. Kirchoff and Mike P. Cook. Jefferson, NC: McFarland & Company (63–88).

Schulze-Engler, Frank, Pavan Kumar Malreddy and John Njenga Karugia et al., 2018. '"Even the Dead Have Human Rights": A Conversation with Homi K. Bhabha.' *Journal of Postcolonial Writing*, 54:5 (702–16).

Sehgal, Parul. 2018. 'A Syrian Refugee Lands in Ireland in *From a Low and Quiet Sea*.' *New York Times*, 31 July.

Sen, Somdeep. 2018. 'Writing the "Refugee Crisis": Proposals for Activist Research.' In *Syrian Refugee Children in the Middle East and Europe – Integrating the Young and Exiled*. Ed. Michelle Pace and Somdeep Sen. London and New York: Routledge (101–12).

Senior, Jennifer. 2017. 'Dina Nayeri's *Refuge* Follows the Reinvention of an Exile.' *New York Times*, 9 August.

Shacknove, Andrew E. 1985. 'Who Is a Refugee?' *Ethics*, 95:2 (274–84).

Shafak, Elif. 2020. *How to Stay Sane in an Age of Division*. London: Profile Books/Wellcome.

Shah, Sonia. 2020. *The Next Great Migration: The Story of Movement on a Changing Planet*. London: Bloomsbury.

Shklovsky, Victor. 1991 [1983]. 'Art as Technique' [1917]. In *Modern Criticism and Theory: A Reader*. Ed. David Lodge. London: Longman (15–30).

Simon, Felix. 2016. 'Chronicling the Refugee Crisis.' *Medium*, 22 June.

Smith, Ali. 2017. *Winter*. London: Penguin.

Smith, Ali. 2020. *Spring*. London: Penguin.

Smith, Erica. 2017. 'Kate Evans, Threads: From the Refugee Crisis – Review.' *Peace News*, 2612, December.

Stonebridge, Lyndsey. 2017. 'Thinking without Bannisters.' *Jewish Quarterly*, 64:1 (18–21).

Stonebridge, Lyndsey. 2018. *Placeless People: Writing, Rights, and Refugees*. Oxford: Oxford University Press.

Tennyson, Alfred. 2006. 'Ulysses.' *The Norton Anthology of English Literature*, Vol. II, 8th edn. New York: Norton (1213–14).

'The 5 Principles of Ethical Journalism.' *Ethical Journalism Network*: https://ethicaljournalismnetwork.org/who-we-are

Tinti, Peter and Tuesday Reitano. 2018. *Migrant, Refugee, Smuggler, Saviour*. London: Hurst.

Tischner, Jósef. 2005. 'The Ethics of Solidarity': www.tischner.org.pl/Content/Images/tischner_3_ethics.pdf

Trilling, Daniel. 2018a. *Lights in the Distance. Exile and Refuge at the Borders of Europe*. London: Picador.

Trilling, Daniel. 2018b. 'Five Myths about the Refugee Crisis.' *Guardian*, 5 June.

Trilling, Daniel. 2019. 'How the Media Framed the Way We See the Migrant Crisis.' *Guardian*, 1 August.

Trilling, Daniel. 2020. 'Greece Has a Deadly New Migration Policy – and All of Europe Is to Blame.' *Guardian*, 27 August.

Tsipane, Outlwile. 2019. 'Outlwile Tsipane Reviews Helon Habila's New Novel *Travellers*.' *The Johannesburg Review of Books*, 2 September.

UNHCR: www.unhcr.org/3b66c2aa10.html

Van Gorp, Baldwin. 2005. 'Where Is the Frame? Victims and Intruders in the Belgian Press Coverage of the Asylum Issue.' *European Journal of Communication*, 20:4 (484–507).

Warner, Marina. 2002 [2001]. *The Leto Bundle*. London: Vintage.

Wiggenhauser, Jana. 2018. 'Storytelling and Political Activism: "Refugee Tales" and Its Call to End Indefinite Immigration Detention in the UK.' *Literaryfield*, 5 November.

Wilson, Janet. 2017. 'Novels of Flight and Arrival: Abu Bakr Khaal, *African Titanics* (2014 [2008]) and Sunjeev Sahota, *The Year of the Runaways* (2015)', *Postcolonial Text*, 12:3&4 (1–14).

Wittenberg, Jonathan. 2019. 'Review: *Refugee Tales* Vol III.' The *JC*, 8 August.

Wood, James. 2017. 'A Novelist's Powerful Response to the Refugee Crisis.' The *New Yorker*, 18 September.

Wood, Morala. 2019. 'Nigerian Writer Helon Habila on the Politics of Travel.' *ZAM Magazine*, 28 November.

Woolley, Agnes. 2014. *Contemporary Asylum Narratives: Representing Refugees in the Twenty-First Century.* London: Palgrave Macmillan.

Young, Robert. 2012. 'Postcolonial Remains'. *New Literary History*, 43:1 (19–42).

Young-Bruehl, Elisabeth. 2004. *Hannah Arendt: For Love of the World*, 2nd edn. New Haven, CT: Yale University Press.

# Index

Thanks to our Patreon subscribers:

*Andrew Perry*
*Ciaran Kane*

Who have shown generosity and comradeship in support of our publishing.

Check out the other perks you get by subscribing to our Patreon – visit patreon.com/plutopress.

Subscriptions start from £3 a month.

## The Pluto Press Newsletter

Hello friend of Pluto!

Want to stay on top of the best radical books
we publish?

Then sign up to be the first to hear about our
new books, as well as special events,
podcasts and videos.

You'll also get 50% off your first order with us
when you sign up.

Come and join us!

Go to bit.ly/PlutoNewsletter